Leapfrogging the Competition

Leapfrogging the Competition:

Five Giant Steps to Market Leadership

OREN HARARI, Ph.D.

Under the editorship of Martha H. Peak

American Century Press
(202) 785–0990

Publisher's Cataloging-in-Publication Data

Harari, Oren
    Leapfrogging the competition : five giant steps to market leadership / by Oren Harari. -- 1st ed.
      p. cm.
    Includes index.
    Preassigned LCCN: 97-72924
    ISBN: 0-9657896-0-8

    1. Management. 2. Strategic planning. 3. Organizational change --Management. I. Title

HD30.7.H37 1997   658
                                     QBI97-40654

To Leslie,
with love

CONTENTS

viii   **Contents**

FOREWORD

As much as their authors talk about openness to change, most business books are substantially alike. Not this one. With all the energy and frankness of his frequent lectures and his 1994 book coauthored with Nick Imparato, *Jumping the Curve*, Oren Harari practices what he preaches in this latest book, *Leapfrogging the Competition.* His brilliant analogies, astute observations and cut-to-the-chase analyses leapfrog over the conventional wisdom of theorists who spend little if any time in the trenches.

This book is not for the faint-hearted, but for the courageous. It is for managers and executives who are still as excited about being in business now as they were in their first days on the job. It is for those who, as Harari puts it, "eat change for breakfast."

If you're lucky, however, you may find that your organization is already taking some Giant Steps. In that case, this book will help you hone your strategies. If the book helps you recognize that your company has not yet moved itself into leapfrogging position and is merely reacting to customer feedback and competitors' moves, you'll find no better catalyst for springing into action.

In clear, no-nonsense language and with plenty of relevant examples, *Leapfrogging the Competition* demonstrates how companies can "lower the cost of failure while simultaneously boosting the returns on successes." That's why I like this book. Harari doesn't just tell executives *what* we ought to do, he tells us *how*, so that we're not left to reinvent the wheel.

Harari speaks the plain truth about the mistakes corporations are making and about what it takes to avoid playing catch-up and instead surge ahead into the information-intensive, hyper-competitive millennium. While contrarian—admonishing managers to rely on intuition and judgment rather than market research for strategic decisions and product ideas, for example—the author's words are weighty and genuine. This is fine-grained wood, not veneer.

"*Exciting, coherent* and *ever-evolving* are the operative words for describing ... the leapfrogging organization," says Harari. To my mind, it is the first chapter, or "commitment," and the last which most strongly support that description. Commitment 1: "Be First, Be Exceptional," might sum up the driving force at Dayton Hudson Corporation, which, today at least, fits the author's definition of a leapfrogging organization. Nevertheless, along with leaders in every other industry, we are susceptible to complacency and must rout out routineness every day. If your company already occupies the leadership position, pay special attention to Commitment 15: "Beware the Danger of Success."

Leapfrogging the Competition is the most compelling argument yet written for being first to market with products and services, and for being first on the all-star list with your customers. Harari dispenses with the commonly held belief that market leaders must constantly study our competitors and fight or dodge their every move in an effort to finally "beat" them. Instead, he issues a charge more realistic for today's marketplace: "Leapfrog" over your competitors and literally redefine not only your organization but the marketplace, as well.

The author's organization of his material into five Giant Steps makes the book—and the prospect of wholesale change—digestible. It matters little whether you read the chapters in order or at random, so interwoven are the principles of innovation, openness, customer focus, relationship-building and the courage to change. So well-told are the stories of failure and success that you are bound to derive value from every page.

This is not a book to be read once and shelved. It is the essential guide to the future of business, in which the concept of permanence is meaningless and in which risk-taking is imperative. With the publication of this book, there is a new axiom in business: It's "leapfrog or languish." And victory belongs to those who leap.

Bob Ulrich
Chairman and CEO
Dayton Hudson Corporation
April 1997

PLAN OF THE BOOK

This book is designed to be clear, logical and pragmatic. It is divided into five main parts. Each part begins with an introductory description of a Giant Step, followed by a set of personal and organizational Commitments which I urge you to use to challenge yourself. The basic premise of this book is that the only way you can position your organization to leapfrog the competition is to be prepared to make—and follow through on—personal Commitments that will change the way both you and your organization think and act and do business.

These Commitments are not "feel-good" homilies; they are not "dare-to-be-great" platitudes. They are tough, challenging, and ultimately rewarding, for they serve as the why-and-how blueprint for implementing the Giant Steps. The book presents 15 vital Commitments in all. In fact, since each chapter represents a specific Commitment, the book is organized and numbered by "Commitments" rather than "Chapters."

For example, the first four Chapters/Commitments illustrate the work needed to achieve Giant Step I: "Catapult Your Strategy over Conventional Wisdom." On page 11, you'll find an overview and discussion of the Giant Step itself. The next four Commitments are relevant to that Giant Step. Chapter/Commitment 1: "Be First, Be Exceptional." Chapter/Commitment 2: "Obsolete Yourself Before Someone Else Does." Chapter/Commitment 3: "Go Beyond Traditional Weapons of Strategic Planning, Competitive Analysis, and Market Research." Chapter/Commitment 4: "View the World with Bifocal Vision." And so on.

Unfortunately, the two-dimensional nature of books requires the Commitments to be presented sequentially. However, please keep in mind that in practice, the Giant Steps and the Commitments are not meant to be implemented sequentially, nor are they listed in any particular order of importance. As leaders, we don't have the luxury of doing anything sequentially. If we are to be successful in leapfrogging the competition and establishing market leadership, we must embrace the idea of at least confronting all five Steps—and every Commitment—during our workday, everyday.

The content of each Chapter/Commitment is selectively drawn from a collection of five years' worth of topical research in articles that I have written for *Management Review*, the flagship publication of the American Management Association. I have integrated, updated and supplemented the information to fit into the framework of this book. If you approach the material as seriously as I believe you will, I predict that you'll find the content of each chapter to be an important aid in your quest for competitive advantage.

ACKNOWLEDGEMENTS

For any author, there is always the temptation to make this section infinitely long by thanking anyone who has ever had any involvement with any part of the book, however minuscule. I'll avoid temptation in this case, but I do want to acknowledge just a few people without whose support this book could not have been completed.

First, I'd like to thank the executives who provided the testimonials you see on the jacket and inside. It's not merely that they took time from their busy schedules to read a draft of this book, but more important, they did it quickly and graciously in order to meet a tight publication deadline. I'm very grateful to Bob Ulrich for writing the Foreword and, for their kind endorsements, I sincerely thank Peter Danis, Michael Dell, J.W. Marriott, Daniel Meyer, Lars Nyberg, Tom Peters, Colin Powell, Scott Shuster, and Douglas West.

The folks at American Century Press have made invaluable contributions throughout this process, and I truly thank all of them. In particular, Kristen Stoimenoff was exceptional in coordinating the perpetual stream of details and shepherding the entire project to fruition.

I am also grateful to my assistant, Susan Darling, who has been wonderful in organizing and keeping me in touch with the daily reality of my calendar, including flight schedules, appointments, conference calls and a mountain of deadlines. Her efficiency, graciousness and, above all, her friendship allowed me the time to create and write.

While in the midst of this project, Mike Childs, a successful entrepreneur and friend, provided me with very practical insights and feedback. In fact, I credit his input for my decision to organize the entire book around five giant steps.

At the University of San Francisco, where I am a faculty member, two individuals merit special acknowledgement. My MBA research assistant, Joshua Engel, has been invaluable in helping me put this work together. Whether using the USF library or electronic databases, whether making phone calls or sending e-mail messages to key individuals, whether poring over hard copy documents or websites, Josh was exceptional at ferreting out the kind of information I need—and often did so at a moment's notice.

I'm also grateful to Dr. Gary Williams, the Dean of the USF McLaren School of Business, where I teach. Over the years, Gary has been extremely supportive of my research efforts with cutting-edge companies and their leaders. He has provided me with the kind of resources and encouragement that has made it much easier for me to write this book as well as my other publications.

Among these "other" publications has been my monthly "Cutting Edge" column in *Management Review*. As noted, I drew from some of the research and commentary in those columns in writing this book. For nearly five years, Genevieve Capowski was my very able editor of those columns. I thank her for helping me keep the writing crisp, clear and succinct.

This brings me to two individuals who in particular stand out, and I'd like to end this section with a special note of gratitude to them.

Martha H. Peak, currently with the New York City Office of Mercer Management Consulting, was until recently Group Editor of AMA Periodicals. Five years ago she invited me to be a monthly contributor at *Management Review* and she has been very supportive of my work since then. I have been so impressed with her skills and acumen that I asked her to be the editor of this book. She did an outstanding job in helping me organize the manuscript and edit the writing, she provided numerous valuable suggestions in style and content and, in general, helped with the myriad things it takes to create a polished end-product. Martha has been so instrumental that I wish to publicly acknowledge her contribution by taking the admittedly unusual step of placing her name on the cover.

Most important, I want to express my profound gratitude to my wife, Leslie, who gave me generous heaps of encouragement and support from the inception of this project. Of course, those are the kinds of words that any author is supposed to write about his or her spouse. But in this case, in view of the fact that our second son was born right in the middle of the process, and in view of the fact that Leslie voluntarily took on the brunt of the childcare responsibilities for both Jordan and Dylan so that I could finish the project on time, I'd say that the laudatory sentiments about her are more than justified. I can't thank her enough, for that and for many other things, and it is to her that I gratefully, and endearingly, dedicate this book.

INTRODUCTION

The world of business today has been described as being in "perpetual whitewater."

It's a good metaphor. Deregulation, globalization and technological advances are generating remarkable upheavals in both organizations and products—upheavals that none of us could have imagined even a few years ago. Markets are becoming less homogeneous and less predictable. They are fragmenting and splintering. Waves of consolidation are routinely followed by waves of divestitures and restructurings. Barriers to entry in industry after industry are crumbling—and new businesses are bubbling up in market arenas that didn't exist just a few years ago. Small wonder that in many industries, convergence and excess capacity are becoming the norm rather than the exception.

All this makes it increasingly difficult for any organization to maintain a preeminent position, either in terms of customer loyalty or market share. Yes, one can point to the Intels, Microsofts and Gillettes as exemplars of domination in their particular industries, but those examples are the exception rather than the rule. (Besides, as we'll discuss later, their success is due precisely to an ever-present healthy paranoia that they'll lose everything tomorrow if they don't act as if they've got nothing today).

The fact is: In every sector, competition has intensified exponentially. With $2 trillion being exchanged worldwide every 24 hours, it's increasingly easy for entrepreneurs to access capital to start a business. Add to that the immense opportunities of global alliances and technologies that allow real-time worldwide linkups, and suddenly everyone—from established behemoth to tiny startup—has the power to be a significant player in any market segment on the planet.

On top of that, the new technologies themselves are becoming potent sources of competition: remote banking software systems threaten conventional retail branches, EDI threatens middlemen in any distribution chain, the interactive potentials of the World Wide

Web threaten everyone. Customers, meanwhile, with an increasing number of vendor options available to them, are continuously raising the bar on the kinds of performance they expect from vendors.

To survive in this whirlpool, organizations themselves are becoming leaner, faster, smarter. The only other option is to perish: Life cycles of both products and organizations are shrinking rapidly (nearly half of the 1980 Fortune 500 has already disappeared). Even organizations that are prospering today still have the uneasy sense that calamity is right around the corner. It doesn't matter how big your balance sheet or press clippings are: There are no guarantees anymore.

What's happening? It's not merely that the rules of the game have changed. The game itself is different. In our 1994 book *Jumping the Curve: Innovation and Strategic Choice in an Age of Transition* (Jossey-Bass), my colleague Nicholas Imparato and I showed that the turbulence in today's marketplace is not just about commerce and business; it is simply one aspect of a more profound revolution. Our entire civilization is going through an immense transformation, the likes of which have not been seen since the Modern Age began 500 years ago. That being the case, we argued, isn't it folly to assume that the management thinking and organizational systems that were appropriate yesterday will be appropriate for tomorrow, or even for today?

Hindsight is 20-20. Fifty years from now students of management will chuckle at our current attempts to comprehend and adapt to this macro-upheaval—just as we chuckle today over tales of Frederick Taylor, armed with clipboard and stopclock, earnestly analyzing assembly-line workers at the beginning of this century. For now, for better or for worse, the only thing we can be sure of is that we are all in the middle of something very big and very different. It doesn't require rocket-scientist logic to conclude that new realities call for new ways of thinking about our business enterprises and the way we manage them.

For the past decade, I have been dissecting this message with clients and audiences around the world. Since the publication of *Jumping the Curve*, I have observed that managers in all segments of the economy have become increasingly receptive to this message, and desirous of confronting it head-on. But while doing so, they have brought an important issue to my attention.

Paradoxically, in a world where the forces of change appear overwhelming in number, what practitioners need more than anything are a few precise, reliable, durable, cutting-edge leadership tools. Too many paths and solutions can themselves become overwhelming. While *Jumping the Curve* presented many practical ways for leaders to address the emerging marketplace, the operative word was "many." Over the past few years, I have often been asked if it is possible to boil down the blueprint for competitive advantage to a smaller, more manageable set of action steps that could serve as a bold compass for visionary leadership.

This is a very legitimate concern, and in response, I have consolidated the findings of my own recent research and consulting experiences into a set of just five steps. I can assure you that these five steps, if diligently and honorably pursued, will most definitely put you in position to leapfrog your competition.

This is why I chose the words for the title of this book carefully. First, consider the word "leapfrog." An organization that can leapfrog is one that can *bound over* a chaotic terrain, flexibly *bounce off* unanticipated hurdles, and *spring forward* to snare any opportunities that fleetingly appear. Competitors? The leapfrogging organization is not obsessed with either imitating or avoiding them. The leapfrogging organization simply *vaults over* them. It does so with explosive speed and outrageous product-service offerings that simultaneously amaze customers and reshape the industry.

These words may sound overly dramatic, but in the emerging millennium they will be the clues to organizational success. In a business world crowded with throngs of jostling competitors and bursting with advances in technology and science, the winners will be those organizations that have both the commitment and the capacity to zoom ahead of the mob. Managing with "me-too" products, "let's-play-it-safe" strategies, and "at-least-we're-no-worse-than-anyone-else" mindsets will be the kiss of death.

Simply keeping up with the competition means consigning your organization to mediocrity. There's nothing wrong with mediocrity per se, except that in the emerging marketplace there will be so many mediocre players that ultimately the act of being just another face in a rapidly growing crowd will doom your organization to nonentity and demise.

But *how* does one leapfrog the competition? How does one create an enterprise that can regularly vault over the morass of mediocrity, and thus stand out above the fray?

I propose five steps. Radical steps. Giant steps. These words hold significance. Giant steps are not small. They are not easy. They are not tentative. They are not faddish. They are not minor variations of conventional wisdom. They are not tweaky extensions of the status quo.

No, they are big, brassy, bold, and occasionally bizarre. They represent the strategic fundamentals of a select but fast-growing group of organizations (a number of which are described in Chapters 1–15) that are already in the process of inventing the future.

The five Giant Steps, the meat and potatoes of this book, can be your path to the future as well. They are as follows:

I. **Catapult Your Strategy over Conventional Wisdom.**
   Paul Handlery, chairman of the Handlery hotel chain, once commented to me that in business, what is revolutionary today is mundane tomorrow. How true. Likewise, what is labeled conventional wisdom today will become anachronistic tomorrow.

   Organizations that leapfrog their competition understand and capitalize on this insight, which is why they insist on doing the unconventional *today*. They start with the premise that the key to competitive advantage is to gear everything—strategic thinking, decision-making styles, employee development, organizational systems, you name it—toward being first to market with exceptional ideas and exceptional offerings. These organizations then ferret out the ordinary in favor of the extraordinary—be it in product, service delivery, distribution or after-sale. Anything that smacks of mundane, vanilla and commonplace is rejected as uninteresting. For leapfrogging organizations, what their competitors are doing today is a quick benchmark to be noted, but not a style sheet that imposes limitations to what is possible.

   That's why these organizations find the courage to deliberately obsolete their on-going products and processes (*especially* if those products are currently successes) regardless of what their competitors are doing. That's also why they do not overly rely on traditional tools such as strategic planning, competitive analysis and market research—all of which reflect today's realities and today's conventional wisdom.

   Companies that adhere to this Giant Step are externally focused, constantly scanning the vast terrain ahead, and seizing on emerging forces in technology, demographics and consumer preferences. They use these forces to fuel their obsession with *leading* the market, not just "responding" to it.

This is why their actions are often deemed weird or outrageous by those who wear the lenses of traditional management.

Finally, the leaders who pilot these catapulting organizations have developed the capacity to view the world not with "vision," but with *bifocal vision*. Every day, in every meeting, in every report they simultaneously attend to today's market realities (technology, competition, customers, etc.) while aggressively anticipating and preparing for tomorrow's.

II. **Flood Your Organization with Knowledge.**
In a knowledge-based economy, smart organizations will be the clear winners. Leapfrogging organizations see themselves not as amalgams of bricks and mortar, but as growing, bubbling cauldrons of interesting, exciting ideas—ideas that can be translated into fast action. They see that competitive advantage is no longer a result of balance-sheet size or press clippings, but of rapid-fire information, expertise and networks that allow people to create what currently doesn't even exist—either in product or process. Organizations that carry out this Giant Step carefully cultivate an ever-growing pool of knowledge as a dominant strategic weapon—and they insure that this knowledge is "flooded" to every corner and every person of the organization.

Unlike many enterprises today, leapfrogging organizations don't drown their people with data, paper and protocol. Instead, they deliberately smash existing barriers to the flow of information, learning and communication—so that employees can access the knowledge and the people they need, when they need it, as they need it. In most organizations, barriers to the flow of ideas are numerous. They can be structural or cultural; such as hierarchical pass-off requirements for even the most mundane of decisions, or policies which restrict financial and strategic information to a chosen few, or an "us-vs.-them" adversarial relationship with suppliers.

Leapfrogging organizations take pains to weaken—if not obliterate—those barriers so that people in every nook and cranny of the organization can draw upon whatever and whoever they need in order to make immediate, informed, creative decisions. This means that information technology becomes an essential tool for everyone, from controller to factory worker. Computers perform the routine work, provide a medium for expert systems, and allow rapid dissemination of ideas. This free-flooding of knowledge is accompanied by rapid applications, tests and pilots initiated by a well-trained workforce, the results of which come full circle and wind up flooding the organization with even more knowledge—again accessible to all. All this galvanizes the organization to continually leapfrog its slower, narrow-thinking, idea-restricted competitors.

III. **Wrap Your Organization Around Each Customer.**
The winning organizations in the emerging millennium will understand—as some leapfrogging organizations already do—that mass markets are dying. Uniform, standardized products and services are dying. Customer patience and tolerance is dying. Leapfrogging organizations begin by vaulting over the standard lip service of "customer is king," and *live* instead by two precepts:

- First, they adhere to a philosophy which states that we are in business *not* to build profit, but to build customers, which means building long-term constructive partnerships with customers. If that is done right, the numbers we all seek—earnings, market share, shareholder value, profit—will soar as the scorecard builds for making the right plays.

  Certainly, the ability to effectively manage costs, assets, cash flow and earnings is a vital component of solid management. (In fact, as we shall see in Giant Step II, it ought to be an important part of everyone's job, not just top management's). The issue, however, is one of priorities. Focusing on the financials at the expense of creating value for customers will concentrate the organization's entrepreneurial efforts on myopic, chess-piece reorganizations and financial sleight-of-hand, which will ultimately diminish both customer loyalty and stock value in an increasingly fickle marketplace.
- Second, leapfrogging organizations commit to tailoring their products and services for each individual customer. They understand that the winning organization will be smart enough, light and limber enough, and fleet and flexible enough to wrap itself around the unique needs and desires of each customer. Personalized service, customized products, turn-on-a-dime responsiveness, and solution-based efforts *to each customer's needs*—these are the passwords of organizations

that follow this Giant Step. By so doing, they leapfrog over competitors that in effect insist that their customers wrap *themselves* around the standardized products, processes and time-frames of the organization.

IV. **Transform Your Organization into a Web of Relationships.**
To leapfrog, you need allies. Organizations that leapfrog their competitors do so with the assistance of a trusted network all around the world. They seek partnerships constantly, because they do not believe for a minute that they—or anyone else—can magically collect and hoard the best talent and all the expertise within the confines of their four walls. In fact, they don't even view their organizations in terms of four walls. They view their organizations as extensions of other organizations—their allies—all of whom have unique expertise and vital talent.

Unsurprisingly, then, they do not define their business environment in terms of insiders vs. outsiders because in their minds there is no "us" or "them." Instead, they view themselves as networks, combinations, clusters and alliances—all open and permeable, where information is freely shared, and where people of all parties freely move in and out of changing boundaries. These "webs" (networks, alliances) are increasingly virtual, usually organically ebbing and flowing, and they hold themselves together by that most intangible of organizational glue: trust.

Visualize the organization not in terms of the traditional heavy, massive, hierarchical pyramid bolted to the ground by the weight of vertical integration. Think of it instead as an ever-multiplying, virtual set of overlapping concentric circles. Visualize an organization that co-contracts (not "subcontracts") every function in which it is not a star player and keeps only that in which it is truly the best. Visualize an organization that looks to any world-class player anywhere—including its competitors and customers—as a potential partner for breakthrough market offerings. Visualize an organization that is unencumbered, perpetually spinning new off-springs in new directions in every corner of the world. In fact, visualize an organization that uses alliances to make the planet its playground—and you'll start to envision an organization that perpetually leapfrogs over heavy, turgid competitors that have no comprehension of what's skyrocketing above them.

V. Eat Change for Breakfast; Serve It Up for Every Meal.

A few years ago, Harry Quadracchi, chairman of Quad/Graphics, explained his company's extraordinary success with a simple statement: "We eat change for breakfast." He meant that his entire company embraces change as a business opportunity, and that the organization is managed in such a way to quickly capitalize on it. I like what he said, and I would extend that advice a bit further:

The leapfrogging organization is one that is mobilized not merely to adapt to change, but to *cause* it. The charge of creating visible, regular, customer-wowing, market-shaking change becomes the personal priority of leaders who are committed to leapfrog the competition. Hence, preparing change for every meal means that corporate leaders quite literally define their management role as *provocateurs* of change.

As provocateurs of change, they proactively seek opportunities to challenge the process *every day*. They "walk the talk" by altering their personal behaviors and calendars to reflect their new strategic priorities. They constantly seek feedback from customers and employees to monitor their progress toward their chosen path. They don't get snookered by management fads-du-jour, not even widely accepted ones like reengineering or TQM. They continuously scan the marketplace with healthy paranoia; that is, they desperately fear the complacency that often follows success. Finally, they understand that this composite of behavior is what really defines leadership, because while everyone loves to talk about change, the fact is that too many people hate the innovator who dares disturb the status quo.

Ultimately, the leapfrogging organization is propelled by individuals who possess both the courage and the perseverance to confront a world of entirely new realities with a daily serving of meaningful change. These are the leaders who turn their organizations into ones that are so fit and fine-tuned that leapfrogging the competition becomes not just a figure of speech, but a real and continuous event.

These are the five Giant Steps, and this book presents the why's and the how's of executing each of them, as well as numerous examples of organizations that are already in the process of vaulting forward. But make no mistake; these are truly *giant* steps—

relatively easy to understand conceptually, but damnably difficult to execute. If you think about it, that's a good thing: If these steps were easy to execute, everyone would be doing it, and that in turn would mean that all of us would be right back in the middle of the pack.

Yet, with courage, commitment and diligence, these five Giant Steps can be successfully accomplished. And when you do so, you will not merely "respond" to the market, you will *lead* it. That is why the subtitle of this book refers to market "leadership." It is market leadership that allows our investors, our customers and our employees to reap the greatest rewards. It is market leadership that spurs our careers. And it is market leadership that creates—and is created by—an exciting, fun work environment.

Buddy Ryan may not have been a particularly successful head coach in the National Football League, but he was right on target when he described competition in terms of a bunch of dogs hauling a snow sled: "If you ain't the lead dog," he observed, "the scenery never changes." I suspect that you have picked up this book because you're not interested in constantly looking at someone else's backside or, for that matter, constantly feeling the breath of someone else behind you. For you, leapfrogging the competition is the most attractive option—in fact, the only option—and this book will help you attain that goal.

Giant Step I:

CATAPULT YOUR STRATEGY OVER CONVENTIONAL WISDOM

As the 1990s end and the next millennium begins to unfold, your company's need to be unique, special and different becomes especially urgent. The explosion of technological advances, competitor entrants and global risk capital coupled with the relentless movement toward free trade means that the worldwide arena of products, services, players, partnerships and ideas is becoming ever more crowded at a frighteningly accelerating pace. The symptoms are clear: glutted markets, indistinguishable products, image and price convergence.

In this high-pressure arena, tepid, ultra-cautious or "me-too" strategies are a prescription for uphill struggle at best, outright failure at worst. If customers and investors can't identify what makes your organization and your products unique, special, and different, you're headed for serious trouble.

Why? Because customers are continually raising the bar on what they expect from vendors. They are demanding more, sooner, better and cheaper—and they expect it all on their own terms and timetables. Think about it: The expectations that you hold today toward your telephone, computer software and hotel services is logarithmically greater than was the case five years ago. And the most ominous part is the sequel: If customers can't get their fickle, unreasonable demands met from you, they'll get them met somewhere else because they've got an ever-increasing number of choices.

Customers in all fields are being bombarded by vendors, options, ads and enticements that they never even considered just a few years ago. To survive and thrive in these circumstances, you've got to be special and unique enough to separate yourself from the din of the mob.

As the future unfolds, this trend will accelerate; tomorrow's customers will be even more knowledgeable and more aggressive than today's. Savvy investors know this, and they know that future earnings depend on your organization's ability to capitalize on this trend.

Unconventional times call for unconventional strategies. Bold actions aimed at being first and being exceptional—that is, first to market with exceptional ideas and unique product-service offerings—create the capacity to differentiate yourself in the marketplace, which in turn create the kinds of customer loyalty, margins, revenues and marketshare you seek. Striving to be first and exceptional also pushes you to innovatively harness today's opportunities for tomorrow's market leadership—rather than relegate you to perpetually playing catch-up to brash, new competitors.

You won't become first and exceptional with hypercautious decisions and bland responses. Nor will you get there with lip-service platitudes that reflect the latest fad or "management speak." Leapfrogging requires daring, *unorthodox* action. Anita Roddick, founder of the Body Shop, and the late Sam Walton, founder of Wal-Mart, represent about as dissimilar a pairing of personalities as I can imagine, but they agreed on at least one thing: To be successful in business, you have to "go in the opposite direction as everyone else" (Roddick) and "swim upstream" (Walton).

Consider this example: To the average individual investor in 1982, the very idea of trading securities electronically without human contact would have seemed a scenario straight out of a sci-fi movie. The aggressive, progressive investor at the time used discount brokers, to be sure, but left the computers to the scientists and techno-nerds. Only a small percentage of Americans had a computer on their desks at work—much less in their homes.

But Bill Porter, founder of E*Trade, was attentive to the emerging trend of decentralized information technology. To him, the idea of using the personal computer to manage an investment portfolio seemed a viable means to achieve total control, immediate responsiveness and save big commission bucks. Accordingly, he persevered in developing and marketing an electronic method of placing trades and his foresight paid off as PCs and on-line services became commonplace mediums for commercial transactions.

That's proved to be just the beginning: "E*Trade carved out an early identity," says James Marks, an electronic commerce analyst at CS First Boston. "They're in a good position to take advantage of on-line media—not only in brokerage services, but in a whole range of financial products." Under the leadership of Chairman Porter and CEO Christos Cotsakos, the company opens a whopping 500 accounts daily, revenues have tripled and trading volume is up 120 percent since last fiscal year, and the stock price has doubled since the company's IPO in August 1996. The start-up has also induced industry giants Charles Schwab and American Express to create their own Internet trading websites and to redefine their own marketing strategies. That's market clout.

When Ted Turner talked about launching a 24-hour news and information station in the 1970s, every particle of conventional wisdom—from market researchers to broadcast professionals to industry pundits—agreed that his vision was crazy, bizarre, guaranteed to fail. But as history proved—and as we shall examine in some detail in Commitment 2—Turner's foray (while admittedly audacious) was actually prudent. The only thing that was "bizarre" was that he catapulted his strategy over convention—and in the process created a powerful global brand that generates 35 percent gross margins.

Nowadays it's riskier to be conventional than unconventional. If you're serious about embarking on a visionary path toward being first and exceptional, this section will be of real use to you. Specifically, this section will present the evidence that the most powerful and enduring results are those that serve to continually create new products, new markets and new futures. Companies as diverse as Benetton, Body Shop, CNN, E*Trade, Federal Express, Dell Computer, Home Depot, Netscape, Nike, Sony and Wal-Mart did not merely "adapt" to the market. They led it—in fact they invented it—with breakthrough products and concepts. They were not market-driven. They *drove* the market. They did not respond to customers. They *pulled* them into the future. Moreover, it is important to note that these companies did not and do not rely extensively on traditional management tools such as strategic planning that are considered sacred in many organizations today.

Traditionally, strategy revolves around consolidating existing heuristics, algorithms, premises and brilliant thinkers in an attempt to "predict" the market, as in formal strategic planning efforts—even though research study after research study shows that the business world today is fundamentally unpredictable. Traditional strategy also revolves around carefully monitoring existing competitors and today's product lines, as in competitor analysis—even though new technologies and unorthodox competitor entrants are being launched daily, out of range of the competitor analysis periscope.

Traditional strategy revolves around tracking customer's existing mindset today, as in market research—even though customers often have difficulty conceptualizing tomorrow's needs, and even though numerous breakthrough products and concepts (from Post-It notepads to Walkmans to 50-cc motorbikes to a 24-hour news channel) initially scored negatives in survey and focus group results. All these traditional tools are inadequate and often futile in today's madcap economy. Moreover, as this section shows, they place artificial caps on the breakthrough possibilities that any company can enjoy.

The examples in this section will demonstrate that a commitment to aggressive action, aimed at being first and being exceptional, will turbo-charge you to leapfrog the competition. Why? First, because it creates your ability to differentiate yourself in the marketplace; and second, because the usual lip-service to innovation notwithstanding, many organizations today (including your competitors) are pre-occupied with maintaining tradition, hyper-caution, and routine practice, all of which generate "being the same and being ordinary."

This section also demonstrates that organizations which leapfrog the competition recognize a curious paradox. On one hand, they continually improve and perfect today's product/service mix. On the other, they continually obsolete and abandon what they're currently doing in order to create a next generation of products and paradigms. Hewlett-Packard and Intel, for example, simultaneously improve and cannibalize their currently successful product lines before they can become commodities amenable to the mass-production economies of scale better left to low-cost competitors.

MCI continually improves its current long-distance voice service via upgrades in technology, enhanced customer service, global expansion, and aggressive marketing. Yet even as it's improving its primary source of revenue, MCI is preparing to abandon it. The company recognizes (and budgets for the fact) that the future of its business is in data transmission, Internet- and intranet-related products, cellular and wireless communication, and bundled service offerings that blend voice, data and image. The breakthroughs—the leaps over current competition— will come in the latter arena, as will the resultant growth, earnings and margins.

True, relying *solely* on paradigm creation is unrealistic. On the other hand, as the companies discussed in this chapter demonstrate, sinking most of your capital into improving products that are already conventional or headed toward obsolescence can only lead to corporate demise. Concentrating on improving products and services that are becoming low-cost commodities is no way to generate excitement or loyalty among either customers or investors. Putting your primary attention on improving internal processes and systems that should be eliminated outright is the height of myopia.

Consultant Tom Brown and I recently concluded that many companies today are reminiscent of a high-level task-force at the turn of the century holding a top-secret off-site meeting to figure out how to reengineer their premier stagecoach. Those who were not trapped by the horse-and-buggy paradigm—those who had the foresight to challenge convention by exploring new technologies and evolving consumer needs—were the ones who were able to catapult both their thinking and their organizations to both dream and take advantage of rpms and horseless transportation.

Parenthetically, I have found that those companies that follow Giant Step I are also those that go beyond convention even in their "continuous improvement" efforts. Too often, companies limit their improvements of current practices to changes in prices and features that are so small that they are either undetected or held to be inconsequential by customers, or so insignificant as to be easily copied by competitors.

Federal Express, in contrast, in responding to the steady inroads of competitors as diverse as UPS, the U.S. Postal Service, fax, and e-mail, is providing customers with more diverse time and delivery options, as well as the technological capacity to track their own packages. These are meaningful improvements from the customer's perspective. Still, FedEx understands that continuous improvement on its own is a slippery slope. That is why, simultaneously, in a paradigm-catapulting process, FedEx is leveraging its technological expertise to reposition itself as a high-value, out-sourced provider of warehousing and logistics services. FedEx's actions insure that the company will not only leapfrog competition, but continue to charge premium prices that customers will perceive as fair in price-value.

This section ends with a personal challenge to leaders: To develop a capacity for bifocal vision, that is, the ability to confront *today's* challenges (demanding customers, payroll, general ledger, quarterly reports) while simultaneously probing *tomorrow's* opportunities—and to do so for every management decision. This doesn't require genetic brilliance. It requires time, practice and commitment.

Audit most leaders' personal calendars and you'll find more than 90 percent of their time is devoted to "right now" problems and "today's crises" activities. Too many managers don't make the tough choice to spend a minimum of 50 percent of their time scoping what the future holds, or projecting how they can leapfrog far ahead of their competitors in that time frame. Nor do they insist that each of today's decisions—in personnel, marketing, product development, etc.—have a bifocal dimension: Demonstrating that the decision will strengthen the company today, and preparing it to be strong in the face of tomorrow's challenges.

In summary, leaders and companies that follow Giant Step I are perpetually reinventing their product-line and persona in terms of bare-knuckle questions such as "what *can* our business be?" and "whom *can* we serve?" To paraphrase strategy guru Gary Hamel, they not only focus on today's market, but on the total *imaginable* market of tomorrow. They truly understand Pixar chairman Steve Job's dictum that the best way to predict the future is to invent it. By truly catapulting over convention, and by insisting that their colleagues do the same, they prepare their organizations to leapfrog the competition.

To catapult your strategy over conventional wisdom, resolve now to make four Commitments that will underlie your organizational strategy and your own daily calendar and decision-making:

- Be first, be exceptional (Chapter/Commitment 1)
- Obsolete yourself before someone else does (Chapter/Commitment 2)

- Go beyond traditional competitive weapons of strategic planning, competitive analysis and market research (Chapter/Commitment 3)
- Look at the world with bifocal vision (Chapter/Commitment 4)

Being first and being exceptional is the Commitment that must underlie both strategy and operations. Commitment 1 reveals clues as to the why's and how's by following the true story of a company that was working hard to move in the right direction, but in fact was mired in the slough of conventional thinking. We can learn a lot from others' mistakes, so see how you and your organization compare with this company.

Commitment 2 introduces the insidious corporate disease I call the "Thomas Lawson Syndrome" and explains how companies that don't obsolete themselves wind up being obsoleted by someone else. This chapter also highlights two prominent CEOs who are making headlines today because they instinctively understand the importance of proactive obsolescence.

Commitment 3 sounds the clarion call for rejecting an over-reliance on so-called sacred tools such as strategic planning, competitive analysis and market research. The byword on all this: Use these tools sparingly to get a quick scan of conventional wisdom, and then concentrate your efforts on leapfrogging by taking advantage of potential alternatives that are much more rewarding.

Commitment 4 calls on you and your organization to develop "bifocal vision"—the capacity and willingness to attack every challenge and every decision with a twin perspective: How the decision impacts today, and how it will impact tomorrow.

COMMITMENT 1:
BE FIRST, BE EXCEPTIONAL

Be forewarned: The first story in this chapter is not about how to put on a better corporate retreat. It's about the fact that so many companies come to accept goals, standards and expectations that are ordinary and mundane. As you read, note that the goals which the company in the story envisioned as groundbreaking were in actuality no more than tepid, same old/same old. My commentary will provide some alternatives that really are "first and exceptional." As you read this, ask yourself which better describes the goals your organization is striving to reach.

This is a tale of a company that seemed to do everything right during its annual corporate retreat, but in reality did almost everything wrong. As Jack Webb in the old *Dragnet* TV series would say: *The story you are about to hear is true; only the names have been changed to protect the innocent.*

It all began innocently enough. The $250-million high-tech company—let's call it Ajax—held its two-day retreat in a pleasant resort hotel. The CEO, the president and the 80-person management team attended. The company hired a consultant (no, it wasn't me) to facilitate the discussions. For two days the managers discussed issues such as competition, emerging technologies and the future of their business. They agreed that at the top of their wish list was the desire to triple revenues in five years, that is, to be a $750-million company by 2002. They also listed their operational priorities for the following year, priorities that would be key to moving Ajax toward a trebling of revenues. They were as follows:

- Improve communications.
- Reduce time to market.
- Optimize resources.
- Reduce functional barriers.

- Change corporate culture.
- Meet customer needs.

Sounds good so far, right? There's more. With the help of the consultant, the 80 participants self-selected themselves into six groups, one per priority. They then focused on developing action plans to help deliver each priority back on the job. Each group agreed to get together after the retreat, write up its list of recommendations and submit it to top management. Top management—in this case, the CEO and the president—agreed to review the recommendations and get back to each group with timely feedback.

Doesn't all this sound eminently reasonable? Doesn't it sound terribly productive? The answer, quite simply, is no. In fact, I propose that this retreat was an exercise in mediocrity, guaranteed to perpetuate everything that leads to corporate stagnation.

Why? Well, let's examine the six priorities, and then you be the judge:

1. *Improve communications.*
   What in the world does this bland motherhood maxim mean? On one hand, it means everything, because in today's Information Age, everything is communication and communication is everything. But from a practical standpoint, it means nothing at all, because it's such a vague, apple-pie item that everyone can nod their heads without really committing to anything— which is precisely what happened at this retreat. If the Ajax managers had really been serious about this issue, they might have prioritized their goal as something like:
       "Develop open-book communication throughout the company." Now that would be something worth talking about. John Case has written eloquently on this subject in his book *Open-Book Management* (Harper Business, 1995). Let me take his ideas a step further to argue that open-book *communication* means that anyone—regardless of job title—can review sales data, quarterly financials, today's income statement, today's quality data, and so on, in the quest toward adding value to the company. It means that anyone can meet with and brainstorm with anyone else in any part of the organization without having to go through myriad preliminary hoops and post-hoc interrogations. It means that leaders share strategies, competitive

analyses, financial challenges, knotty operational problems and market opportunities with all hands, both face to face and electronically—on a regular, collaborative problem-solving basis. It means no barriers, no turfs and no hoarding when it comes to information and "intelligence."

That's the kind of environment that is emerging in successful businesses as diverse as Springfield Remanufacturing (engine overhaul), VeriFone (credit card authorization) and Oticon (hearing aid products). What these companies are doing is confronting the nanosecond demands for intelligence in today's business world by obliterating cultural and structural barriers to information exchange. Their open-book efforts represent a helluva lot more than what most companies—including Ajax—refer to when they say they want to "improve communications."

2. *Reduce time to market.*
   Oh, dear. That's like telling a 400-pound man that he ought to lose some weight. It's pathetically insufficient, and it doesn't carry nearly enough urgency or compelling purpose. The real key to competitive success is not to simply *reduce* time to market, but to be *first* to market—be it in product (think about ongoing breakthroughs from Hewlett-Packard, Johnson & Johnson, Merrill Lynch, Nike and 3M) or concept (think about the core ideas underlying the launch of CNN, Charles Schwab, Dell Computer, FedEx and Home Depot). The research is clear: Being first is the most effective path toward gaining the profit margin and market share we all crave.

   Just as important, being first can generate a learning infrastructure. That is, the pathfinding organization can leverage its premier technologies, people and systems in a way that perpetuates its position with next-generation breakthroughs—which is the trademark of companies like HP and Schwab. Being first is also the most effective means of preparing for the future, because one is not worrying about "predicting" or "responding to" tomorrow's markets; rather, one is acting to create those markets. The company that is first gets to define customer expectations consistent with its own capacities, and it can charge a healthy premium in the process. The company that is first also gets a lock on valuable partnerships and alliances that serve as a critical mass for future endeavors.

Ajax managers would have been well-advised to concentrate on what they need to do to position their firm to address these issues vigorously; specifically, what they need to do today in order to lead tomorrow. In a world where the life cycles of products and technologies are compressing dramatically, a company that is satisfied with merely "reducing time to market" is a company that is doomed to playing perpetual catch-up.

3. *Optimize resources.*
   This is a bit of a no-brainer, isn't it? Doesn't every manager "get" the idea that his or her job includes efficient allocation of resources? Once again, the goal is reasonable, but in today's madcap economy, "reasonable" is unreasonable.

   In their book *Reengineering the Corporation*, Michael Hammer and James Champy were specific: The changes they were calling for were, in their words, "fundamental," "dramatic" and "radical," not gradual or incremental: "Reengineering is about beginning again with a clean sheet of paper ... about inventing new approaches to process structures that bear little or no resemblance to those of previous eras." Heady words.

   But among the hue-and-cry lip service that so many companies give to "reengineering," Hammer and Champy's warnings are often ignored. Instead, "optimizing resources" within the current structure, as was the politically correct goal in the Ajax retreat, passes for real change. Lip service has no impact other than making a few internal people feel good.

4. *Reduce functional barriers.*
   "Reducing" them means they still exist. How about eliminating them altogether? That would have been a much more valuable goal to discuss at the Ajax retreat. Companies today no longer have the luxury of subsidizing a chain of horizontal pass-offs. They're slow and costly—and they inevitably foster warring fiefdoms.

   In contrast, Lee Gammill Jr., executive vice president of New York Life Insurance, in November 1992 described in *Management Review* what happens when departmental barriers are eliminated: "Actuaries, lawyers, underwriters and investment analysts—as well as product, marketing and sales experts—sit on management teams. All work with the understanding that nothing is sacred or taboo, and that no parochial interests are allowed." The results? "We analyze market forces more quickly and deliver more responsive products and services. The time required for many products has been reduced by half."

Amen to that, and if Ajax was really serious, it would have sent its managers to visit successful companies like Nypro (plastics manufacturing) and Merix (circuit board assemblies)—companies that apply the concept of obliterating barriers to their customers and suppliers, respectively. These companies often share production plans and databases with "outsiders," a practice that puts to shame the typical functional gang warfare among "insiders."

5. *Change corporate culture.*
   Once again, this is too tepid a goal. When applied to corporate culture, the word "change" implies tweaking, tinkering, fine-tuning—all mild, timid responses. UCLA's Wellford Wilms and his colleagues attribute the extraordinary success of NUMMI (New United Motor Manufacturing), the Toyota-GM joint venture in Fremont, Calif., to a virtual "transformation" (their word) in corporate culture. The new culture includes just three job classifications for the entire unionized labor force (a reduction from more than 80), significant gainsharing pay plans, heavy investments in cross-training, genuine self-management and peer discipline, and open dialogue between managers and "workers" on production and quality decisions that used to be the sole domain of management.

   When Ajax managers blithely talked about "changing" culture during their retreat, were they prepared to take on the magnitude of change that managers at NUMMI did? Wilms quotes NUMMI managers who are frank in admitting that nothing short of a sheer overhaul in corporate culture would have allowed the plant to meet external competitive pressures. I'll wager that the same statement can be applied to most organizations today—Ajax included.

6. *Meet customer needs.*
   This is perhaps the surest road to flat revenues and earnings. Nowadays, "meeting" customer needs merely allows a company to play in the game. But if that's all it can do, it is unlikely to

emerge a survivor, much less a victor. Today, customers are more demanding, more aggressive, more impatient and more astute than ever before—and worse, they have more choices from competing vendors than ever before. They're becoming increasingly fickle, and they're continually raising the bar. A company that simply "meets" customer needs provides the bare minimum of value to them, which means that it inspires little loyalty.

Less loyalty, as researchers like James Heskett and Frederick Reichheld have independently demonstrated, yields less repeat business, lower margins and less word-of-mouth referrals—and, hence, significant reductions in profitability, market share, and "share of customer." Loyalty emerges when companies exceed customer expectations with market-leading concepts, cutting-edge products and "knock-your-socks-off" service.

Think of Charles Schwab carving out a new market in discount brokerage, and then think of E*Trade carving out yet another market in computer-driven, broker-free discount brokerage. Think of Mpath Interactive redefining the computer gaming industry by making it possible for customers to interact with one another over the Internet with flight simulations, sports and war games. Think of Pacific Bell creating an electronic commerce application that allows a customer to, say, arrange a flight and pay for it with digital cash over a personal communication system on a wireless network. Think about small retail businesses like Boston's ScrubaDub car wash, where computer databases on individual customers yield personalized services, and where regular customers receive a three-day guarantee, complete with the promise of a free rewash if the weather turns rainy or dusty.

Think of the Century Plaza Hotel in Los Angeles offering guests "cybersuites" with a huge screen Web access, voice-activated electronic butler (who closes curtains and turns out lights), cellular phone in addition to regular phone access, virtual reality games, and teleconferencing capabilities. Think of American Standard developing a bathtub with features including a touch-tone speaker telephone system, a stereo and a remote control for household appliances.

These companies go much further than merely meeting customer needs. Often, in fact, they go so far that they create "needs" that customers didn't even know they had. That's why they engender a strong customer following, yielding the kinds of returns that most organizations merely fantasize about.

Now comes the finale of this little tale. If the six priorities above are problematic, the very process within the retreat itself compounds Ajax's difficulties. Here's why:

First, a once-a-year all-hands discussion of issues like emerging competition, technologies and markets is grossly inadequate. When people get back to the job, they get right back to their normal routines. Thinking about the future, and meeting with colleagues to discuss the future, must itself become the daily routine. Most of the time, this sort of activity is absent in management life. Strategy gurus Gary Hamel and C.K. Prahalad argue that this near-absence is striking even within executive circles.

And what about the notion of top management at Ajax receiving the specific action-plan proposals from middle management, and then responding with yea or nay? I can't think of a better way for a company to reinforce a debilitating command-and-control structure and induce passivity among its managers. Suppose that instead, Ajax managers had used the retreat to come to consensus on some broad legal and financial boundaries that would apply to everyone, and then agreed to leave it to the six teams to take full responsibility for both developing action initiatives and executing them. No passive waiting for "approval" required, which, by the way, is what "empowerment" is all about.

Finally, there's this business of tripling revenues in five years as the top organizational priority. What sort of priority is that? Sure, concrete growth objectives are helpful as performance benchmarks, but saying that it's the top priority of an organization is like saying that the primary purpose of your life is to grow your net worth. If that really is your main goal in life, I feel sorry for you. Besides, even in business it's a myopic goal.

CEOs as diverse as Paul Allaire (Xerox) and Robert McDermott (United Services Automobile Association) have emphasized that the numbers are not the *raison d'etre* of a business, but the consequence of doing things right in terms of products and customers. (More on this in Commitment 7.) It would have been a lot more productive for Ajax managers to have concentrated on questions like: What are we best at? What are we world-class great at? What makes us unique? How are we going to serve our customers in such a way that nobody else can? What "wow" products and service can we offer? What are we going to do, perhaps in alliance with other world-class greats, that will lead the market? If we can execute the answers to those strategic questions, we'll be successful over the next five years, and maybe we'll even hit that desired $750-million mark as a result of our efforts.

Ajax is a good company. It's staffed by competent, conscientious managers. But as with any company, there's no guaranteeing that it will even be around five years from now. Strategic thinking can move a company toward breakthrough action or toward mediocrity. As you prepare for the future, you may wish to contemplate these things. Let's check in five years to see what has happened to Ajax.

COMMITMENT 2:
OBSOLETE YOURSELF BEFORE SOMEONE ELSE DOES

When a Southwest Airlines executive reckons that in five years more than 50 percent of ticket bookings will take place via the Web, I hear a funeral dirge start to play for conventional travel agents. But Philadelphia-based Rosenbluth Travel is already capitalizing on this relentless technological trend by developing software systems that will allow its corporate clients to surf travel sites on the Web more easily and, in partnership with Rosenbluth, create their own travel deals. Rosenbluth is an exception. Too many companies wind up waiting for someone—or something—to obsolete them. Don't become a fragment of yesterday's news.

"Toward dawn on Friday, December 13, 1907, the sailing ship *Thomas W. Lawson* sank off the Scilly Isles in the English Channel." So begins McKinsey Director Richard Foster's excellent book *Innovation: The Attacker's Advantage* (Summit Books, 1986).

The *Thomas Lawson*, a huge, unwieldy seven-masted ship, was the Rube Goldberg-like product the sailing establishment put forth to compete against the new steam-powered vessels that increasingly had taken cargo business away from sail. The last-gasp effort to deny technological advance was futile, of course, and as Foster observed: "The age of commercial sail ended with the *Thomas Lawson*, and steamships began to rule the seas."

It's been over a decade since Foster wrote his book, yet the *Thomas Lawson* still sails among us. The affliction I call the "Thomas Lawson Syndrome" is the tendency for organizations to tenaciously prop up current products, services and processes in the face of technological advance that often spells the obsolescence of what the organization is currently protecting. By hindering managers from discarding the old technologies and embracing the new, the Thomas Lawson Syndrome prevents organizations from transcending the status quo and looking ahead to the future.

The Syndrome can afflict any firm, but it is especially pernicious among organizations with successful products and enviable balance sheets. Foster describes how Du Pont clung to nylon, its cash cow, in the early 1960s, despite the scientific evidence that a new product—polyester—was superior for tire cords, and despite the fact that Goodyear, its leading customer, had publicly come out in favor of polyester. Meanwhile, Celanese, a competitor whose position in the tire industry was small relative to Du Pont's, faced far fewer internal barriers to polyester. Celanese had no nylon investments to protect, no nylon tire-cord facilities whose cost had to be justified. Nor, I suspect, did Celanese have managers and researchers whose career success, reputation and egos were tied to nylon. While Du Pont poured R&D money into improving nylon, Celanese—unencumbered by its past—began to turn out polyester tire cord. The product was quickly adopted by tire manufacturers, and within five years Celanese had captured more than 75 percent of the market.

Think about this history lesson: The market research was clear, the test data were clear, the technology was available, and Du Pont had the resource base befitting a market leader. Logic would predict that Du Pont would quickly adapt to market realities and blow Celanese out of the water.

But the Thomas Lawson Syndrome is an insidious disease. It blocks both logic and vision. It causes managers to tenaciously cling to the geese that laid yesterday's golden eggs even as the geese are reaching the end of their life cycles. Consistent with the Du Pont-Celanese case, MIT's Jim Utterback found that in 32 of 34 companies he investigated, the market leader " ... reduced investment in the new technology in order to pour even more money into buffering up the old."

Even when market leaders are not closed to new advances, the Thomas Lawson Syndrome paralyzes their ability to apply them. Researchers Arnold Cooper of Purdue and Clayton Smith of Notre Dame note that even " ... where established firms enter threatening young industries, they do not pursue the new product aggressively, and they continue to make substantial commitments to their old product even after its sales begin to decline." Researchers attribute this trend only partially to lack of technical expertise. The more significant causes are internal politics, managers' comfort zones, habit and the need to justify sunk costs.

Thus, even though Du Pont "explored" the possibilities in polyester, the result was inevitable. The difference between "exploration" and "commitment" is the difference between market failure and success.

I recently reviewed two cases cited in *Jumping the Curve*— IBM and Time, Inc.—and realized that both had their roots in the Syndrome. In the 1980s, IBM labs produced breakthroughs in microprocessors and PC software, but as one pundit observed: "IBM had all the technology ... but they fell back reflexively protecting their own mainframe world." Peter Drucker, in fact, noted that "top management [of IBM] practically forbade the PC people to sell to the potential mainframe customers." The Time case, in turn, showed that the Syndrome can emerge when managers' comfort with an existing process or technology blinds them to new business possibilities. Prior to the Time Warner merger, Time, Inc. was undervalued by $6 billion, a phenomenon which many Warner people found perplexing. One Warner executive told me that with CNN and HBO, Time had the muscle to dominate the emerging information and entertainment sectors, "but Time management grew up in print and saw the world in print. They didn't understand the revolution in technology."

Along these lines, the Syndrome is notorious for blinding even "creative" people to the revolution in technology. Seymour Cray's dogged persistence in pursuing a next generation Cray-3 supercomputer was questionable because the machine was obsolete while still on the drawing board. The massively parallel processing architecture offered by companies like Hitachi, nCube and Tandem is cheaper and offers greater performance potentials than do the "big iron" products that Cray once innovated.

Apart from the blinders it puts on vision, the Thomas Lawson Syndrome induces operational tactics that are guaranteed innovation-depressors across the board. When the Syndrome is in effect, for example, it is not uncommon for the in-house champions of the new technology to be required to report to defenders of the old guard. This step not only deflates the morale of the champions, but also ensures that aggressive product development and marketing will be undermined by entrenched powers who feel threatened by the change.

Thus, the polyester proponents at Du Pont were apparently required to report to the heads of the nylon division, and transistor activities at RCA in the 1950s were placed under the "helpful" wing of the vacuum tube division. In both cases, the old-guard dominant group slowed the machinery by continually calling for still more studies and still more evidence. The result was perpetual delay and deflation of entrepreneurial spirit.

Even when champions are not officially required to report to the old guard, they are often placed in a subservient position within the organization's political pecking order. In the 1980s, Motorola's in-house bias toward its successful 68000 microprocessor led to top-level decisions that guaranteed insufficient budgeting, staff and visibility to proponents of the faster, simpler reduced instruction set computing (RISC) technology. The fact that the champions of the new technology lost numerous internal battles to defenders of a successful older one led to a significant delay in Motorola's RISC introductions, which in turn led to major customer defections to vendors including Intel and Sun Microsystems.

Unsurprisingly then, the Thomas Lawson Syndrome often causes those who appear to be best positioned to get into a new business to actually be among the worst. This often yields huge opportunities for new-entry competitors and entrepreneurs who are burdened with less old baggage.

Companies like Apple Computer and Sun Microsystems were born because their founders became frustrated at trying to sell concepts like personal computers and workstations to established firms whose roots and profit margins were embedded in products of the past. The Chicago upstart CCC Information Services has grown to well over $100 million during the past decade by leapfrogging over existing technologies in the auto collision estimating market. While much larger established competitors were content to "continuously improve" the traditional print mediums ("blue book" and "red book" auto value publications) and manual systems (adjustors filling out and mailing spec sheets), CCC introduced a set of entirely different service paradigms. With computerized used-car databases and collision-estimating software systems that operate on portable computers, CCC has significantly reduced errors in data transmission, turnaround time, and clients' fixed costs.

The CCC story is important because it shows that the Thomas Lawson Syndrome is just as applicable to service industries; just ask CCC's competitors. Consider a few of the ominous technological challenges (and opportunities) looming over the horizon for other service companies. Overnight mail deliverers are experiencing painful dents in their revenues because of fax, e-mail and Web delivery. Insurance brokers, car dealers, stock brokers and travel agents are realizing that advances in information technology are such that many of their services can be duplicated by smart customers who can access the same database and come to their own informed conclusions. Universities are seeing interactive computer and telecommunication technologies as well as electronic self-paced learning options begin to obsolete much of their traditional class-lecture formats. Airlines are concerned that rapid improvements in teleconferencing capabilities may preclude the need for some current business travel.

Middlemen in a wide variety of distribution chains are learning that their old-boy connections and customer service skills don't count for much in the face of Electronic Data Interchange, which eliminates the need—and expense—of many of their current services. Ad agencies' traditional delivery formats in TV commercials and magazine spreads may soon be rendered ineffectual by digital interactivity.

What all this implies for service providers is a call to abandon the *Thomas Lawson* ship. It is a call to seek and absorb the opportunities inherent in new technologies. This is nothing less than a call to re-create the business with the kind of cutting-edge technology-driven services that really add value to tomorrow's customers.

That is a tough but necessary challenge for any leader in any business. As noted earlier, even when companies are in distress and *know* they must change, the Thomas Lawson Syndrome induces either paralysis or "more of the same" responses. At troubled Eastman Kodak, "continuous improvement" of the core film photography business may be necessary for surviving, but it is surely insufficient for thriving. The company's salvation is much more likely to result from breakthrough applications in digital imaging. The challenge for CEO George Fisher is to scuttle the *Thomas Lawson* and get his crew to focus on the fast-moving technologies in the electronics field while, simultaneously, creating support structures (manufacturing, distribution, marketing) for those efforts. The talent and technology is already within Kodak; the challenge is to overcome—you guessed it—the dreaded Syndrome.

On the other hand, if the organization is prosperous, the Thomas Lawson Syndrome can be doubly insidious, for it sabotages even the desire for change. Apple Computer, the company that made computers cool and the term "user-friendly" a non-oxymoron, became fat and happy by the mid-1980s. The snazziest technology, the most recognizable brand name, and the sweetest margins in the microcomputer business all conspired to generate complacency and arrogance.

Accordingly, the operating system went without a major rewrite for years and, in a disastrous decision by then-CEO John Sculley, Apple refused to license its technology to non-Apple clones. Why share the crown jewels? Why fix it if it ain't broke? But had the company done so, Macintosh technology would have become the universal PC standard and Windows 95 would have been stillborn long before reaching market.

For the last few years, in the post-Sculley era of Michael Spindler and Gilbert Amelio, Apple has been tightening costs, streamlining processes, pruning payroll, and fine-tuning current products. All well and good, but then what exactly do you do to really grow your business? At this point, both customers and investors are none too optimistic; Apple's market share and stock value has languished, and a slew of its more renegade managers and designers have left for greener pastures.

Ironically, the company that Apple used to mock in the 1980s—IBM—has been making a steady turnaround over the last three years. The reason is that under Lou Gerstner's helm, it seems to be confronting the Thomas Lawson Syndrome head-on. No more stuffed-shirt self-importance, no more smugness in responding to small startups and alternative technologies, no more clinging to old habits and past glories.

The lesson is clear. When executives believe they are impervious to market realities, or when they start believing their own press hype, the emergence of the Syndrome is a sure thing. Today's numbers are a reflection of yesterday's decisions; tomorrow's numbers are a reflection of today's decisions. There's always a delay in the marketplace, and actions that led to success today may not lead to success tomorrow. Fighting tomorrow's battles with yesterday's successful products and services is not a prescription for corporate success, regardless of the organization's size or reputation.

NB: As of the final printing of this book (July 1997), the dissatisfied Apple board had let Gilbert Amelio go.

Of the 1980 Fortune 500, 230 (46 percent) no longer even exist, in large part due to their anachronistic responses to the pressures of relentless free-market forces. Small wonder that Peter Drucker has argued that one of the deadliest of business sins is "slaughtering tomorrow's opportunity on the altar of yesterday."

So I leave it to you: Is your company sailing the *Thomas Lawson*? If so, are you ready to lead the call to abandon ship?

Hindsight is 20/20. It's easy to look back and recognize that wooden sailing ships couldn't stand a chance against iron-hulled steamships. But what about the technologies that are sailing along today, unmindful of their nimbler, more futuristic competitors? What follows is a story of two businesspeople who aren't afraid to abandon ship. Regardless of the industry we're operating in, we can learn valuable lessons from them.

"You don't need a weatherman to know which way the wind blows," Bob Dylan sang years ago. The changes in society, economics, technology and politics—which seem revolutionary to us when they do happen—are not sudden at all; the forces that caused them existed long before the actual changes occur. Just as we can hear the vibrations on a train track before the train comes into view, the emerging phenomena around us are perceivable to those willing to stretch their comfort zone and step out of the paradigm in which they currently reside.

I.   Mr. Turner, Meet Mr. Kuhn.

Consider this example. In the 1970s, three TV stations—CBS, NBC and ABC—owned nearly 90 percent of the viewing market. The news was delivered at 7 p.m. in half-hour segments by venerable anchormen including Walter Cronkite and David Brinkley. Billboard advertising executive Ted Turner was astute enough to take seriously certain societal changes that those in the television world did not. First, the traditional family unit was fraying. With two parents working to support often-blended families, there was less time to dutifully gather around the TV set to watch the 7 p.m. news.

Second, people increasingly wanted news and information on *their* time schedule, and in whatever locale their jobs and interests might take them. In other words, any time, any place. Third, the advent of cable was a potentially serious threat to the near-monopoly status enjoyed by the Big Three. One could argue that in view of these demographic and technological changes, Turner's decision to launch CNN in 1980 was a prudent risk, not the insanity that conventional wisdom derisively labeled it at the time.

The real question is, why didn't the established companies launch these innovations themselves? Why didn't ABC, for example, create a 24-hour news service? Why didn't NBC unroll an all-information alternative viewing option? Why didn't CBS aggressively pursue the cable market? One would assume that the giants could easily preempt any move by a pesky outsider like Turner. One would even assume that the big boys, by virtue of their formidable market presence, financial strength and technical know-how, would be more likely than any newcomer to pilot a new product in a new delivery system.

In fact, the opposite occurred. In most cases, big market positions yield entrenched thinking, as I noted in describing the Thomas Lawson Syndrome. Big players are no smarter and no dumber than new entrants. The problem is that they are burdened by historical baggage: the psychological comfort of the status quo and the financial necessity to justify sunk costs. Moreover, even though yesterday's market conditions may be entirely different than today's, and even though tomorrow's opportunities may diverge from today's conventions, established companies like to point to (that is, cling to) prior successes with the current products as a reason for maintaining a dogged commitment to them.

This commitment is so pervasive that even when they do enter young industries, established companies do so almost reluctantly, without a full-court press. As noted earlier, IBM labs turned out important breakthroughs in microprocessors, microcomputers and PC software in the early 1980s, but the company's "soul" remained firmly entrenched in mainframes, allowing feisty newcomers like Apple, Compaq and Microsoft to aggressively capitalize on the new developments. Likewise, Smith-Corona's "soul" remained in typewriters, even in the face of a 10-year trend toward computerized word-processing. The company eventually came out with a series of computer-like typewriters—curious, clumsy hybrids with limited appeal—thus hastening the demise of that venerable organization.

Back in 1962, Thomas Kuhn predicted this phenomenon in his classic book *The Structure of Scientific Revolutions* (University of Chicago). Kuhn is the scholar who introduced the concept of paradigm shifts to the public consciousness. How and when paradigms change is virtually impossible to predict, Kuhn said, but who changes them is almost invariably the young or newcomers to a field. Why? The young and the new are not burdened by the mental constraints that limit the vision of those whose successes have been built on the past.

Like the child in "The Emperor's New Clothes," it is often the newcomer's innocence that is his or her greatest asset. At Xerox's Palo Alto Research Center in the 1970s, scientists were creating the precursors to today's PC (mouse, icons, miniature screens, keyboards) for in-house usage. The corporation higher-ups, applying conventional financial projections, could not see commercial application of these contraptions that would justify capital investment into the unknown. It was young outsiders like Apple co-founders Steve Jobs and Steve Wozniak who had the passionate vision that these innovations could one day be shaped to form the dominant tool on everyone's desk.

According to Kuhn, decisions on whether to stay or leave a paradigm are usually not based on data per se (else Xerox would have inaugurated the PC revolution). Further, says Kuhn, choosing how we look at a given paradigm is often not a matter of appealing to deductive proofs and rigorous methods. Instead, our decisions, and how we see a given situation, are based on the weight we place on certain values, or what philosopher Hans Gadamer calls our "prejudgments."

In 1980, the television veterans were not able to transcend the prejudgments that had brought them success. That is why they ridiculed Turner when he launched CNN. They couldn't move beyond the awareness that the forces which brought them to power no longer had monopoly status: Divorce rates were up, both parents were working, cable television was diversifying the viewer's choices, people wanted more news and information than one-half hour every 24 hours, and they didn't want to wait until 7 p.m. to get it. Of course, all these trends were public knowledge; the TV veterans had access to the same information and technology that Turner did. The difference was the way they saw, interpreted and acted on the data. As Kuhn noted, by clinging to paradigms that no longer represent reality, defenders of the old are often left to the side.

Like Ted Turner and Steve Jobs, Federal Express founder Fred Smith and McDonald's founder Ray Kroc were able to use existing paradigms as jumping-off places for further progress. Each of these individuals had less commitment to defending the old system than organizations such as CBS, IBM, the U.S. Postal Service, or the old-time funky hamburger joint. They realized it is not by repeating the tried-and-true, but by making new choices given all the available knowledge, that ensures progress in their field. Choosing and innovating are rational activities that challenge rather than refine an old paradigm.

Naturalists have verified that within any species, certain ambitious animals are constantly roaming from their adapted environment, stretching their comfort zone to take up homes where they don't traditionally reside. Guided by what could be best described as vague desire or curiosity, some coyotes will go too far north, some mockingbirds too far south. They stay, they adapt, and in time a new breed emerges.

Wired magazine editor Kevin Kelley, in his book *Out of Control* (Addison Wesley, 1994), describes how one species of finch learned to pick up a cactus needle to poke for insects. The finch opened up a new niche for itself and ultimately for its species. Like the coyotes that sniff out new areas to live in, or birds who test the limits of new behaviors, business innovators create change that affects a whole population. Kuhn notes that while the aesthetics of a recent development " ... often attract only a few scientists to a new theory, it is upon those few that its ultimate triumph may depend."

II. Mr. Kuhn, Meet Mr. Gates.

It's official: Microsoft has teamed with NBC to create an all-news channel. Folks at Fox are doing the same. Well, welcome to the party, 15 years late. These are all exceptional companies, but the key to business success is defining the market by being first with something ground-breaking—not waiting until all presumable kinks have been worked out by someone else and then assuming that one can make a leisurely entrée into the field by virtue of one's name. In fact, there's a certain arrogance in presuming that just because one is a master in one business, one can take over another.

If I were a CNN executive, not even the magic moniker of Microsoft would be enough to make me shiver. I have the utmost respect for Microsoft and its chairman. Nevertheless, free markets have a way of cutting everyone down to size, and until recently, Microsoft has been as much a prisoner of its own paradigm as the big TV stations were 15 years ago.

The most significant development in the world of software—and arguably in the world of business as a whole—is the Internet and its graphical subsidiary, the World Wide Web. In the face of this development, the paradigm that has fueled Microsoft's phenomenal success from its inception is slowly crumbling. In fact, Microsoft's paradigm over the past decade can be broken down into five basic "old realities:"

1. Programs and word processing packages are written for a particular kind of hardware (say, a Mac) and operating system (say, Windows 95). Customers are forced to choose sides among differential and incompatible standards.
2. Once they make a choice of standards, customers are locked into purchasing a constant stream of upgrades and ever-beefier packages from their vendor of choice. They find it necessary to buy new hardware at regular intervals to handle the advances in the software.
3. The vendor has to pour substantial resources into building compatibility into new products. Microsoft, with an installed base of 100-million computers on Windows, has to invest big bucks—and lots of program code—to insure that each Windows upgrade is compatible with its predecessor. Those costs are built into pricing and marketing.
4. Computers are "personal," products are proprietary, vendors act alone, the marketplace is individualistic, hostile and combative.
5. Product development is a secretive, under-wraps, two-year affair at best (Windows 95 actually took four years). Customers, held captive to the vendor's current product, wait breathlessly for the unveiling of the next; competitors, their cries of "foul!" notwithstanding, simply fall back because they can't keep up.

Under this paradigm, Bill Gates' initial Internet strategy was pretty straightforward: attach on-line access to existing Microsoft products, methodically develop new "bloatware" (ever-expanding upgrades and features), assume that Windows customers will dutifully sign up for a proprietary Microsoft on-line service, shield development efforts from outsiders, and systematically knock off any competitors. Unfortunately (for Microsoft, anyway), Silicon Graphics CEO Ed McCracken was correct when he declared that "the Internet is subversive." In the new world order, initially spearheaded by Netscape, Sun Microsystems and Oracle, the counterpoints to premises 1-5 above are becoming the realities of the new paradigm:

1. Commonality in standards is the name of the game.
2. You can buy what you want, when you want it, right from the Web. Often, you can download it for free.
3. Compatibility is not as consequential as it used to be.
4. Personal computing becomes social computing. Collaboration is "in."
5. No more captive audiences, no more two-year product development cycles. It's all public and ongoing.

Gates, who has admitted to being blindsided by the new realities, quickly backpeddled from his initial strategy. Microsoft found itself in a hitherto unthinkable position of having to play follow-the-leader with the likes of previous unknowns such as Netscape and previous non-factors such as Sun. While one can never discount a company that owns 80 percent share of current operating systems software, many agree with Eric Schmidt, who argued when he was chief technology officer at Sun that Microsoft would not be able to achieve similar dominance in the emerging Internet world: "It's a very different beast. The strategies and tactics that worked so well in the PC markets are not strategies that work on the Internet." We shall see what strategies Schmidt uses to tame the Internet beast now that he has been tapped to be CEO of Novell.

III. Mr. Gates, Meet Mr. Turner.

What, then, finally causes the defenders of the old paradigm to move?

Often, states Kuhn, they don't; they slowly die off. Those who succeed re-create their existing paradigms before somebody else does. In the words of McKinsey consultant Richard Foster, the winners challenge and change the existing order rather than protect the existing cash flows.

For practicing managers, the paradox is to deal with today's reality—pleasing investors, meeting payroll, improving current products, serving customers—and simultaneously listen to the approaching train. But be forewarned: It is very difficult to straddle two paradigms simultaneously. This is a lesson that many established companies—from Eastman Kodak to Xerox—are grappling with. Kuhn says that full commitment, with a risk of being wrong, is the price of significant scientific advancement. The more entrenched a company is in old routines, the harder it will be to take on that full commitment and fully capitalize on new possibilities. The ability to even see the emerging forces in a field often seems to be inversely proportional to one's investment in that field.

Ultimately, one must choose, for today's paradigm-maps should not be mistaken for permanent "reality." The key for leaders and organizations is to encourage the qualities of flexibility, adaptability, open-ended learning, risk-taking, creative thinking and personal responsibility so as to capitalize on the forces that are all around us, rather than staying comfortable with what is familiar.

If any established company can do it, Microsoft can. Some observers think it already has. Bill Gates is driven by his acute awareness that no software company in history has ever pioneered two revolutions.

What about CNN? In the face of new competition from myriad entertainment, software and communications titans, will it also be able to abandon the paradigm that brought it fame and fortune and thereby reconstruct tomorrow's reality?

We'll know the answers soon, for in his joint venture with NBC, Mr. Gates formally meets Mr. Turner in the marketplace arena. The software genius who loathes being second in anything will confront the iconoclast who commented on Fox Chairman Rupert Murdoch's decision to unroll an all-news channel: "I'm looking forward to squishing Rupert like a bug."

I don't know how the final outcome will pan out, but for us customers at ringside, it'll be a very, very interesting show.

COMMITMENT 3:
GO BEYOND TRADITIONAL
COMPETITIVE WEAPONS

Going beyond conventional wisdom requires going beyond traditional strategic weapons. Let's start with competitive analysis. Sure, competitive analysis will help you track your rivals' movements. But if you truly want to leapfrog the competition, don't rely on the data as the cornerstone of your competitive moves. If you do, you're relegating your company to being just another bland face in the crowd. Here's why:

"When Blockbuster and IBM announced last spring that they'd developed technology that would allow record stores to make their own CDs, therefore bypassing the traditional record distribution system, the recording industry huffed and puffed about how they hadn't been apprised of the development." So began a lead article in the *Gavin*, a trade publication in the radio and record industry.

Two quick questions, if you please: Why should those huffers and puffers have been "apprised" of anything in a free market? And, more important, why didn't those big recording labels—supposedly the elite group with all the prerequisite connections and "core competencies"—brainstorm this development on their own and develop the new technologies and alliances themselves?

The first question is rhetorical, of course; but I'll attempt to answer the second. The record companies focused their attention on each other's movements to such an extent that they became oblivious to the possibilities of radical new delivery systems and the innovative movements of nontraditional competitors who were prepared to quickly capitalize on them. "Competitive analysis" of each other's strengths, weaknesses and management decisions mesmerized the record labels into acting as if the traditional distribution system were inviolable.

"What's to stop customers from one day making their own CDs, paying for and pulling digital information off satellites, cables or fiber-optic lines and using laser printers to spit out a CD jacket," asks rock critic Ben Fong-Torres? Indeed, what's to stop artists like Madonna or the Rolling Stones from completely bypassing the record companies by recording their own songs, putting them on the Net, and allowing consumers to download what they want and pay for it electronically?

The answer: nothing! Anything's possible in today's wild world of business. The gumption of entrepreneurs coupled with the 24-hour electronic flows of capital they can access worldwide means that competitors suddenly turn up out of nowhere, and traditional barriers to entry in any business fall like bricks in an earthquake.

All this is why I confess to a mixture of surprise and amusement when I read reports that conclude, as one did recently, that "competitive analysis is the cornerstone of effective strategy formulation and implementation." It ought to be anything but the cornerstone.

Effective strategy formulation and implementation relies on concepts like uniqueness, differentiation and standing out in a very, very crowded marketplace. Ineffective strategy formulation and implementation relies on concepts like imitation, caution and blending in with the rest of the pack. Competitive analysis does a great job in fostering the latter.

Let me say right up front that I have no problems in performing a quick, occasional scan of what today's competitors are doing. That is just plain prudent management. It ought to be done sparingly—but yes, it's a good thing to do. The problem is that executives can easily wind up sinking big resources and becoming hypnotized into tracking the movements of today's "official" competitors—who themselves are often lodged in yesterday's solutions for yesterday's customers. And when all these gyrations start seriously influencing strategy, the end is in sight. New sources of competition (read: opportunities) become slighted (the way Digital Equipment and IBM reacted to microcomputers, software and related services in the early '80s), or they become treated with arrogance (the way the Big 3 TV networks treated the emergence of Fox, TNT and other cable companies).

Let's face it: If one assumes that the 1960s' and 1970s' corporate world of mainframes and centralized MIS will go on forever, then IBM's decision to continue focusing primary attention on the actions of other mainframe providers made perfect sense. And if one assumes that the 90 percent market share held by the Big 3 networks in the 1970s would go on forever, then their single-mindedly obsessive concerns with imitating each other's programming and promotions also made sense.

But the world doesn't stand still for one second anymore. Great news for consumers; spooky news for vendors. Think about it. You're a successful record label executive. Your marginal costs on making CDs are near zero, and you get to sell the doggone things for a nice, fat $15 a pop (even more abroad). You not only do a regular analysis of your competitors, heck; you know many of them personally. It's a nice club. Comfy. Predictable. And then out of the blue, huge storm clouds emerge, threatening to capsize everything you and your familiar competitors have built.

Back in the 1960s, American tire companies—all bias-ply producers—concentrated so much on each other that they were blindsided by the powerful left hook coming from Michelin and its radials. A few years ago the Baby Bells, having so carefully analyzed the movement of other local telephone providers, wound up—in the words of one business publication—"shocked" at the first indications of the AT&T-McCaw Cellular merger, a marriage that would allow the steadily increasing number of cellular users to bypass Baby Bell lines (and the $14 billion in access fees) altogether. Meanwhile, AT&T analysts initially had no earthly reason to track oil hauler Williams Company until one day they woke up to learn that Williams had decided to use their pipelines to carry fiber-optic cables, thus immediately becoming an important participant in the phone wars.

What I'm driving at is that traditional competitive analysis is often short-sighted in depth, range and possibility. This is true even in the very definition of "competitor." The world of radio, for example, is so fragmented that if a station gets 5 percent Arbitron share (meaning that 95 percent of potential listeners choose not to listen), the general manager is hailed as a hero.

What, then, should a radio station consider as a "competitor"? Other radio stations having the same format—country, classic rock, jazz, etc.? Other radio stations in any format? Perhaps any other source of information, education, diversion and entertainment—including TV, audiotapes, movies, reading, theater, tennis? Other technologies (like Web venues and CD-ROM) and distribution systems (television and videocassettes) that can serve as alternative means for record labels to get new releases out to

potential listeners? To an increasing number of concerned, visionary radio people who are thinking about tomorrow's ominous realities, the answer to all of these is an urgent yes.

Similarly, who should a large bank consider as a "competitor"?
Other big banks, both domestic and foreign? Small regional banks
that offer speedy, specialized community-based services?
Brokerage and financial services firms like Merrill-Lynch (which not
only offers secured loans but is a giant in the world of mutual funds,
money market funds, personalized financial portfolios and investment banking)? General Motors, whose GMAC financing division is
one of its few truly profitable entities (leading British philosopher
Edward de Bono to comment that General Motors is really a bank
that uses cars as incentives)? AT&T, whose joint venture with Wells
Fargo on the Mondex electronic purse card is aimed at setting the
standard for on-line Internet payments? Individuals themselves,
who as a result of disintermediation no longer require the services
of banks to access money market funds? Currently unknown,
totally unanticipated sources of competition?

The answer to all these questions is, of course, *yes*. And banks
can also be a source of new competition to non-bank institutions;
many banks have entered hitherto alien sectors of brokerage, personalized financial services, mutual funds and insurance.

Whether it's radio, banking or anything else, how could you
possibly analyze all conceivable competitors, even if you actually
wanted to? Ex-IBM Chairman John Akers once remarked that IBM
has about 50,000 competitors. If one considers that IBM has
20,000 partnerships in every pocket of the world in the computer-
electronics-telecommunications-education-entertainment arena,
50,000 competitors sounds about right. Conducting and analyzing
scans on each one of those competitors sounds suicidal to me,
especially when, like weeds, new ones are sprouting as you read
these very words.

What all this means is that if you're spending a lot of valuable
time tracking your competitors' movements, you're not only running
in circles, but you're probably paying too much attention to the
wrong guys. It's the folks that you can't track—the ones that don't
exist yet either as competitors, or even as companies—who are
your real problems. That's because they're not worrying about
tracking you. They're moving ahead with new offerings, redefining
and reinventing the marketplace as they go along.

Glen Tullman, the ex-president of CCC Information Services, which appeared from nowhere in 1980 and revolutionized the auto collision estimating market, is quite blunt: "We didn't want to imitate our competitors. We wanted to change the rules of the whole game." As described earlier, CCC did, with radical new software, networks and decentralized technology that upended the traditional manual and mainframe approaches that had been the industry norm for years—and in the process took away significant revenues and market share from venerable established competitors 10 times CCC's size.

In summary, seeking future organizational success while wearing the glasses of conventional competitive analysis is, at best, myopic. It is tantamount to driving a car on the highway looking side to side at "competitor" cars while ignoring the road ahead. At worst, it influences an organization to imitate the movements of well-established players that are unknowingly becoming obsolete. Thus, those who argue that competitive analysis is the "cornerstone" of successful strategy are simply dreaming.

Of course the successful organization conducts brief periodic environmental scans that include what today's official competitors are doing, but the primary attention is on doing whatever it takes to lead the race. The blinders of competitor analysis limit our capacity to capitalize on the vast unchartered terrain before us.

Like the hypnotist who mesmerizes people by having them follow the pendulum-like watch, competitive analysis hypnotizes us to look only side to side, back and forth, and even worse, makes us believe that what lies ahead is the same as what we're looking at back and forth, back and forth, back and forth. ...

As long as we're barbecuing sacred cows, let's look at market research. Just as traditional analysis amounts to studying competitors' cars on the same stretch of road, market research amounts to so much time spent looking in the rearview mirror. Take the case of Mercedes-Benz.

In 1900, Mercedes-Benz completed a market research study that "estimated that worldwide demand for cars would not exceed one million, primarily because of the limitations of available chauffeurs," notes social commentator Stewart Brand. But by 1908, the Model T had democratized the automobile and by 1920, more than 8 million cars were rolling on the roads of America.

Relying on market research for strategic decisions and product ideas is like driving a car while looking only at the rearview mirror. Market research is always a step behind. It provides yesterday's solutions to today's problems, or today's responses ("conventional wisdom") to tomorrow's opportunities. This is why Mercedes-Benz came up with the market findings it did, and why over the past decade so many companies with huge market- and consumer-research budgets—including Digital Equipment, GM and Kmart—produced reams of reports and still managed to misread the tea leaves.

The radio and TV industries obsessively fit this description. These brutally competitive businesses are haunted with every nuance of every number. The data of Nielson and Arbitron surveys determine stations' programming, promotions, investments, and peoples' career prospects. Yet critics, myself included, have argued that these obsessions stifle creativity and perpetuate bland "me-too" similarity among stations. Program directors and general managers in radio, for example, are frustrated at having to subjugate their industry experience and creative instincts to a "research-based" playlist that does little but provide a financially unstable, angst-producing, 3 percent market share (the norm) for their stations.

Does this mean I would throw out all market research? No, of course not. But use it cautiously. It should supplement but never replace peoples' intuitive judgment and sense of creative experimentation. At its best, market research taps into user preferences and desires given what they *currently* know and expect of the industry. To make business decisions based on market research leaves organizations struggling along with the pack of known competitors, offering variation-on-a-theme products and service. Logic dictates that vendors provide what consumers "want," and consumers "want" what they're accustomed to wanting based on past experiences. It's a vicious, self-perpetuating cycle.

The *Economist* has editorialized that "carmakers are among market research's biggest fans, as the dull similarity of modern cars testifies." Breakthroughs in the auto business have almost uniformly deviated from the conventional wisdom tapped by market research.

MIT's Peter Senge quotes one Detroit executive who commented, "You could never produce the Mazda Miata solely from market research. It required a leap of imagination to see what the customer might want."

Similarly, designer Hal Sperlich initially couldn't sell Ford on the concept of the now-wildly successful minivan, and thus moved to a more receptive Chrysler. His experience led him to note a fundamental flaw in Detroit's product development paradigm. Market research probed likes and dislikes among existing products: hence executives didn't believe there was a market for the minivan because the product didn't exist. "In 10 years of developing the minivan, we never once got a letter from a housewife asking us to invent one. To the skeptics, that proved there wasn't a market out there," said Sperlich in *Fortune* magazine.

At 3M, one of the major roadblocks to the release of the Post-It notepad was none other than the marketing department. Nobody was calling up the company asking for semi-sticky little yellow pieces of paper, and nobody would have known what to do with them if asked in a research sample. Therefore, there was no hard data suggesting a viable market for them. Today, along with paper clips and staples, Post-It notes are one of the most commonly used office products. 3M's capacity to crank out new product applications, including Post-It greeting cards, calendars, stationery and trainers' sheets, helps the company generate a cool $600 million in a market they invented and that nobody asked for.

The movie *MASH* and the television programs *All in the Family, Hill St. Blues,* and *Cheers* were all characterized by two things: negative initial viewer reactions and a dogged commitment to those programs by producers Robert Altman, Norman Lear and Stephen Boccho. (I have always liked business start-up specialist Philipe Viller's definition of entrepreneurism: "Unreasonable conviction based on inadequate evidence.")

If one counts the TV spinoff and residuals, *MASH* made more money for 20th Century Fox than any other single movie made for any studio—well over $1 billion. Yet according to Robert Altman, the only reason the movie wasn't buried at the outset is because he dragged Richard Zanuck to a sneak preview, where a wildly excited audience of 1,200 people belied the lukewarm results of the research sample. Sums up Altman: "I always say that *MASH* wasn't released. It escaped."

Market research does have some value. It can provide a snap-shot overview of the current lay of the land, which can be useful in periodic small dosages. If you're a retailer, assessing the age and income demographics surrounding a current or potential locale is good common sense. If you're a ski resort operator concerned about dwindling baby-boomer visits, tracking the tastes of young snowboarders becomes a prudent step. If you're a Ben & Jerry's, monitoring the changes in peoples' ice-cream preferences à la fat content becomes essential.

During a recent visit to Israel, I noticed highway billboards and magazine pages blanketed with Pepsi-Cola ads. Pepsi was moving aggressively to end Coke's stranglehold in the Israeli cola market. The ads featured young, virile men and women in military fatigues, because market research had indicated that Israeli youths admired young, virile soldiers. It made perfect sense to gather and apply these data in product promotions.

However, there was nothing unique or proprietary about the data; they were available to Coke, and for that matter, any vendor of any product who did market research in Israel. But if everyone is accessing the same data and if those data are driving the busi-ness, then "me-too" strategies, promotions and products are inevitable. Vendors become indistinguishable from one another, fighting desperately for ephemeral bits of earnings and market share, and in the process blinding themselves to breakthrough possibilities.

That is why market and consumer research have the same lim-itations as public opinion polls. "[Polls] simply rediscover conven-tional wisdom, which is a blind alley," says economist Jude Wanniski. An organization that wants to strategically differentiate itself from the pack cannot be satisfied with a reliance on conven-tional wisdom. It must strike out boldly in unchartered areas—even if the initial unfamiliarity and discomfort on the part of the con-sumers yield negative market research results.

With research models and computer technologies becoming more sophisticated and more readily available, many managers will be highly tempted to base critical decisions on "the data." Apart from the problems already listed, the danger with this approach is that one becomes "market driven," and thus simply reactive. When this occurs, preparing for tomorrow's opportunities is sabotaged, for as consultant Tom Kelley points out: "Research can only reveal what people like and dislike today, not what may appeal to them tomorrow."

Even worse, an over-reliance on research means that "latent needs" and "deep discovery" don't surface. These are important concepts. Peter Senge argues that for competitive success, "companies need to understand and meet the 'latent needs' of the customer—what customers might truly value but have never experienced or would never think to ask for." Market research simply cannot access these sorts of needs effectively. For this reason, a Boston Consulting Group partner urged audience members at a conference I attended in Oslo, Norway, to move toward deep discovery. "Deep discovery starts where traditional market research stops," he said.

Quality guru W. Edwards Deming once noted caustically: "No customer ever asked for electric light or photography." And customers didn't line up en masse demanding CD-ROM and desktop publishing, either. Originally, most of today's customers of these products and services didn't even know they "needed" them.

Intel Chairman Gordon Moore—whose company supplies the microprocessors to most of the 100 million PCs on the globe today—confesses that as late as the mid-1970s, he was asking, "'What is a personal computer good for?' And the only answer was that a housewife could keep her recipes on it. I personally didn't see anything useful in it."

Thus, my advice is simple. Just as you have to look in the rearview mirror occasionally when you drive, so do occasional market research as you feel you must. Analyze the data quickly. Discuss aggregate trends quickly. And don't take the findings too seriously. Concentrate instead on the vast unchartered road ahead. Concentrate on tapping into "latent" opportunities and offering exciting products and services that exceed customers' expectations. Concentrate on moving ahead of the pack and defining the market-to-be. Concentrate not on reacting to markets, but in creating them. This means don't be led by customers; lead them. It means don't be market-driven; drive the market. In short, go beyond market research.

Here are four points to ponder if you're serious about vaulting over the potential pothole of market research:

1. Use research primarily to monitor people's reactions to your innovative actions *after the fact*, not as a means to determine

what products and services you should launch. TCI and GTE test-market their new digital formats in selected venues. Makes sense. Similarly, executives at Benetton, MCA Music, Rubbermaid and Seiko eschew traditional market research. Instead, they solicit quick consumer feedback on merchandise and features that they have already introduced. The feedback allows them to quickly make revisions in product features and provides valuable information to move to the next step.

The advice, therefore: Concentrate less on market research and more on factors like quick flexible design and manufacturing, and on corporate cultures where pilots replace proposals and action replaces hyper-analysis. Within that context, some *quick, post-hoc* market research—short feedback loops—can be very helpful as a means to monitor progress. Keep in mind that at Seiko and Benetton, not all launches are successful, but their systems and cultures have dramatically lowered the cost of failure while simultaneously boosting the returns on successes. It's all a question of getting your organization focused on tries—more tries, more successes.

2. Have people focus on the market, not on market research. Peter Drucker notes that the reason that the Japanese took the lead on fax machines is because they did not ask what market research said about the machine itself. Rather, they asked themselves, "What is the market for what this machine does?" The market gives alert managers clues every day. *The Miami Herald's* successful Spanish language spinoff *El Nuevo Herald* emerged as a result of clues about demographic shifts in southern Florida, not because market research told managers that subscribers would buy a sister newspaper.

3. Insist that everyone on the payroll get involved with lots of "naive listening" to customers as an official part of their job requirements. (More on this in Commitment 14.) Then provide mechanisms—from open dialogue to newsletters to groupware—that allow people to share their impressions and come up with ideas for product and service innovations. The key to naive listening is not to ask customers, "Would you buy this?" or "Would you buy that?" The key is to hang out with them on project teams, on-site visits or in bars, if that's where you'll find

them, listening to their issues and problems, noticing what frustrates them on the job, staying alert to what they get excited about, and observing what they wish they had to make their lives easier. By doing this, you'll get plenty of food for fresh creative ideas, you'll know what they'll respond to before they themselves do. Companies as diverse as Interim Services (healthcare), Intuit (software) and Weaver (popcorn) function this way.

A final payoff of good listening is that you'll start reacting to customers as individuals, not as "markets." By building relational databases, as Banc One and Mirage Resorts do, you begin the process of transforming "market research" to "person research." (More on this later.)

4. A few years ago, I asked Tom Peters about his thoughts on market research. His reply is worthy as a final piece of advice: "John Sculley came to Apple after having the job of president of Pepsi-Cola. [Pepsi-Cola] is absolutely driven by the most infinitely minute market research. Yet Sculley's comment was, looking back at his career at Pepsi-Cola, that he had never seen a good marketing decision that was made based on the data. Sure, you need the data. Sure, you read the data from the systemic market research. But at the end of the day it is a very, very healthy dose of intuition that leads you to invent something that's a little bit special. ... You have to have the guts to try things that are a little bit different."

In short, remember that market research is, at best, simply one of many tools in the arsenal of an effective manager. Don't ever let the numbers replace entrepreneurship based on hands-on feel for the market. If numbers alone were adequate for business decisions, software would replace leadership. Thank goodness that's not the case.

> *Now let's look at that sacred cow of management, strategic planning, which provides neither steak nor sizzle. How can we set the table in anticipation of a tomorrow unlike anything we've swallowed thus far in our history? One solution may be the most radical step of all: Replace traditional strategic planning with high-precision strategic conversation.*

Let's start with the bad news. Read it and weep.

- "No battle plan survives contact with the enemy." *(General Colin Powell)*
- "A good deal of corporate planning ... is like a ritual rain dance. It has no effect on the weather that follows, but those who engage in it think it does." *(Brian Quinn, Dartmouth)*
- "Strategic plans are forecasts of historical trends and rarely anticipate new opportunities." *(an Arthur Andersen director)*
- "If you start planning, you blind yourself to opportunity." *(Harry Quadracchi, Quad/Graphics)*
- "Business plans may be great for bankers and investors, but if companies really followed them, you might never have heard of Compaq, Lotus or Ben & Jerry's." *(Inc. magazine)*
- "Tonight, I'd like to tell you about strategic planning at General Electric or, more specifically, why we no longer do strategic planning ... " *(Lawrence Bossidy, at the time a senior vice president at GE)*

You get the drift. Traditional strategic planning is harmful. It's rigid. It's static. It's overly complicated. It's detached. It's uninspiring.

It's also arrogant. The assumption is that smart, degree-studded people armed with software and algorithms can forecast the nonlinear discontinuities of the future in a linear systematic manner. Nobel laureate Frederich Hayek called this assumption "the fatal conceit" of managers. Writing in the *American Economic Review*, Hayek argued that "economists must understand that the complex phenomena of the market will hardly ever be fully known or measurable, unlike most of the factors that determine events observed in the physical sciences."

Most managers will ruefully agree with corporate intelligence expert Herbert Meyer, who noted that "no sooner do you conclude what the prevailing circumstances are than your conclusions begin to lose their validity." The reason is simple: The planning process relies on certain premises about technology, capital markets, competitors, customers, cash flow, inflation, market value, sales, geopolitics—all of which may be appropriate today but irrelevant tomorrow.

That, by the way, is why another pet premise of strategic planning is false: the idea that endless analysis of current data will somehow yield brilliant predictive insights and groundbreaking decisions. In fact, the opposite occurs: The mountain of analysis invariably yields vanilla "me-too" strategies. Analysis is a useful tool for any rational manager, to be sure, but researchers like McGill University's Henry Mintzberg have persuasively argued that it is creative synthesis—of information, resources, people's creativity and commitment—that makes the difference in terms of successful strategic action. In other words, it is collaboration, teamwork and collective entrepreneurship that generate business success.

As flawed as strategic planning is, its execution is frequently worse. Planning is often done by one of three groups: corporate staff groups who are out of touch with the fluid, day-to-day realities faced by line managers; top managers who themselves are out of touch with the prevailing realities faced by "real people" in the trenches; or conventional assembly-line consulting firms that are out of touch with everyone but still manage to crank out a pseudo-customized boilerplate, which guarantees that the client's strategy will be basically the same as everyone else's. Regardless of the source, the final "plan" is then hierarchically imposed on everyone else, generating neither commitment nor understanding within the organization. It soon gathers cobwebs on a shelf anyway.

But the damage it does before it hits the shelf can be mind-boggling. Writing in the November 1993 issue of *Fast Company,* Mark Fuller notes: "Think of it as Joe Stalin visits corporate America." Once the ringing commitment to meet the goals of the "plan" are heralded, the fun begins. Continues Fuller:

"Companies then decompose pieces of their strategy into separate projects and assign them out to different people in different places—people who have never worked together, never even met each other. In fact, these people were hired, promoted, motivated and rewarded in ways that trained them not to like each other, not to trust each other, not to help each other, not to speak to each other. They were trained not to work together."

Is all this depressing enough? It ought to be. Strategic planning as we know it is as sacred a management cow as one can imagine—and it can be downright dangerous to your company's health. Well, never fear, because the good news is right around the corner.

Back in 1985, McKinsey's Frederick Gluck showed prescience: "Management by remoteness, management by the numbers, and management by exception are dead. Management by involvement is in," he wrote in the *Journal of Business Strategy.*

Why involvement? Because as Ticketmaster CEO Frederic Rosen says: "The only rule to the '90s is how innovative can you be." Innovation does not come from any one "plan," nor solely from a few people sitting in top management suites. Innovation is an all-hands, everyday effort, regardless of whether the "boss" is around or not.

If you take this notion seriously, then you will accept the idea that a culture of innovation occurs when every person on the payroll transcends his or her current role in order to assume the role of "businessperson" or "owner." This means that people approach their work activities as if they owned the business. Which, in turn, means that every person takes on the responsibility not of performing a fixed, static job, but of adding value to the organization.

Thus, strategic planning done by a select few is yesterday's paradigm. In the new paradigm, strategic thinking and execution become the job expectations of everyone. Each individual "comes to work" with the goal of thinking of opportunities, and seizing opportunities, in the arenas of cost reduction, product enhancement, quality and service improvements, niche marketing and new sources of revenue growth—and then working collaboratively with like-minded souls to develop those ideas and take action. The question now is: How do you create such an environment?

My suggestion: First and foremost, start visualizing strategy as *conversation.* Imagine strategy not as a plan but as a process: a perpetual set of conversations aimed at developing an exciting, coherent, ever-evolving "motion picture" of the organization and the business. *Exciting, coherent* and *ever-evolving* are the operative words for describing the strategy of the leapfrogging organization:

1. *Exciting*, as in: What can we do that's world-class and market-dazzling? How can we execute it in such a way that we "knock the socks off" of customers and investors?
2. *Coherent*, as in: How do we maintain a clarity, commitment and consensus among all hands as to our priorities, values and directions?
3. *Ever-evolving*, as in: How do we ensure that our priorities, et al., do not stagnate? How do we insure that we move and change as quickly as the marketplace does?

The answers to these three questions reside not in a strategic plan, but in *strategic conversation.*

Your conversation is your picture, your picture is your strategy—and it's never complete. To do this, you'll need to address three issues with your team(s): purpose, uniqueness and values. The list on these pages encompasses some questions that you can draw on to stimulate the discussions you will hold.

AMMUNITION FOR LEAP-FROGGERS

Purpose

1. Why do we exist? Why should we?
2. What is our purpose?
3. What exactly is the business we're in? Now and three years from now?
4. Who exactly are our customers, or intended beneficiaries? Now and three years from now?
5. Who are our competitors?
6. What, specifically, are the changes (domestic and global) in technology, capital structures, demographics, socio-political trends, and science that we must be especially attentive to?
7. What are we doing to stay abreast of and capitalize on the above changes?
8. How do we define "success"? How should we?
9. How will we know we are succeeding or failing over the next two to three years?

(continued next page)

10. What, if anything (our structure, our culture, our habits), is preventing us from moving in the right direction? What do we need to do to change?

Uniqueness

1. How are we different from any other organization?
2. What's unique and special about our organization?
3. In what unique way do we add value to our customers? How do we amaze them? What benefits can we offer them that will allow us to sharply boost our share and returns in the future?
4. Why should customers come to us rather than to any-one else?
5. What are we better at than anyone else?
6. What are we doing today to ensure that we remain bet-ter and unique?
7. What, if anything (our structure, our culture, our habits) is preventing us from moving in the right direction? What do we need to do to change?

Values and Norms

1. What do we stand for? What is our philosophy?
2. What are the values we should live by?
3. What do we really care about?
4. What are we striving for? Who do we serve?
5. How do we define success? Now and in the future?
6. How will we behave toward one another and toward our customers and partners in the process?
7. What do we need to do to ensure that we can all rally around a common purpose and common values?
8. What are we doing to ensure that our behavior, systems and processes are aligned with our values and ideals?
9. How have we changed our roles and behaviors as a result of this process? How should we change them?
10. What, if anything (our structure, our culture, our habits), is preventing us from moving in the right direction? What do we need to do to change?

These questions are meant to fuel problem-solving conversations that you—the leader—drive and orchestrate. The discussions are open and freewheeling, but you're at the helm. You push and direct the process. You demand commitments and accountabilty. Your priorities are coherence, excitement and evolvement vis-à-vis the big goal lines (strategic priorities, business imperatives, corporate philosophy) and the broad sidelines (financial, legal, ethical, cultural) that everyone plays in. The discussions define the "business game," which means that your people must be fully aware, and involved, in the financial, strategic and ethical "rules of the game" (more on this in Commitments 5 and 6). The discussions are a mixture of pragmatism and business theory. They instill in people a common purpose, language and viewpoint.

As Arie de Geus, former chief planner at Royal Dutch/Shell has noted, the real purpose of effective strategy is not to make plans but to change people's "mental models." The conversations I suggest can provide a framework to evaluate alternatives and make the strategically "right" choices every day as they quickly create and capitalize on new opportunities.

Most important, these discussions are not a one-shot deal. They're ongoing. You do them with cross-disciplinary and diagonal slices of the organization. You periodically invite partners, lead users and key suppliers as bona fide participants. You insist that your direct reports follow your lead. This is crucial because, as a group, you need to constantly refine your direction, address problems and build ongoing consensus so that people's strategic thinking and entrepreneurial action are in alignment with the strategic "motion picture."

"What!" you say. "Repeat the same discussion over and over?" No, I mean you initiate strategic conversations over and over, not the "same" conversation repeatedly. Create your own questions. Choose among the questions from the list as appropriate. Adapt them to your needs; for example, perhaps your concern is two to three months ahead, not years. Use the conversations as a vehicle to explore business issues, generate "best bets," probe alternatives, applaud commitments, critique decisions, bless new initiatives, share learning, address implementation problems. If, after all this, you find yourself having the "same" discussions, you know nothing new or interesting is happening in your organization. Which means you're in deep trouble. You want your organization bubbling with creative ideas and audacious pilots.

If this process generates a charter, a mission, a vision statement or even a rough document called a "plan," well and good. But these things are not end products in themselves because there is no end product. They are simply temporary by-products of a never-ending chain of conversations.

Keep in mind that I am not calling for "democracy." Conversation is not an excuse for putting strategic options up for ballot-box voting. Nor is it another word for "employee involvement," though clearly, involvement is central to any legitimate dialogue. Leaders must still lead. You, the leader, have the responsibility to drive the conversation and focus mindset. What conversation allows is to generate reality checks on everyone's thinking (including yours), collectively ponder alternatives, clarify ambiguities, confront inconsistencies, gather ideas for execution, challenge the process, pinpoint accountability, heighten excitement and perpetually raise the ante.

Some will find it difficult to accept this idea. They are still wedded to the notion that strategy is a document, or that strategy is somehow their private fiefdom. To them, I say: Change or perish. Other doubters will insist that, at the least, big-ticket corporate strategy—like acquisitions, alliances and asset management—must remain a top-level domain.

Why? If you can't talk about—and justify—big-ticket corporate strategy with your general managers (and their direct reports) using the questions on pages 53 and 54 as a reference guide, then I am frankly suspicious about your company's use of shareholder investment.

In sum, your job as a manager and executive is to initiate perpetual conversations about strategy, which then create the arena for people to proactively implement the fruits of their discussions. Strategy is exciting, dynamic and organic, just like business. And if you want people to act as businesspeople and think strategically every day, you drive the conversations in that spirit. Do it with sincerity and persistence and, trust me, your payback will be huge: a wealth of ideas, opportunities and initiatives that will yield organizational transformation and market leadership.

COMMITMENT 4:
VIEW THE WORLD THROUGH BIFOCAL LENSES

Ever wonder why otherwise well-meaning managers focus on quarterly results to the exclusion of tomorrow's needs? Ever wonder why everyone is in favor of vision exercises, but nothing ever seems to get accomplished? Maybe the reason is a lack of "bifocal" vision. Consider the following:

My colleague Chip Bell tells me that when he was growing up on a Georgia dairy farm, one of his chores was to herd the cattle in the evening. In order to be successful at this, he had to learn bifocal vision, that is, he had to acquire the capacity to monitor each and every one of the cattle while in the midst of them while simultaneously looking ahead to where he needed to move them next.

The young farmboy can teach us a lot. Management gurus tout the importance of vision for leadership, and one cannot argue with that. But vision as it's usually presented—unidimensional, static, overgeneralized—is not enough. In order to really help the organization meet today's business requirements and prepare for tomorrow's, vision must be pragmatically and unabashedly bifocal: it must simultaneously paint a picture of the opportunities today and the "best bets" of tomorrow—and, when push comes to shove, it must prioritize the latter.

In *Jumping the Curve*, Nicholas Imparato and I briefly introduced the concept of bifocal vision. Since then, I've come to realize that we underestimated its importance. Here's why:

To meet responsibilities to today's customers and investors, the leader must insist that today's products and services be continually improved and perfected. At the same time, in order to successfully prepare for responsibilities to tomorrow's customers and investors, the leader must insist that the company aggressively pursue the development of tomorrow's products and services—which means investing in riskier ventures that draw budget away from existing procedures and cash-cow outputs. It is a simultaneous process:

building on the status quo while de-emphasizing it in pursuit of bigger opportunities.

It sounds paradoxical, if not schizophrenic, but the symptoms of bifocal vision are demonstrated in a number of successful companies. The $3-billion Rosenbluth International (3,500 employees, 1,000 offices in 40 countries) improves today's travel agency business with better telecommunications processes and customer service. Simultaneously, it is fast-forwarding into tomorrow's travel business, where customers will do much of their own bookings via the Internet. Rosenbluth has already taken the lead in developing cutting-edge software and Web-based tools that allow corporate and individual customers to create—alone and in tandem with Rosenbluth—the cheapest, most customized travel packages on a real-time basis.

MCI and Telecom Finland Ltd. prudently invest in improving their long-distance market via technology upgrades. Yet both these companies recognize that their dominant product—wired, long-distance voice transmission—is rapidly becoming a low-margin commodity, and that the future of the business is in high-speed, high-band width digital network products like ATM (asynchronous transfer mode) as well as applications which can integrate the output of the most advanced PC's, phones, pagers, conferencing tools, and wireless communication systems. That's where the serious capital and attention are now invested.

Walt Disney Co. invests in improving its flagship theme parks, and, despite some EuroDisney disappointments, the company is planning to build new and better parks, both domestically and abroad. Simultaneously, the company is relentlessly applying its core skills in entertainment to a broad array of integrated niches, including movies, athletics, children's online software and services, TV, cable, and video entertainment, arenas that Disney executives expect will offer even greater opportunities tomorrow.

Personally, I find the idea of "bifocal vision" appealing. I'm skeptical of all the hype about "vision" and the mega-consulting industry it has spawned. All too often, "vision" becomes a chic buzzword that leads to pleasant corporate retreats facilitated by nice consultants, resulting in fluffy overgeneralized statements that adorn company walls and have little impact on management decision making.

Bifocal vision is more gutsy, earthy, dynamic and utilitarian. It requires managers to address today's business realities while they position themselves for tomorrow's. It requires daily discipline in looking at now and looking ahead at the same time, at interpreting events, choices and decisions in terms of their impact on today's prerequisites and tomorrow's bigger picture expectations. It's an active everyday nonstatic process rather than a one-shot deal.

In practical terms this means that you—the leader—should insist that every important meeting agenda, document and decision should explicitly consider dual impacts: On today's marketplace, and also on tomorrow's. Whether it's product development, marketing, personnel or capital budgeting—all should be approached bifocally. Before you hire or promote that individual, or spend the money on that particular project or acquisition, make sure you can justify how the decision helps you succeed today, and—even more important—how it will help you succeed given tomorrow's realities.

At first, your people will complain: "How am I supposed to know how decision XYZ will impact tomorrow's customer?" Insist, then, that they do over-the-horizon thinking beforehand. Insist that they pay attention to what Gary Hamel calls the "discontinuities in technology, lifestyles, work habits or geopolitics that might create opportunities to rewrite the industries' rules." And then—and only then—come to a decision today.

This is not easy stuff. It requires a great deal of practice. The paradox of bifocal vision is that it requires attention to the "now" and the "later" at the same time. It can be done, but it is a competency that does not occur naturally; it must be learned as a discipline. The micro-dynamics of bifocal vision are akin to what professional foreign language interpreters call "shadowing," the skill necessary to listen to a speaker's comments and translate them right now while simultaneously listening to what he or she is saying a few sentences ahead. Interpreters have to master this challenge by initially learning to "shadow" another speaker's comments in their very own language even before attempting to do it with two languages in play. Try it, and you'll see that the skill is devilishly tough to learn. Unsurprisingly, shadowing demands lots and lots of practice. So does bifocal visioning.

Wayne Gretzky is not the biggest, strongest or fastest player in the National Hockey League, but he is arguably its greatest player ever. According to consultant William Carey, Gretzky was once asked the reason for his success. Here is a player who obviously must concentrate on the rapid movement of the puck every moment of the game, yet he replied: "When I get on the ice and play begins, everyone else on the ice goes where the puck is. Me? I go where the puck is going to be."

In an eerie parallel to that sentiment, a newspaper story recently described Microsoft's Bill Gates as someone who not only administers a business efficiently but, more important, " ... is a master at knowing where the market is going and getting there first." Whether it's hockey or software, those who view vision and strategy through bifocal lenses strike gold.

I predict that leaders who intend to leapfrog their competition will find the practice of "bifocal vision" more relevant than "vision" alone. It won't be easy. It's much easier to participate in a one-shot vision exercise. It's much harder to do daily bifocal visioning. But if a hockey player and a Georgia farmboy can learn to do it, I think the rest of us can too.

GIANT STEP II:

FLOOD YOUR ORGANIZATION
WITH KNOWLEDGE

In the book *President Kennedy*, author Richard Reeves describes how John F. Kennedy and Soviet Premier Nikita Khrushchev would argue over the relative merits of communism and capitalism. They were not alone. For 40 years after World War II such arguments were commonplace. Today, of course, we know the final act of the drama: Adam Smith won and Karl Marx lost. Yet I submit that within the din of this argument and the aftermath, a subtle but crucial fact has quietly emerged: Many of the traditional arguments among economists of all persuasions, then and now, have become increasingly irrelevant.

The reason is that the traditional building blocks of economic analysis—land, labor and capital in particular—have become less salient in a world of business and commerce that can best be described as brain-based. Today, knowledge—or, more colloquially, expertise, intelligence, imagination and ingenuity—is the key determinant for economic and business success. The most important factor of production in an economy is no longer the interplay of land, labor and capital that Kennedy, Khrushchev and the rest of us haggled over. Likewise, the key success factor of an individual business enterprise is no longer its sheer size or the number of tangible assets it controls. In both cases, the critical factor is knowledge.

The concept of *knowledge* leaves many managers uninspired. It's a very intangible, soft concept, and conventional thinking in economics, accounting and finance emphasizes the hard, tangible "stuff": size, physical assets, balance sheets—all variations of the land, labor and capital theme.

Of course, for years we have seen evidence that undermines the premises of conventional thinking. We've seen, for example, a stampede away from vertical integration in favor of downsizing, outsourcing and partnering. We've seen small underfunded resource-deficient companies significantly outperforming venerable giant firms on any yardstick (compare returns and growth rates of the Fortune 500 with those on the Inc. 500 and the Forbes 200). We've seen small countries with few natural resources outperforming big resource-rich countries (compare the fortunes of Singapore, Taiwan and Hong Kong to those of Nigeria, Russia and Bolivia). We've seen asset-tiny companies like Microsoft attaining a stock market value exceeding asset-huge companies like Boeing and Eastman Kodak.

We've seen exceptional growth in so-called "mundane" companies like Rubbermaid and Coleman because of their ability to apply knowledge. Rubbermaid, a company in the exotic world of garbage cans and dustpans, cranks out one nifty new product per day. As one observer noted, "Rubbermaid is not a rubber company. It's an innovation company." Similarly Coleman offers more than 100 different models of ice coolers in numerous color combinations and sizes—and has the capacity to quickly vary the design or color of a cooler to meet specific retailer needs either domestically or internationally. We've seen new spinoffs attain market presence by their ability to apply new knowledge to familiar products. The value-add of Lucent Technologies, for example, becomes its ability to take discrete commodities like voicemail, e-mail and fax and bundle them into a single unified message system that is both cost-effective and convenient to the customer.

We've seen the market valuation of companies in general grow to a significant multiple of their book value because of soft, intangible reasons variously defined as goodwill, brand equity, corporate reputation, market potential, quality of management, and so on.

For the organization that leapfrogs the competition, this entire discussion is crucial. As Thomas Stewart notes in his book, *Intellectual Capital* (Doubleday, 1997), it is people's capacity to excel in tasks like sensing, judging, creating and building relationships that define the most valuable assets of the organization.

Hence, as Imparato and I first pointed out in *Jumping the Curve,* the size of the organization's "body"—its tangible assets, its personnel size—is less important for competitive advantage than the size of its "brain"—its collective value-adding intelligence and expertise.

Now, let us go a step further. All other things being equal, I propose that the bigger an organization's body size, the less likely the possibility that it can leapfrog *anything.* That's basic physics. The priority for any organization, therefore—even successful large corporations like GE, AlliedSignal and Rubbermaid—is perpetual weight loss and brain gain, a continual pruning down of sheer mass and crusty hierarchical structure, and a continual expansion of the knowledge base.

Writing in *The New York Times* on February 12, 1997, Thomas Friedman captured the spirit of this discussion: "As globalization gives everyone the same information, resources, technology and markets, a society's [*author's note:* or organization's] particular ability to put those pieces together in the fastest and most innovative manner increasingly separates winners from losers in the global economy."

All this has significant implications for your organization, for the question now becomes: How do you create an organization that is characterized by the kind of knowledge-richness and knowledge-in-action that will provide the fuel to leapfrog the competition? Visualize, if you will, an organization with a steadily growing "brain"; with a body-structure so light and fluid that it is no longer constrained from jumping over competitors whose bodies are encumbered by the weight of fixed assets and sunk costs. The leapfrogging organization obsoletes the traditional model of organization, which revolves around the premise of big body/little brain.

The conventional big body/little brain premise is represented in the omnipresent organizational pyramid, including all of its current "progressive" variations. When all is said and done, knowledge is still primarily concentrated and hoarded at top management levels and among specialized professional staff. Think about where expertise (high-end technical, functional, strategic thinking) and information (profit-and-loss data, policy and systems analysis, strategy and business development) really resides. Think about where the decision making authority and accountability for initiating innovative decisions based on that expertise and information *really* resides. You know the answers, and I've illustrated them, and the alternative, as follows:

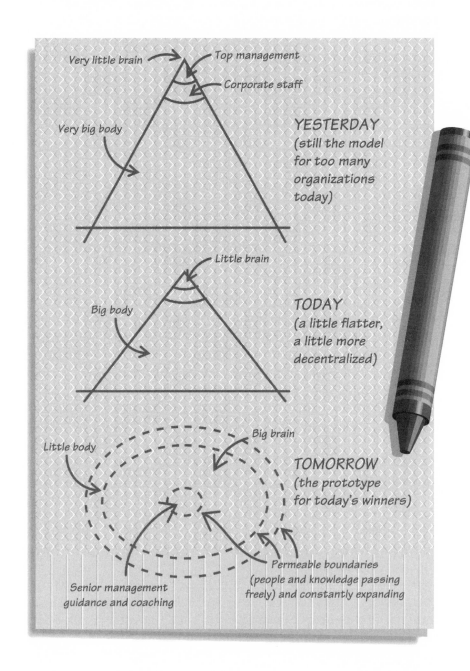

Very little brain → Top management

Corporate staff

Very big body

YESTERDAY
(still the model for too many organizations today)

Little brain

Big body

TODAY
(a little flatter, a little more decentralized)

Big brain

Little body

TOMORROW
(the prototype for today's winners)

Permeable boundaries (people and knowledge passing freely) and constantly expanding

Senior management guidance and coaching

Obviously, these three models represent gross stereotypes, but the point they make is real. Leapfrogging organizations move away from big body/little brain and toward big brain/little body. They understand that the successful organization of tomorrow is no longer automatically the one which acquires the most land, labor and capital. Rather, the successful organization of tomorrow (read: today) is the one which can continually harness and augment knowledge.

In the race for market share and profitability, there is an increasing awareness that "smart organizations" are the horses to bet on. Companies as diverse as Buckman Labs, Chaparral Steel, Oticon, Physician Sales & Service, Quad/Graphics, Springfield Remanufacturing and VeriFone instinctively connect to this big-brain metaphor. That's why for them, training and job enlargement is *de rigueur*, because everyone on the payroll continually expands their skills, contributions and responsibilities in order to help the organization attain its mission and goals.

Everyone has access to information, expertise, learning opportunities, fast decision-making authority, and accountability. Information and data that were previously hoarded now become dispersed; people with ideas freely cross permeable boundaries within and beyond the organization. Expert systems, electronic databases, and open telecommunication systems proliferate.

Whoever or whatever function is in the organization is part of the big brain—the core competency, knowledge-growing, value-adding part. Otherwise, it is sourced to outside partners or it is eliminated entirely as value-detracting. Non-brain body weight is kept to a bare minimum.

The manager in this kind of organization is no longer a "boss"— it is self-defeating to put an artificial cap on knowledge. Nor is he or she an "organizer"—knowledge changes so rapidly that it quickly obsoletes any structure or system that has the slightest whiff of permanence. Nor is he or she an empire-builder—in a hierarchy-less, de-massed organization, playing power politics and even attempting to hoard talent and information for self-aggrandizement becomes downright absurd.

Likewise, employees are no longer order-takers who expect good things to occur if they keep their noses clean. In fact, those sorts of people are the first ones downsized in a brain-based organization because, as Xerox executive Barry Rand declared to his people: "If you've got a yes-man or yes-woman working for you, one of you is redundant."

In this section, we will see that organizations that leapfrog their competition use knowledge in two ways: One, they understand that a perpetual flow of great ideas depends on people's capacity to freely access knowledge. Hence, they deliberately smash barriers to the free flow of knowledge—barriers such as multiple management layers, narrowly focused functional silos, rigid job descriptions, numerous sign-off requirements, obsolete technologies, meager training, and corporate cultures marked by secrecy and one-upmanship.

Two, they liberate employees to harness and use knowledge in order to create fresh value for customers and shareholders. In this environment, employees continually grow their knowledge base, use state-of-the-art information technologies as their servants, take on an attitude of "how would I act if I owned this business?", and take full accountability for the rapid decisions they're encouraged to make at all times.

Flooding the organization does not mean drowning people with paper and data. It means having an enormous wealth of knowledge for people to access as they see fit. Flooding the organization with knowledge gives people the fodder to use intelligence to perpetually transform corporate processes and products—and thus transform organizations in such a way that they can leapfrog the competition.

Flooding your organization with knowledge means that you turn your organization into a big brain/small body entity that can more easily vault over heavier competitors. In short, it means creating an organization where *mind* matters more than anything else. In order to achieve this Giant Step, you'll want to make two crucial commitments:

- Obliterate current barriers to the flow of ideas (Chapter/Commitment 5), and
- Don't empower your employees; liberate them (Chapter/Commitment 6)

Obliterating current barriers to the flow of ideas will require courage and persistence, for these barriers are the sacred cows of many organizations. Commitment 5 tells how to do it: First, by carrying out several specific actions that will turn your organization into a hotbed of exciting, value-adding ideas. Second, by creating a corporate culture of openness, such that opening the doors and sharing the truth becomes a business necessity, not merely the subject of Sunday morning sermons.

When barriers are obliterated, decisions are made faster, better and more creatively. But there's even greater payoff: Employees become more powerful. Knowledge is power. More knowledgeable employees are more powerful employees. More powerful employees make for a more powerful organization—one that can spring over competitors.

Accordingly, Commitment 6 challenges you to go well beyond traditional notions of "empowerment." First, via a "Dear Abby" response I gave to a question posed to me by a reader of my "Cutting Edge" column in *Management Review*, I argue that in the new economy, it's inappropriate to "empower" employees, because that retains the hierarchical mode that serves best to control passive underlings. The trick is to create an environment in which employees make *themselves* more powerful by freely taking hold of knowledge in order to make the cutting-edge decisions that will allow you to leapfrog your competition.

This requires big shifts in how most organizations deal with their people. As we will see, it also requires big shifts in how most organizations implement their technology. The trick is to let the computers—not the people—be the bureaucrats. When computers are bureaucrats, routine gets accomplished faster and without error, leaving peoples' minds free to perpetually figure out ways to help the organization spring forward, and over, today's competition.

COMMITMENT 5:
OBLITERATE BARRIERS
TO THE FLOW OF IDEAS

There are many reasons to obliterate barriers in organizations, but the main one is that by doing so, you morph your organization from a hotbed of internal politics to a hotbed of ideas. Knowledge is power, and people who share knowledge can create incredible things. With that precept in mind, here's how to create a "power-full" organization.

When he was chief financial officer at ARCO, Ron Arnault delivered the following challenge to a group of fast-track managers: "The challenge is to do something different. What are the new value-creating ideas? All I can tell you is, if we don't come up with them, the competition is going to get nastier."

Arnault was absolutely right—only he didn't go far enough. It is no longer enough to think of organizations as an amalgam of bricks, capital and bodies, but rather a perpetually growing reservoir of ideas. In a brain-based economy, the winning organizations will be those that can generate the greatest number of interesting ideas, take rapid-fire action on them, and then disseminate immediate feedback to everyone so as to generate yet more ideas. By repeating this cycle over and over and over, throughout every nook and cranny of the organization, the organization's intelligence grows, and thus its efficiency, creativity and competitive vigor increase as well.

I propose that the best predictor of a company's future earnings is its capacity to generate, consolidate and use ideas from every possible source: employees, customers, suppliers, partners, outside experts and myriad databases. In a knowledge- and brain-based organization—that is, an organization that is continually growing its idea base—managers always ask two related questions: How do we develop into an organization where everyone has access to, disseminates, uses, creates and applies the knowledge of ideas? And how do we develop into an organization where ideas flow and grow freely?

Managers who are interested in turning their organizations into a bubbling, churning cauldron of ideas can do so by applying five basic principles.*

1. **Spread information everywhere.**

   The goal of Principle No. 1 is to create an environment where everyone can quickly access any information needed for rapid, creative decision making. Immediate availability is essential. The charge for you, the manager, is not to carefully, benevolently filter out information to people. Nor is it to overwhelm people in a deluge of paper and data. Rather, the key is to create an environment where a huge wealth of knowledge and information exists, and is available to people to draw upon, and add to, as they see fit.

   Consistent with the notion of "open-book" management, everyone must have immediate access to "real" information: strategy updates, income statements, balance sheets, sales and quality data, and current status of customers, suppliers and partners. The quicker that people can access critical information on their own, without having to depend on the goodwill of others, the faster they can add to the idea pool, and the more innovative their decisions will be.

   Companies that spread information everywhere draw from a wide range of both high-tech methods (group software, local area networks, expert systems) and low-tech methods (interactive newsletters, bulletin boards, face-to-face interchanges). These provide employees the tools, resources and authority necessary to obtain and use information effectively.

   Information equals power. When information is spread everywhere, people become more powerful, which means the organization becomes more powerful. It should not be surprising that at a successful high-technology firm like Sun Microsystems, all information (from product line to consumer

---

* For those who are interested, these five principles are presented in some depth in my video "Mind Matters," distributed by CRM Films in Carlsbad, California.

feedback to financials) is on the company's intranet and available to any Sun employee.

But I'm more intrigued with Springfield Remanufacturing Corporation, an engine rebuilder staffed primarily by what are traditionally termed "blue-collar workers." CEO Jack Stack's candid goal is to create an organization in which everyone thinks and acts like a CEO. That is why open information is a fundamental strategic priority at the company. Everyone learns to dissect a financial statement that sometimes exceeds 100 pages. Daily operations numbers, weekly income statements and regular cash flow reports are shared and openly discussed. Work teams analyze variances and determine production plans and schedules. The result is that in a mature industry noted for razor-thin margins, Springfield Remanufacturing has turned its balance sheet around and been consistently profitable; as of last year, annual sales exceeded $100 million, earning a $6-million pretax profit, and this year, the company has a goal of $135 million in sales.

2. **Challenge sacred cows in pursuit of bold goals.**
   The goal is to create a corporate culture that is characterized by two attributes:

   - There are no sacred cows other than the most fundamental of corporate mission and values (and even those are examined periodically).
   - Everyone on board sees their charge as continually challenging the existing process in order to strive for quantum leaps in performance and market offerings.

   Dramatic upheavals outside the organization call for radical changes inside. Tweaking and improving the current systems and processes is no longer enough. A "no sacred cows" culture treats everything that is currently done (policies, procedures, structures, methods, meeting agendas) as an experiment. This means that everything is open to challenge, testing and renewal.

   Pewaukee, Wisconsin-based printer Quad/Graphics is a good example of Principle No. 2. A $1-billion privately held company that has an annual growth rate of 10 to 15 percent,

Quad is honored throughout the industry as a cutting-edge benchmark of quality and innovation. As Chairman Harry Quadracchi puts it, "Change is our bread and butter. We see change as our job security. That's why in almost every department of our printing operation, there is virtually no similarity to the way things were running six months ago." Can you say the same about your organization?

To foster this sort of atmosphere, companies that challenge sacred cows follow five "to-do's": First, they encourage everyone to ask "why" questions. Why are we doing things this way? Why are we doing this at all? Would a customer pay us to do what we are doing? Would a customer prefer that we automate it, delegate it, outsource it, or eliminate it entirely? What currently prevents us from doing things that we know we ought to—listening to our customer, collaborating with people in other divisions and other world-class companies, starting a project team, making a decision quickly and then holding people accountable for results?

Second, they constantly shed old goals and set new extraordinary ones. Leaders in these companies set broad decision boundaries (financial, strategic, ethical "rules of the game"); then, within those boundaries, they insist that people regularly set new goals and standards that are bold—even impossible—by current standards. As divisions in companies as diverse as Motorola, Nellcor Puritan Bennett, United Airlines and, of course, Quad/Graphics have found, letting people set "impossible" goals (like a 70 percent reduction in cycle time) becomes possible only if they are allowed the freedom and accountability to revamp existing systems so as to attain those goals. Ordinary goals produce ordinary efforts and ordinary results—a kiss of death in a frenetically competitive world economy.

Third, companies that challenge sacred cows liberate people to take action. Liberating people means enabling them to act, which means getting out of the way and, when necessary, helping people overcome organizational hurdles that currently prevent them from taking immediate action. If employees lack the power to ask tough questions, form an exploratory task force, or visit outside the organization for more facts, the idea pool shrinks. Companies that liberate try to get people to adopt a start-up, entrepreneurial mentality when they look at the business, asking themselves: "what would I do if this were my business?"

Fourth, these companies teach everyone business literacy. Chaparral Steel, Physician Sales & Service, Quad/Graphics and Springfield Remanufacturing teach people how to "keep score." Employees throughout these companies learn the fundamentals of running a business: strategy, cost accounting, systems applications, computers, income statements, market research, statistical process control, how to run a meeting. Whatever the organization's purpose and vision, people must have the skills and expertise necessary to move it toward that end. This is why organizations that try to live Giant Step II place few caps on their investment for brainpower. And that's why Quad/Graphics' employees take classroom education weekly (literally), and why Chaparral Steel workers have the opportunity to take educational sabbaticals to augment extensive in-house training.

Finally, companies that expect people to challenge sacred cows on behalf of bold goals make certain, in return, to challenge their own sacred cows of conventional compensation. Brain-based organizations do not simply pay people to come to work in exchange for a set wage or salary. Significant performance-based variable pay—gainsharing, profitsharing, equity ownership—becomes a key part of compensation. At Chaparral Steel, where productivity is triple the worldwide industry norms, gainsharing is universal and stock ownership is nearly so (over 90 percent), while two-thirds of employees voluntarily opt to allocate portions of their paychecks to buy additional shares each month.

At Microsoft and Physician Sales & Service, the variable pay plans not only attract and retain top talent, but also—as executives in both companies proudly note—create a slew of wealthy employees, from software engineers to truck drivers. At Microsoft, one in 20 employees is a millionaire, and at Physician Sales & Service the ratio is one in ten. Companies like Chaparral, Microsoft and Physician Sales & Service understand that ideas will continue to flourish if employees who invest their brain capital into the company are rewarded with the same spirit as are the outsiders who invest their financial capital.

3. **Create a permeable organization.**

In June 1994, Bob Ulrich, CEO of Dayton Hudson Corporation, sent a memo to the heads of the company's operating divisions and staff groups. In it, he reminded everyone of a primary goal of the corporation, to wit: " ... to create a boundaryless organization where the divisions constantly benchmark each other and encourage the sharing of ideas, successes, resources and people from one operating division to another. I believe that to make our corporation a truly world-class structure, we need to aggressively break down any barriers among divisions, and to create an organization without boundaries." I submit that this commitment to permeability—the easy, smooth in-and-out flow of information, expertise and minds throughout any organizational boundaries—is one of the main factors underlying Dayton Hudson's successes under Ulrich's helm.

Permeable organizations try to minimize boundaries in the first place. They understand that if employees must butt heads against vertical ceilings or functional walls, then information can't easily spread, and the idea pool stagnates. Even those boundaries that remain are not taken too seriously because results are more important than turf or ego. Companies like Chaparral Steel, Enterprise Systems (medical software) or startup Custom Clothing Technology Corporation (a garment manufacturer recently purchased by Levi Strauss) are particularly aggressive exemplars of permeability because they put into action four important prescriptions:

First, they break down adversarial relationships among colleagues and partners into ones based on trust, openness, collaboration and mutual problem-solving. Second, they aggressively flatten the organizational structure because they know that each layer of management simply allows someone to delay, distort and politically massage information before passing it on. Third, they crush functional turfs by redesigning work so that it can be done by interdisciplinary work groups. Fourth, they create an environment where insiders are outside (say, engineers working with customers at a customer site) and outsiders are inside (say, suppliers are invited to work with in-house folks in solving a knotty operational problem). With permeability, traditional concerns like rank, hierarchy and turf become quaint anachronisms. Traditional barriers to information flow become irrelevant. Permeability turns on the spigot to a rapid sharing and cultivation of ideas.

4. **Cultivate a culture of curiosity.**
   In the conventional paradigm, people are hired based on their specific technical skills and experiences. They are expected to contribute within the narrow scope of their job definition, and within the even narrower scope of "here's how we do things around here." Ideas they might develop outside their particular "jobs" are discounted or are plain unwelcome.

   In the new paradigm, the charge for the leader is markedly different: to cultivate an organizational culture that supports universal curiosity. Southwest Airlines, Manco (adhesives), Chaparral Steel, Custom Clothing, Enterprise Systems, and Quad/Graphics have found that the most effective way of doing this is to start right at the beginning: Hire curious people. That is, hire eager-to-learn people, adventurous people, people who question things, people who want to understand, people who aren't afraid to stumble or take risks. The idea, as Southwest Airlines CEO Herb Kelleher insists, is to make curiosity and related attitudes a more important criterion for hiring and promotion than length of resume or service.

   Once they hire curious people, these companies try to keep them curious. They support and reward those who are willing to ask, experiment, stretch boundaries, share learning in teams, and take responsibility for actions. They view curiosity as an appreciating asset. As mentioned earlier, they make serious investments in training, education and development.

   At industrial manufacturer EG&G Electro-Optics Division, creating an environment where blue-collar workers were encouraged to *request* the training they needed was crucial in generating the kinds of grass-roots ideas and initiatives that fueled the company's turnaround efforts. At Manco, employees can enroll in any outside course—business or basket-weaving—and be fully reimbursed as long as they pass. CEO Jack Kahl's rationale is revealing: "It lets people know ... that one of the highest values in Manco is to be curious and allow curiosity to take place."

   Companies that cultivate curiosity make sure "fail" is no longer a four-letter word. They protect curious people. More important, they encourage mistakes as an important part of competitive advantage. Wood Dickinson, CEO of the Kansas-based Dickinson Theatre chain, tells his property managers that he wants to see them making "intelligent failures" in the pursuit of service excellence. Not thoughtless, sloppy mistakes, but the kind of stumbles that occur in the pursuit of innovative "stretch" goals. This philosophy is shared by Stan Shih, CEO of Taiwan-based Acer, the seventh largest computer company in the world. If a manager at Acer takes an "intelligent" risk and makes even a costly mistake, Shih is prepared to write the loss off as tuition payment for the manager's education. Both Shih and Dickinson emphasize the educational element of error. That is why Dickinson argues that it is essential to share the learning points that emerge from the stumbles, so that everyone can benefit. At Buckman Labs and VeriFone, the learning byproduct of errors is welcomed and disseminated electronically. The presence of thoughtful mistakes suggests that people are experimenting with, and learning from, new ideas.

5. **Insist on perpetual learning.**
   Arie de Geus of Royal Dutch/Shell once sagely observed: "The ability to learn faster than our competitors may be our only sustainable competitive weapon." In an organization committed to Principle No. 5, the expectation in the air is that everyone, up to and including the person behind the CEO desk, takes part in continuous learning so as to augment skills and expand thinking—and hence grow the reservoir of ideas.

   Obviously, per Principle No. 4, the organization must do its part by providing opportunities for learning. But the key to Principle No. 5 is that perpetual learning is an individual responsibility. Ultimately, the onus falls on the individual to seek out opportunities for continuous evolvement of the mind.

   The advice is basically this: Don't wait for someone else to hand you education. In the emerging world of flattened, shrunken organizations, career mobility will no longer be found in vertical promotion. Reengineering guru Michael Hammer correctly observes that it will be found in "mastery." I suggest that those who continually master new skills necessary to add value in new ways will have more freedom, more interesting work and better pay than those who simply do a routine set of tasks well. They will also have more marketability should they decide to move on.

The "masters," therefore, will pursue learning. They will enroll in courses. They will volunteer for task forces and project teams to build their skills. They will seek new responsibilities, they will form new networks with people who have different competencies. They will learn from diverse sources, from on-line services to their own mistakes. They will do this without reservation, because intuitively they understand that career growth will depend on their capacity to be a major contributor in a perpetual chain of new ideas. They are determined never to be obsolete, never to rust. An organization that can fan the flames to this sentiment will be the one to bet on in the future.

To view organizations in terms of ideas rather than bricks and mortar is a big challenge. All the companies mentioned above are all in various stages of development in trying to meet that challenge. But try they are, because, to paraphrase ARCO's Ron Arnault, it's the value-adding ideas that will separate the also-rans from those who leapfrog over them. It's safe to say that in the emerging economy of brains, mind does indeed matter.

The best intentions, the most sophisticated technology and the biggest training budget in town will have only marginal impact if your organization's culture sanctions secrecy, distrust and closed-door decision-making. If you want to flood your organization with knowledge, you'll need to create a culture marked by candor and straight talk. Consider these decision-makers who did just that:

I fly a lot in my work. Over the years I've learned to work on airplanes, sleep on them, even enjoy the edited movies on them. But I've got a confession to make. I'm one of the first to get white-knuckled when the plane starts going through what the pilots euphemistically call "turbulence." And therein lies a story, with, I hope, some important implications for leaders who are themselves trying to navigate through the turbulence in their own businesses.

Two years ago I left Copenhagen on an SAS flight to Newark. A few minutes after takeoff, at about 17,000 feet, something interesting happened—*interesting* as in the Chinese curse, "May you live in interesting times." Rather than use my own layman's terms to describe the experience, let me quote from an in-house SAS Bulletin. This document describes an event that had occurred on another, earlier SAS flight, but it was similar to what happened during my flight.

"Just after liftoff ... the right engine stalled twice with a very loud bang and the aircraft yawed violently. ... An EGT overtemp warning was displaced. ... A mayday call was sent and after a short circuit a single engine overweight landing was made."

The Bulletin even had a thoughtful sidebar called "What is an Engine Stall?" Quoth the Bulletin: *"An engine stall occurs if, for some reason, the engine is unable to 'swallow' the air it has ingested. The pressure buildup through the compressor collapses and air is expelled with a pressure wave the 'wrong' way out of the compressor. This is accompanied with a bang and sometimes also with spectacular flames."*

I can do without all that.

But you know what was truly exceptional about this little experience? During the 25 minutes it took us to get back to friendly earth, I was quite alert—to say the least—but surprisingly, I was not nearly as anxious as I have been about a jillion other times on flights that were frightfully choppy but nevertheless completely safe. What made the difference?

The difference was the Danish captain, Ebbe Starcke, who did something unique: During our descent, he never stopped talking to us (in both Danish and English, by the way), never stopped informing us about what was happening. He didn't sugarcoat our predicament, but gave us reassurance that he had things under control. His voice was not detached and mechanical, either; it was genuine and conversational. His demeanor was focused but not panicked. For 25 minutes, until our touchdown, he never stopped communicating—what was happening, what probably had caused the problem (he described and explained every possibility from ice and lags in vane system functions to birds being sucked into the turbines), what he was doing step by step ("you'll notice that I'm banking off to the right; the reason is ... "). Step by step: "Eight more minutes, folks ... four more minutes folks. ... "

By the time we landed, that pilot was our hero. And get this: When we arrived at the terminal, he actually came out to greet us. In fact, he waved us in for a huddle, and a big bunch of grateful travelers crowded around this man, who continued to amaze us.

First, he was genuine. His first words: "Boy, I need a cigarette." Even the hardcore nonsmokers urged him on. Then he told us that the phone calls he had just completed confirmed that over the past few months SAS and other European carriers had experienced some problems with a Pratt & Whitney 4000 model engine that was being overhauled by a certain shop in Zurich. In fact, he observed that similar incidents had occurred twice before (as noted above in the SAS Bulletin that he was kind enough to share with me when I talked to him privately thereafter). He told us that SAS had just grounded all 767s like the plane we were on until the problem was fully rectified. In an industry notorious for outright lying to its customers (any business traveler will know exactly what I mean), Captain Starcke's honesty was a stunning breath of fresh air.

In contrast, I can't tell you how often on other flights I have wished that the captain, silently entombed behind closed doors in an aircraft being tossed and plummeted by fierce winds and lightning, would do what Captain Starcke did—even a little bit. And that made me think. What exactly did Captain Starcke do? Not much, really, except that he opened the doors and told the truth. I felt included, I felt like a partner, I felt "empowered" with information, I felt—strangely enough—loyal to him.

I won't bore you with more of the details, nor will I use more space justifying my decision to fly SAS whenever I have the chance from now on. The point is that the reason I was calm and focused in a dangerous situation is that the leader of our "organization," the airplane, kept all of us informed and involved.

And therein lies the lesson for those of us who want to leapfrog the competition. I believe that one of the most self-defeating actions managers can take these days is to work behind closed doors, literally and figuratively. Closed doors inevitably yield a culture of secrecy, "for your eyes only" information hoarding, and sugar-coated partially-true communication to those outside.

Among the "insiders," closed doors create the delusion that they are in control and in the know, and that their decisions will be quickly understood and eagerly endorsed by those outside. Among the "outsiders," closed doors generate the kind of paranoid fantasies that can paralyze an organization. How often have managers, employees and staff anxiously wondered about the discussions and goings on behind closed doors? "What are they talking about?" or "What do you think they will decide about the budget, the product, the pay scale, the downsizing, etc. etc.?" Closed doors, not surprisingly, create a workforce that feels powerless, alienated from the ultimate decisions, and skeptical about the veracity of the communications— and the communicator—thereafter.

I submit that in a brain-based global economy, where competitive advantage results from an organization's ability to quickly gather, spread and exploit knowledge, behind-the-door behavior— literally or figuratively—is flat-out destructive. It delays, distorts and hence corrupts information and the decisions that are based on it. Where decentralized information technology should allow everyone on your payroll to communicate immediately with everyone else and to quickly access unfiltered information for rapid-fire decision-making, closed-door behavior creates barriers that diminish decision efficiency, accuracy and speed.

In a marketplace where your greatest assets are human beings who take on the mantle of proactive businesspeople concerned with the fate of the entire organization (not just with their job description or their department), a behind-the-door culture diminishes personal accountability in favor of passivity, dependence and a cover-thy-butt mentality. In an environment where collaboration and shared expertise become crucial for market leadership, behind-the-door thinking generates a culture of turfism and egocentric self-aggrandizement. And in a corporate world where credibility is fast becoming both the glue and fuel for the success of any important intervention, be it a product launch, process reengineering, or organizational restructuring, a behind-the-door culture diminishes trust and makes a mockery out of words like "empowerment" and "teamwork."

After my experience with Ebbe Starcke, I can't say whether Danes have a genetic predisposition to openness and honesty, but I find it ironic that the reason I had been in Copenhagen in the first place was to learn more about an extraordinary company called Oticon. This $160-million company has revolutionized the hearing-aid industry and is two years ahead of its competitors, including multibillion-dollar giants Panasonic and Siemens, in product development. With its first-to-market obsession and its cutting-edge product line, which combines state-of-the-art digital technology with fashion-like, multi-hued designs, Oticon boasts more than a doubling of revenues since 1991 and a 10-fold increase in operating profits.

For a company like Oticon, CEO Lars Kolind sees little value in mass production of conventional, low-margin, commodity-like hearing aids ("let the big companies do that," he says). Rather, he sees Oticon's competitive edge as "fast and creative integration of all existing expertise in the field," including chip development, circuitry, anatomics and audiology. Accordingly, the sharing and exploitation of knowledge and information becomes vital. That is why the company organizes itself around multidisciplinary project teams that are so egalitarian and intertwined that Kolind describes Oticon's organization as a "spaghetti structure."

Unsurprisingly, barriers to open communication are nonexistent—literally. For starters, it's not merely that people don't have offices to close doors to, they don't even have desks to hide behind. Yes, desks do exist and each is equipped with necessary materials such as a computer and telephone, but a desk can be and is commandeered by anyone who needs it. Instead of a permanent office, each employee—including Kolind—has a personal caddie cart, which is basically a little file cabinet on wheels. One wheels one's cart to wherever one is working that day—usually where one's project team is gathered—and takes over a desk as needed.

On the day I first met Kolind, he had just returned from a two-week business trip, and he was informed by a clerical person that her team had moved his cart to another floor. Apparently, her team had required the desk he had been using. Kolind shrugged. Business as usual. No closed doors. No hierarchical power trips. No barriers.

Kolind told me that as a result of a joint software development project with Hewlett-Packard and Andersen Consulting, all incoming mail is now scanned into computer and, with few exceptions, anyone can access anyone else's mail, including Kolind's. His calendar is also accessible to anyone; the software allows an individual to seek an appropriate block of time, which Kolind has designated as available. It's not just mail; any document is accessible to anyone. In fact, project teams are encouraged to tap into each other's files whenever possible. Expertise that flows and grows is the key to Oticon's creativity, and Kolind makes sure to nourish and reinforce that process. In his most recent letter to me describing Oticon's progress, he jotted this note on the cover of the annual report: "Don't be surprised. Knowledge-based organizations do work!"

So as I tip my hat to the Great Danes Starcke and Kolind, I wonder why the rest of us don't get it. We're all in constant turbulence and choppy air in our businesses. If we want to leapfrog the competition, that's all the more reason to open the doors and tell the truth. People in your organizations can cope with the truth, however unpleasant. In fact, they hunger for honesty and inclusion. If you're straight with them, they'll help you fix the problem, or help you take advantage of an opportunity. It's not the turbulence that upsets people, it's the feeling of helplessness—of not knowing what's going on behind the closed doors.

So let's stop treating people with condescension. Smash down the barriers, and make a vow that there will be no more secrets. Join with Starcke and Kolind and others who seem instinctively to understand that a commitment to openness and truth is not just the morally right thing to do but, when advances in technology ultimately render secrecy a futile prospect, it's a savvy business thing to do as well.

COMMITMENT 6:
DON'T EMPOWER YOUR EMPLOYEES,
LIBERATE THEM

Flooding your organization with knowledge makes sense only if your people have the capacity to absorb it and the capability to do something with it. Otherwise, your efforts at flooding will simply overwhelm and drown them. What's the leader's task then? As this open letter shows, it's not to "empower" people. The challenge is much more dramatic—and powerful—than that.

Dear Dr. Harari:

I recently received a promotion to be general manager of a radio station. In many ways, it's my first real management position. I find your opinions very helpful in challenging my own thinking about management, but as I take over this new position, I am worried about something. I want to empower my people, but how can I be sure that the decisions they make are the right ones? I can't be looking over their shoulders all the time. What should I do?

Sincerely,
Joe Jones
(name changed)

Dear Mr. Jones:

Your questions are so reasonable that you may be shocked when I tell you if you don't change your thinking right away, you'll be out of a job soon and your station's ratings will be plunging south all the sooner.

There is more to this than meets the eye. For example, what exactly do you mean by the "right" decisions? Do you mean the decisions you would yourself make if you were in their positions? Do you simply want clones of yourself? The right decision made by someone else may be different than the one you would make. It may be more innovative, more up-to-date, more appropriate to the current situation (not the situations you previously dealt with) and more appropriate to the style and capabilities of the decision maker. Giving your people the message that the right decision is *your* decision, or the one *you* would make, is a surefire way to diminish motivation, creativity, accountability and morale.

Let's take it a step further. You're absolutely right that you can't be looking over their shoulders all the time. Would you want to even if you could? For one thing, your people not only have a more intimate bird's-eye view of their immediate environment, they're also probably smarter than you. After all, if you're hiring the best and brightest, as you should be, they are by definition experts in programming, disc jockeying, sales, administration and so on. Why put a leash on their talents? Intel CEO and cofounder Andrew Grove, a brilliant engineer himself in the 1950s, has freely admitted that, given the explosive advances in science, today's 21-year-old engineering graduate knows a lot more than he does. He's happy to hire these young upstarts and set them free to experiment. Not a bad role model if you know anything about Intel's track record over the past few years.

In fact, to be an effective leader, you don't have to be a hero with all the answers, and you don't have to be a cop overseeing clones of yourself. Instead, imagine that your job is to create an environment where your people take on the responsibility to work productively in self-managed, self-starting teams that identify and solve complex problems on their own. If you concentrate on doing this, you'll find that your people will need you only for periodic guidance and inspiration, which frees you to spend your time confronting big-picture, common-fate sorts of strategic and organizational issues. Can you see the opportunities in that scenario?

With all this as a background, let's now get down to the nitty-gritty: the "empowerment" thing. Look in the mirror, and ask yourself how sincere you really are. Can you see that your comment, "I want to empower my people, BUT ... " is a self-canceling phrase? I hear that big "BUT" all the time, and that BUT is why the word "empowerment" has turned into a slick, glib, hypocritical concept in many organizations: Managers say they're committed to empowering people, but the people who are supposedly empowered know it's a con.

I'll wager, Mr. Jones, that you are a responsible adult who raises kids, pays the mortgage or rent on time, buys clothes and food and other consumer goods, participates in community affairs, plans vacations and in general is a responsible productive citizen. And somehow you manage to accomplish all this without the help of a supervisor. Yet, when you go to work, someone immediately insists that you "report" to someone else—and then starts talking about "empowering" you! Doesn't that strike you as somewhat contradictory?

I confess that I have always failed to understand the pseudo-complexity of empowerment. Why is it so difficult to allow rational, well-trained adult human beings to make their own decisions without being second-guessed and yanked around, possibly by someone who feels a need to justify his or her own position? In too many organizations I've found an inverse relationship between the amount of talk about empowerment (hot-air memos, splashy empowerment leadership sessions) and the amount of empowerment that actually goes on. It's really not all that complicated. Consider Peter Drucker's cogent observation that "much of what we call management is making it very difficult for people to do their jobs."

Okay, I suspect you're still a little skeptical. Fair enough. Hopefully you're willing to consider the possibility that you don't want clones, you don't want to play hero or cop, and, therefore, you no longer want to play the "empowerment, BUT ... " scam. On the other hand, you don't want to adopt a laissez-faire attitude that simply tells your people to do whatever the hell they want to do, purpose and consequences notwithstanding. So what can you do? As a reward for stoically tolerating my abuse, I will now share three secrets with you.

Secret #1. While waiting for my appointment with a particular manager, I became impressed by what two of her young clerical assistants were doing. Periodically, one of them would pick up the phone and call a customer and ask how the customer liked the company's product, and then jot down the response. I nodded in approval; no wonder this manager had such a good reputation. When I finally met with her I offered congratulations on her ability to delegate the customer service task to her staff.

"What are you talking about?" she asked, bewildered.

"Why, your secretaries are calling up customers on their own," I replied.

"Oh, really? Is that what they're doing?" she said, laughing.

Now I was the bewildered one. "You mean you didn't delegate that task to them?"

"No," she said. "I didn't even know they were doing it. Listen, Oren, my job is to get everyone on my team to think creatively in pursuit of the same goal. What I do is talk to them regularly about why we exist as a company and as a team. That means we talk straight about our common purpose and the high standards we want to achieve. I call these our goal lines. Then we talk regularly about some broad constraints we have to work within, like budgets, ethics, policies and legalities. Those are our sidelines. Once we agree on the goal lines and sidelines, I leave it to them to figure out how to best get from here to there. I am available and attentive when they need feedback. Sometimes I praise, sometimes I criticize, but always constructively, I hope. We get together periodically and talk about who's been trying what, and we all give constructive feedback to one another. I know that sounds overly simplistic, but I assure you it is my basic management philosophy.

"And that's why I don't know what my assistants are doing, because it's obviously something they decided to try for the first time this week. I happen to think it's a great idea because it's within the playing field and it'll help us keep high standards for being Number 1 in our industry. I'll tell you something else: I don't even know what they intend to do with the data they're collecting, but I know they'll do the right thing."

She leaned forward and, with a little smile, continued: "Here's my secret: I don't know what my people are doing, but because I work face to face with them as a coach, *I know that whatever it is they're doing is exactly what I'd want them to be doing if I knew what they were doing!*"

How's that for a statement of trust? I recommend that every manager paste it on his or her bathroom mirror and repeat it three times before going to work each day. And if you buy it but you're still worrying about exactly how you'll be able to "let go" effectively, listen to the second secret.

Secret #2. While working with an agricultural laboratory, I witnessed a fascinating story unfold. A director of one small division became enamored with the idea of empowerment. He read articles on empowerment, he talked about it frequently and, by George, the man wanted to empower like crazy. But despite his noble intentions, he simply couldn't "let go." Although he and I agreed fully about the futility of creating clones, cops and "empowerment, BUT ... ", he agreed only in theory. Bottom line: he couldn't walk his talk.

One day, he sadly told his boss that he would have to leave the company because serious family matters required him and his wife to move to another state in six months. His boss, in the spirit of flattening the organization, decided not to replace him. The director was thus given the task of organizing the four functional groups which reported to him in such a way that they could fully take over his job. So for the next four months this man worked with the four group heads in reorganizing, streamlining and leading his shop. He did one-on-one coaching, he hired trainers, he helped his direct reports revamp the processes and systems. And after only four months he told me proudly that his direct reports and the newly reengineered division were now able to successfully take on all the tasks and responsibilities that he once used to grapple with on his own. (To tell the truth, I found out that the new four-person management team of the division was able to perform much better than he did under the old system.)

A few days later, this director came to the office in a state of shock. He had just found out that he didn't have to leave town after all. He wanted to stay on with the company, but as what? He had effectively worked himself out of a job. I told him that he had done the company a great service, and it was now up to him to create a new job for himself, one that would truly add fresh value. The company needed his experience and expertise, but it was up to him to figure out where.

After a little hand-holding and reassurance from his boss, this man rose to the challenge. He started a new division to tackle a niche market he felt that the company had neglected in the past. As it turns out, he was delighted with the move, as was his boss once the revenues began to roll in. Finally, his brainpower was being put to optimal use.

The only reason that this director was able to "let go" was that he knew he was going to leave. Just knowing that neither he nor anyone else was going to be around to supervise led to the kinds of actions that all the prior platitudes about empowerment had failed to engender. So here's the second secret: *Pretend you are leaving the company in six months with no replacement, overhaul your organization and train your people to take over your job, and then find a new way to add value.* And be prepared to repeat the cycle, over and over again (maybe with different employers) until you retire.

Secret #3. Mr. Jones, I'll now share with you the last and most important secret of all: *Your goal is not to empower, but to liberate.* Liberation involves freeing people from the organizational constraints (including you) that inhibit their willingness to take proactive action and accountability. Power is a feeling, an experience. It is the consequence of liberation. To put it succinctly, one successful manager was quoted as follows: "You know what good leadership is? *Tell 'em the rules of the game, train the dickens out of them, and then get the hell out of the way.*" That's liberation. Feelings of power follow.

All this empowerment stuff is a con because you cannot confer power on human beings. You cannot make anyone powerful. What you can do is create a condition where people will feel powerful, a condition where people choose to create power for themselves.

In short, as you get ready to face an unforgiving business world, please stop trying to empower people. It's a demeaning and futile task. Concentrate on offering your people the gift of liberation from the shackles of the organizational bureaucracy and from your own "helpful" intrusions. Liberate them from the protectors of the old guard. Do that and those delicious feelings of power will emerge among your people, as will productivity and organizational success. I can also assure you that you won't have to look over anyone's shoulders or worry about their making the "right" decisions. Perhaps the nicest thing of all is that you'll never have to use that condescending word *empowerment* ever again.

Best of luck,
Oren Harari

To leapfrog the competition, liberated employees need technology to be their servant, not their master. Technology can take over the routine as the organization is flooded with knowledge; technology can help unleash peoples' initiative and brainpower. But beware: Just as a real deluge changes the landscape of a flooded valley forever, technology, if used properly, will also change the landscape of your organization forever.

Your job is dying. All the eleventh-hour mouth-to-mouth resuscitation of restructuring and "empowerment" won't save it. It's doomed because the economy of the emerging millennium has no room for it. Your only hope is that you can hold off the inevitable until you retire—a rather forlorn wish. Or you can start confronting the future today by preparing to obsolete your current work before it obsoletes you—and then re-inventing it.

We are moving from an economy where intangibles like speed, flexibility and imagination are more important predictors of business success than tangibles like mass, size and physical assets. Accordingly, hitherto sacred principles like volume, economies of scale, experience curves, mass production and mass marketing are becoming less and less useful if we're interested in competitive edge. Rapid collaborative application of intelligence is where it's at.

Some companies get it. Like Microsoft. Some argue that Microsoft's slashing, aggressive moves into the world of Internet are due primarily to Bill Gates' ego. In a word, that's absurd. In 1990, Microsoft achieved a 38 percent quarterly sales boost by adding $90 million to its top line; in 1995, that same 38 percent standard required Microsoft to generate $800 million in new business. Today, the bar is raised even higher. Where's the new business coming from? Economies of scale? Cost reductions? Rubbish. It has to come from market-leading, customer-pleasing products. Microsoft has to generate at least $15 million a day just to break even. Without heaps of speed and imagination, it's dead.

Likewise, to say that Rubbermaid's success is due to its efficiencies in production and distribution is ridiculous. Cost-efficiencies are necessary for the survival of any organization, to be sure, but Rubbermaid's corporate success is due to its capacity to develop and launch one new interesting product every day in a supposedly humdrum, mundane business. It is speed to market and ingenuity in both product-development and marketing that create wealth for Rubbermaid.

To say that EDS is successful because of its sheer size in manpower is to again miss the point. EDS is successful in spite of its size. The company is smart enough to break down its 90,000-person workforce into independent micro-teams which work directly with individual clients—often on client sites—on creative business solutions. EDS recognizes that the key to business *success* lies not in high-volume mass services, but in the capacity to create customized value-adding product-service mixes for smaller and smaller segments—ultimately reaching market units of one: me and you and every other individual who responds to intelligent personalization. (More on this in Commitments 7 and 8.)

These corporate trends are both reflected and accelerated in the new knowledge economy, where competitive advantage is—according to a random sampling of pundits' comments—based on factors like "breakthroughs," "exploration," "mental flexibility," "production of ideas," and "curiosity as deep as it is boundless."

Now, let's take this a step further. Where do all these intangibles—breakthroughs, exploration, ideas, etc.—come from? Who's going to supply them? Who'll take responsibility for seeing them to fruition? In the old big body/little brain hierarchical model (that is, the one most corporations are still comfortable with), the answer is clear: a few smart people, like senior managers, staff experts and consultants. Everyone else, by and large, executes. It's a nice neat process: Logical, sensible, practical—and ultimately suicidal.

In yesterday's economy, hierarchy and centralization worked fine. In the new economy of intangibles, the old way of management is a monumental barrier to information flow, initiative, collaboration, creativity and speed. And the worst of it—and underlying every symptom listed above—is that the old way of management is fundamentally evil. It's evil in that it coarsens people's humanity by robbing them of their imagination and curiosity and turning them into bureaucrats. In a brain-based economy, bureaucracy kills.

Now we get to the crux of the matter. Yes, lots of routine work in organizations exists. Thus, there is a big place for bureaucracy in any organization. However, in the successful organizations of the future, those that leapfrog successfully, bureaucracy will be non-human. Specifically, it will be your information systems, and the bureaucrats will be your computers.

Right now, computers have the capacity to do almost every routine task you can do: they can check, monitor, search, scan, view, review, request, locate, list, gather, record, retrieve, edit, transfer, store, access, select, replicate, duplicate, assemble, combine, file, categorize, mail, dispatch and, of course, compute. In a narrower sense, they can organize, allocate and project. And they can do it a lot better, a lot cheaper, and a lot faster than people can.

Yet·the tasks described above are precisely the tasks that define many peoples' jobs. These are the tasks that people spend much of their daily calendar time doing at their desks or on the shop floor. This fits nicely into the hierarchical model, but when people spend much of their time doing routine (including the routine of waiting for directives), there is not much time (or initiative) for ingenuity and unconventional thinking. There is not much time to provide customers with personal attention and imaginative solutions. There is not much time for learning, either, even though in the new knowledge economy, working and learning are equivalent. In short, there is not much time to figure out how to leapfrog the competition.

This brings us to consultant Harry Dent, who makes a provocative point: Computers can now do the analytically detached, bureaucratic routine at lightning speed. If computers are thus the ultimate bureaucrats, why use people for that sort of work at all? (Even if you're smart enough to outsource such work, the question can still be aimed at the supplier). Asks Dent: Why not use the computer to do the bureaucratese in order to free people to think, to imagine, to create, and to serve customers in a breakthrough manner?

It's a very valid question. In the emerging economy, there will be less and less space available for bureaucracy in jobs. Yes, there'll always be a need for a travel agent or an insurance broker, but if they're simply providing routine, commodity-like services, they'll be obsoleted by computers. Likewise, looking inside our organizations, we need to ask how we can afford to carry the overhead of bureaucratic jobs if competitive advantage results from the intangibles. Even now, companies as diverse as GTE, Dell, and Rosenbluth are finding that giving front-line people the technology, the training and the authority to make decisions without the need for further handoffs dramatically reduces cycle time and improves quality. Bureaucratic conduit-jobs, those that are based on pass-offs and reviews of passed-off work, are rapidly disappearing.

The trends are quickly accelerating for a simple reason: information is power, and technology democratizes and universalizes the availability of information. Hence organizations will no longer be able to subsidize processes and jobs which glorify hierarchical control but turn off the spigot on knowledge-flow.

I recently attended a conference where futurist George Gilder eloquently described an emerging world where the economy is based on sand, glass and air. Sand is the silicon used to make microchips, the building blocks of computing; and use of that building block is growing exponentially. The performance of microchips doubles every 18 months. The most recent $300 Nintendo computer videogame has more computing power than a $20 million supercomputer used by the Pentagon 25 years ago. The near future will see the power of 16 Cray supercomputers on one Pentium chip for less than $100.

Then there's glass, which is used to make optical fibers, thin as human hair, carrying a thousand times more information than phone lines. And air, which is the medium for wireless communication technologies. These technologies converge to shrink the planet, eliminate time and distance from communication, and make us more powerful than any king or queen in history. Create a collaborative culture using a networked computing system, and your power goes up exponentially. Gilder calls it the "law of telecosm: *n* computers in the network yield *n*-squared performance."

Put it all together and you're talking, in Gilder's terms, about technologies "flinging intelligence to the far reaches of the globe, overthrowing centralization, pyramids and hierarchy." You're talking about any individual anywhere being able to instantly access anyone, or any hitherto proprietary information. You're talking about accessibility of anything, where walls of secrecy and hoarding and ego-status come tumbling down.

In a world where information is a flood accessible to everyone—and where nothing is secret or proprietary—the only organizations and managers who will thrive are those who can quickly wade into the water, harness what they need, and then add value to it through speedy, innovative business decisions.

The 1995 White Paper of the World Gold Council put it nicely:

> *"In tomorrow's marketplace, information—gathered and transmitted through a vast network of interconnected computers—will be the most valuable currency of business. The companies that win will be those who most efficiently collect and use information to rapidly test new products, identify best-selling items, replenish stock and match marketing efforts to new consumer demands."*

There's no place for human bureaucracy in this scenario. The sheer volume of information and knowledge available to any individual (and any competitor) will mean that talent, resourcefulness, energy and ingenuity will necessarily become an all-hands, collaborative affair, the responsibility of everyone on board. Bureaucracy will thus fill the job description of the computer, not the human being.

Some social thinkers view this trend with alarm. They point to factories where robotics has replaced mind-numbing manual labor, and offices where telecommunication systems eliminate the need for people who mechanically take messages. And instead of feeling hope, they despair, painting a picture of a world where only a few human beings have jobs at all. Jeremy Rifkin, in his book ominously entitled *The End of Work* (Putnam, 1995), writes: "We are entering into a new period in history where machines will increasingly replace human labor in the production of goods and services. Although timetables are difficult to predict, we are set on a firm course to an automated future and will likely approach a near-workerless era, at least in manufacturing, by the early decades of the coming century."

I respect Rifkin, but in this case he's only half right. We'll see not a decline of jobs in general, but a decline of bureaucratic jobs. At the last turn of the century, anxiety was expressed about all the farming jobs that were going to be lost. And indeed, they were lost; the industry which accounted for 85 percent of the jobs in 1900 today accounts for about 5 percent of them—and the industry is so productive that it can still feed the world. Likewise, 50 percent of the jobs that existed in 1955 no longer exist. So what? Just as new jobs (and new industries) were born then, new ones are being born as we enter the next millennium. Some projections suggest that the majority of jobs in the early 21st century have not yet been invented. Whatever they are, these new jobs will be more fulfilling and more rewarding, because the beasts of mental burden will be the computers.

Parenthetically, the number of computers currently in your organization says nothing about whether your organization is currently preparing for success. Computers are ubiquitous in every corporate setting nowadays, but as Paul Saffo of the Institute for the Future observes, most of the time they are used in a way that merely "paves the cowpaths." Or, as George Gilder says, today's computers are like a car stuck in the middle of a jungle. In other words, computers are not fully integrated into the new market realities that I've described. They are adjuncts to the conventional routine work that people continue to do. In fact, argues Carol Bartz, CEO of Autodesk, computers simply perpetuate old hierarchical processes in many organizations.

The challenge, therefore, is to create an organizational infrastructure that attaches routine and hierarchy to technology, not to human beings. This requires a new social order within organizations, a new definition of what jobs are and what people do. You won't give people computers and then continue to restrict information à la "for-top-management-eyes-only" or "go-through-me-before-you-can-talk-to-her." You give people computers and expect them to access anything and anyone, period. Likewise, you don't give people computers and then tell them what to use them for; you give them computers and let them devise the applications necessary to add value to the organization.

I began by arguing that your job is dying. I mean that much of what many of us do is still bureaucratic. This, I suspect, helps explain why studies of both Price Waterhouse and the Boston Consulting Group have suggested that 75 to 95 percent of steps and processes that currently go on in organizations add little or no value to the customer. People are doing the tasks that computers can do better. Even worse, they are fighting the computer by spending their time delaying, distorting and hoarding information. That's human bureaucracy in action.

But in the organization that floods itself with knowledge, there is no place for these activities. To those who are serious about leapfrogging the competition, a major corporate challenge today is to prepare our organizations in such a way that the technologies do the bureaucracy and the people do the creating. Our personal challenge is to prepare ourselves to fit into that reality, and if we're not CEOs, to lobby for it with our current employer, or to move to a place that is heeding the wake-up call. Do we have the managerial courage to face these challenges?

GIANT STEP III:

WRAP YOUR ORGANIZATION
AROUND EACH CUSTOMER

If you give them the opportunity, customers will gladly provide you the clue as to where and how to leap. Thus, first and foremost, organizations that leapfrog the competition are genuinely obsessed with customers. Managers in these organizations are fanatics when it comes to really understanding their customers—their needs, wants, lives, experiences, challenges, businesses. They do this not only to provide customers with outrageous service today, but also to get insights about what they might want or need tomorrow.

Managers at all levels in these organizations are preoccupied with collecting and disseminating customer anecdotes, warehousing and scrutinizing qualitative and quantitative customer data, talking about customers extensively in management meetings, allocating significant capital toward addressing emerging social-technical issues that might be of interest to customers, working collaboratively with customers on projects, and "hanging out" with them to learn one-on-one what makes them tick.

These sorts of behaviors are quite different in tone and integrity from the empty "customer is king" lip service that accompanies everyday customer neglect in so many organizations. Leaders that are committed to Giant Step III show behaviors that reflect their willingness to go beyond lip service in order to wrap the entire organization around their customers.

Kinko's Copiers Chairman Paul Orfalea is, frankly, a fanatic when it comes to customers. His ignition of a "wraparound" customer obsession at Kinko's has resulted in outcomes well beyond friendly, personal customer service—outcomes like state-of-the-art photocopy and computer technology that business customers want; outcomes like 24-hour service, pickup at home or office; outcomes like the total transformation of the Kinko's storefront from a passive copying facility to a complete telecommunications and graphic design center, and a complete office-away-from-the-office operation.

The wrap-around customer obsession has a literal physical dimension as well. The success of companies like EDS and the architectural firm CRSS is in no small means due to their willingness to send small teams to actually camp out and "live" with customers at their businesses, working jointly on customer problems. In the healthcare arena, Baxter and Interim Services often locate their people in offices situated right in hospital-customer sites.

These sorts of healthy preoccupations lead managers in any company to the realization that each customer is unique, and that nowadays, the smart, knowledge-rich, technology-loaded organization can address the unique needs of every single one of them. Hence, the next stage in this process is that the thriving organization is one that can wrap itself not merely around "customers," but around *each individual customer*. Competitive advantage in the emerging knowledge based economy is no longer dependent on mass production, mass marketing, mass distribution, uniform policies and economies of scale.

That's because the keys to business success lie in addressing each customer's unique idiosyncracies. It's a fundamental way to differentiate yourself from competitors, to forge relationships and thus engender customer loyalty, and to transform commodity products and services into genuine value-add.

Customers themselves are increasingly defining "quality" as the ability of the vendor to provide high-level solutions. Hence the quality value of a vendor's output will be directly proportional to the extent to which it alleviates or solves the unique problems that each customer faces.

It makes sense to capitalize on economies of scale whenever you can get them. But as markets become more splintered and customers become more demanding, strategies that generate standardized products and services within uniform delivery systems are strategies that will inevitably generate flat earnings—even if the output is efficiently produced and certifiably TQM defect-free.

Companies that grudgingly offer customers a few options in products and services still miss the point. The challenge today is to focus on market units of one, and to create flexible responses to each customer's unique problems. Thus, at NCR, Mirage Resorts, First Direct Bank (Great Britain) and K. Barchetti retail stores, rich computerized customer profiling is analyzed extensively to help salespeople and other personnel individualize their customer service.

At Pittsburgh-based K. Barchetti Shops (retail clothing), salespeople use software to track a customer's purchases and stated preferences, to generate a psychographic analysis, and to pop up reminders for themselves to call customers who have not been in the store for some time. Salespeople use the data to create unique ensembles for individual customers, and if appropriate they go to the customer's site to demonstrate this clothing—at a time convenient to the customer, of course.

At northern California industrial packaging distributor Conifer Crent, centralized truck routes are being eliminated in favor of decentralized routes run by self-managed cross-disciplinary teams of truckers, accountants, and sales and support people who electronically link with their assigned customer segment for two-way order and after-sale communication. Why? So that Conifer Crent can profitably deliver *any* volume at *any* time to *any* customer.

Already, companies as diverse as Houston-based Vallen (safety equipment), San Jose-based Cadence (electronic design tools), Unisys and General Electric are determining that the products themselves are only one element of a total package they offer, and that steep rises in both margins and earnings will come from selling the organization's *expertise* to individual customers' specific problems. Thus, GE sees its future in servicing each hospital-customer's medical equipment (including competitors' wares) and by working with the people in that hospital to improve services like X-ray imaging, rather than by only selling medical equipment in a "mass" market. Similarly, Cadence CEO Joe Costello pointedly says that his company has significantly benefited from a major strategic shift, to wit, a shift from selling product and making transactions to selling expertise and developing solutions—for individual customers.

Even the products themselves are becoming customized. MCI offers customers the opportunity to tailor a bundle of leading-edge services including e-mail, fax, on-line shopping, Internet access, videoconferencing, real-time document sharing, and news-wire search. A customer can create a personalized search profile by selecting one of 23 industries and then ranking their level of interest in each of 14 industry concepts, for example. Search matches are delivered to the customer via e-mail twice daily, with up to 10 news flashes per day.

In a similar vein, Andersen Windows is leapfrogging the very notion of just-in-time inventory management because ultimately it will have no real product inventory to manage! The "inventory" will be listed in an electronic catalog that customers (contractors and homeowners) will use to customize their desired window products. Andersen provides each of its dealers with a PC, Oracle database, and proprietary software (about a $4,000 price tag). Once the customer delineates his or her specs, the computer checks them for structural soundness and feasibility, and then generates a price. State-of-the-art flexible manufacturing and electronic linkages allow Andersen to respond to each request without having to keep countless variations of windows in stock. Last year, Andersen generated nearly 200,000 different products this way with minimum inventory.

This section will show that in today's knowledge-based economy, organizations that can wrap themselves around each of their customers will be able to vault over their competitors by sharply redefining the whole notion of "customer service," by snaring new niches and by perpetually reinventing their businesses. In order to effectively leave the paradigm of mass markets for that of market units of one, organizations have to be incredibly smart and agile— precisely the qualities needed for leapfrogging competitors.

The days of a vendor offering products with limited features and service marked by uniform procedures at designated hours and locations—all convenient and cost-efficient to the *vendor*— made sense in a world where competition was limited and customers' alternatives were few. That world is fast fading, and the organization that seeks to leap over competitors aggressively is building corporate systems and cultures to wrap itself lovingly around each and every customer.

To leapfrog the competition, we've got to break away from two beliefs that are bedrock in conventional management: One, that our primary attention ought to be in making profit. Two, that mass markets exist and hence salvation lies in cost-efficiencies of standardization, routinization and economies of scale. In contrast, the two commitments that will allow you to wrap your organization around the customer, and thus leapfrog the competition, are:

- Obsess about customers, not profits (Chapter/Commitment 7)
- Focus on market units of one (Chapter/Commitment 8)

Commitment 7 is quickly stated; the chapter offers a short, empirically grounded statement of business philosophy: Profits are a scorecard, they are not the game. Certainly, you've got to pay close attention to financials. You've always got to be concerned with them. The issue is what you choose to obsess on. Obsession on your customers will most likely yield higher financials. Paradoxically, obsessing on the financials will most likely yield the opposite result.

As this section will demonstrate, leapfrogging organizations begin with the philosophy that they are not in business to make a profit, but to make—that is to create and maintain—customers. If they do that well, their long-term profitability will most likely shine. If they don't do that well, all the financial and restructuring wizardry in the world will only serve to keep the wolves at bay in the short run.

Commitment 8 takes this a step farther. It will challenge you to think *strategy* whenever you think *quality;* quality is not merely meeting specs and delivering error free—it encompasses the individual customer's entire experience with you and your organization. Using a seemingly ordinary story about the construction of a backyard fence, the chapter takes the moral further: If mass markets are indeed withering, if technology and competition force us to consider each customer's special needs, then we are compelled to take certain steps to start redefining our entire business in response to each customer.

As mentioned earlier, economies of scale should be capitalized on in both manufacturing and service delivery; but in the new economy, they will not be the precursors to competitive advantage. To leave the world of mass markets and economies of scale in favor of market units of one is a huge commitment to make, but it is the essence of leapfrogging far beyond competitors who are still trapped in the logic on uniformity and mass.

COMMITMENT 7:
OBSESS ABOUT CUSTOMERS, NOT PROFITS

> *It's a paradox: The more you concentrate on profits, the less likely it is you'll achieve them. But focus your primary attention on your customers, and the profits and all the other good things will follow. Here's why.*

What do the following CEOs have in common other than a successful track record: Paul Allaire (Xerox); Edward McCabe (McCabe and Company); John McConnell (Worthington Industries); and Robert McDermott (former CEO of United Services Automobile Association)? If you're stumped, here are some clues:

Paul Allaire: *"I have to change the company substantially to be more market-driven. If we do what's right for the customer, our market share and our return on assets will take care of themselves."*

Edward McCabe: *"You think I want my tombstone to say, 'He had 27 offices'? What's important to me is that our company did outstanding advertising. ... The numbers are not achievements in themselves, but the results of achievements."*

John McConnell: *"Take care of your customers and take care of your people, and the market will take care of you."*

Robert McDermott: *"The mission and corporate culture of this company are, in one word, service. As a company objective, service comes ahead of either profits or growth. Now profits and growth do matter ... but I submit that it's because service comes first at USAA that profits and growth have been so healthy."*

Before continuing, let me tell you why I developed this quiz. David Fagiano, president and CEO of the American Management Association, wrote in *Management Review* in September 1991 that "profit is not the mission of any company that wants to be around for the long haul." He was promptly blasted by irate readers who considered his comments to be worthy of the antichrist. Perhaps he shouldn't have been surprised at the reaction. In 1987, Ernst and Young surveyed 154 CEOs about their top priorities. Profits and growth topped the list; service—for all the lip service it garners—came in eleventh. In any event, Fagiano responded to his critics with an article titled, "Are We in Business to Make Money?" It should be required reading for every MBA student.

I've never met Fagiano and it is clear that he does not need my help. What intrigues me is that in a premier business magazine published by the American Management Association and read by progressive, enlightened managers, there was even a need for follow-up defense of what should have been an obvious truism.

There's more. Not only is Fagiano correct in asserting that profit should not be the primary goal of any business, but the same statement can be made about stock value. Many managers in the United States still operate under the twin fictions that their most important stakeholders are shareholders, and that their primary purpose in management is to enhance shareholder value. Whether this is true from a legal perspective in the case of publicly traded firms is worthy of debate; but from a strategic and operational perspective, it is dead wrong for *any* firm—publicly traded or privately held. Organizations that leapfrog the competition understand that a business does not exist primarily for the benefit of investors, nor should it be run under that premise.

In the words of Harvard's Ted Levitt: "The purpose of business is to get and keep customers." Similarly, Peter Drucker has argued for years that the only justification for an organization's existence is the extent to which it can service the needs of a particular constituency in society called "customers." In other words, though it sounds heretical, the primary allegiance of any organization ought to be to that constituency, not to its shareholders—a conclusion that, by the way, is formally institutionalized in the corporate credo of Johnson & Johnson. Those CEOs I quoted above know this lesson well, and it is precisely because they have learned this lesson that their organizations—and therefore, their shareholders—have prospered.

Obviously, the interests of shareholders—particularly the large institutional investors that control more than 50 percent of U.S. companies' equity capital—should be a significant concern to any executive. Just as obviously, profit—and the need to reinvest it for the purpose of improving the company—must be a crucial goal for anyone in business; even nonprofit organizations have to declare a surplus over expenses in order to survive.

Moreover, any organization that hopes to be successful must be adept at managing cost, debt, cashflow and assets. In fact, a publicly traded organization would also be wise to gain proficiency in managing earnings in such a way as to maintain consistencies and reduce unpleasant surprises to investors.

Clearly, therefore, astute financial management must be a given for any organization that wants to compete effectively. The issue becomes one of priority. Paying attention to the numbers is good, effectively manipulating the numbers is good. But where do the numbers come from? What is the source of the big, steady boosts in revenue, margins, cashflow stock price? I have found that long-term financial success depends primarily on leaders' abilities to capitalize on globalization and technology and to launch dramatic breakthroughs in innovation, quality, service and teamwork. That ought to be the top priority. Committing to wrapping one's organization around the customers, as well as committing to the other four Giant Steps, is the way to realize these goals.

Hence, the problem is not management's concerns with financials. The problem occurs when financials such as profit and shareholder value become the primary goals, and when they are viewed not as the consequence of effective strategy, but as the *raison d'etre* of the business itself. At that point, an intriguing boomerang effect takes place: Profit and shareholder value go down—if not quickly, then certainly over time.

Why should this be? Well, let's consider what happens in an organization or business unit when the top managers seriously adhere to—or manage as if they seriously adhere to—the premise that profit and stock value are the main business priorities. Certain trends inevitably emerge:

1. *Managers learn to become emotionally and analytically detached from their business.*
   When the company becomes simply an expedient tool toward the more "important" goals of profit and stock value, opportunism replaces a commitment to growing a business. When the primary commitment is to turn a profit, notions like love of product, careful cultivation of customer relationships, and mind-blowing service delivery become quaint anomalies. One middle manager of a struggling firm once complained to me: "You know what the problem is around here? Nobody cares. Management speaks numbers, dollars, cents. Nobody speaks vision, passion, being the best."

Analytical detachment has a ripple effect throughout the organization. It is hard to sustain excitement and enthusiasm among employees if the only things that senior executives seem to care about are the returns—and inevitably, this focus means that the organization will be hard-pressed to retain top talent. As noted earlier, companies that leapfrog the competition share financial information and financial gain with employees, but even that's not enough. Increasingly, the high corporate performers today—from Sun Microsystems to Coca-Cola to ESPN—are noted for providing their employees not merely "jobs," but a "cause," a "calling."

Anita Roddick, founder of the hugely successful, environmentally focused cosmetics enterprise Body Shop, put it this way in the *Harvard Business Review*: "Most businesses focus all the time on profits, profits, profits. I think that is deeply boring. I want to create an electricity and passion that bonds people to the company. Especially with young people, you have to find ways to grab their imagination. You want them to feel that they are doing something important. I'd never get that kind of motivation if we were just selling shampoo and body lotion."

University of Southern California's Ian Metroff has concluded that one of the main reasons that the Big Three American auto manufacturers lost dramatic earnings, market share and, more important, competitive positioning to foreign rivals is because their underlying assumption in the 1960s and 1970s was illustrated as follows: "GM is in the business of making money, not cars." This was why ex-Chrysler Chairman Lynn Townsend, who presided over the unraveling of his company, could deride an investor's concerns about quality with, "The only thing that people care about are the stock splits."

2. *Managers become obsessed with short-term financials, or "meeting their numbers."*
This obsession takes on various forms.

First, managers plunge into regular cost-cutting frenzies by spending more of their time looking inward than outward. Customers are put on back burners as managers spend their time and attention on variance adjusting, paper chasing, paper-clip-counting and innumerable endless meetings to review progress on those fronts. Creative accounting becomes *de rigueur*, especially in the last few days of the quarter. These activities usually have an immediate, though marginal, impact on costs and cash flow. However, they also ensure that management remains buffered from employee frustrations, daily shifts in markets and the regular infusion of fresh competitors who you can bet are entering the playing field with interesting products and services.

Second, managers who focus on the short-term financials are more likely to employ sweeping meat-cleaver approaches to head-count reductions—approaches that often are not carefully thought out and integrated into operational efficiency and long-term competitive strategy—but which serve well as quick fixes. It should not be surprising that, according to American Management Association research over the past decade, few downsizing efforts across American businesses have yielded lasting increases in productivity and profitability.

Third, the notion of "patient capital" becomes a self-canceling oxymoron, which leads us to the next point:

3. *Managers become overly cautious and conservative.*
   Managers become less apt to take risks and make necessary investments in new products or services, comprehensive, organization-wide reengineering, capital improvements, unchartered market niches, training, significant quality and service initiatives, and research and development. (Ironically, per No. 2 above, it is well-executed reengineering and quality enhancements that can significantly reduce costs.)

   Instead, analysis paralysis and worship of algorithm become norms. Fast, guaranteed returns are implicitly expected from new ventures. Intuition becomes suspect; net present value proofs become a prerequisite to action—which means little action takes place. A barrage of stringent control mechanisms—both financial and hierarchical—are regularly imposed on managers in the name of fiscal responsibility, thus further eroding their creativity, initiative and accountability.

4. *Buying success becomes preferable to earning it.*
   The implicit motto becomes, "If you can't manage one company, buy another." When one's primary orientation is profit and

stock value, management commitments requiring patience, risk, unflashy fundamentals and pain—all necessary to growing a business—become less attractive. With profit as the dominant driver, it appears a lot easier to consolidate balance sheets with another firm than to go through the mundane grind of developing a product line and workforce. The excitement of financial sleight-of-hand while "doing the deal" yields more gratification than visiting suppliers and sitting in on customer focus groups.

Certainly, some acquisition and divestiture activity can make for prudent strategy, but managers who rely on portfolio strategies for market share and earnings growth are more likely to drive their company's profits and stock value down, as the research of Harvard's Michael Porter has shown. And as the raiders of the '80s were delighted to discover, executives' obsession with wheeling and dealing for quick profits over the prior three decades led to the development of grossly undervalued empires ripe for the plucking. The final irony is that the purest examples of "buying success" strategies—the conglomerates—have consistently underperformed the Standard & Poor's 500-stock index.

5. *To boost sales and revenues, the organization beats up on salespeople and tries to buy customers.*
   Since a commitment to quality, service and innovation is basically lip service (after all, "profits are why we are in business"), then the ways to enhance sales are twofold:

   • Use big carrots and big sticks to get sales people to meet their numbers any way they can, no questions asked. Let those people in the field figure out how to sell square pegs to reluctant customers holding round holes. Apart from the fact that this strategy no longer works well, a couple of additional byproducts emerge. One, the salesforce is removed from operations and strategy, which lowers both operational efficiency and market-driven innovation. Two, after-sale service inevitably becomes de-emphasized, which, in turn, depresses customer loyalty and word-of-mouth marketing.
   • Attract customers by buying their affections via regular price slashes and big money promotions and advertising blitzes. This approach automatically shrinks margins and, as car

manufacturers have learned, simply causes shrewd customers to postpone buying decisions until the next low-price
promotion appears. Moreover, as Eastern Airlines found
during the final stage of its corporate demise, cheap tickets
cannot repair a reputation for shoddy service.

As numerous magazines have learned, glitzy promotions
and incentive giveaways to new subscribers may boost circula-
tion and cash flow in the short run, but in the long run often
lead to a spiral of cost increases necessary to maintain "soft"
uncommitted subscribers and prospect for new ones to replace
the dropouts. With tactics like these, it should not be surprising
that the head of one major media organization—a gentleman
who publicly declared his business strategy to be to "increase
thy profit margin"—presided over an empire that lost $100 mil-
lion in profits during his tenure.

6. *The "heroes" become the wrong people.*
    The heroes become those who count and analyze things
    rather than those who make and sell things. They become
    those who restructure and rearrange boxes rather than those
    who operate and develop them. They become those who count
    beans rather than those who grow them. They become those
    who say "no" to risk rather than those who inspire others to try
    something new. Financial wizards and "paper entrepreneurs"—
    along with their ever-increasing and expensive staffs—attain
    the highest status and most power. Champions of quality and
    entrepreneurship take a back seat when significant manage-
    ment decisions are made.
       One additional clue: Tell me who attends senior manage-
    ment meetings and I'll tell you the caliber of decisions that are
    being made. In many large American manufacturing firms dur-
    ing the '70s and '80s, for example, financial and legal folks sig-
    nificantly outnumbered manufacturing and engineering folks in
    top management meetings. With the wrong heroes, the priori-
    ties and activities of the firm become distorted, and the com-
    petitive vigor of the organization slides accordingly.

Back in 1988, I predicted Eastern Airlines' bankruptcy in a series
of speeches. I am no soothsayer; I simply observed that Eastern

management scored high on each of the six trends listed above. There was no one more financially adroit and profit-conscious than CEO Frank Lorenzo but, to quote consultant J. Daniel Beckham: "Eastern is a tragic monument to what happens when an organization has a vision based on nothing more inspiring than a deal-maker's spreadsheet."

What is the bottom line of all this? Leapfrogging organizations operate by the principle that profits are the resultant scorecard of good management. They do not define good management. Companies that focus on creating value for their customers yield the highest total returns to investors. The story is the same when it comes to preparing for the future. David Aaker of the University of California at Berkeley studied 248 businesses and determined that the top-ranked assets and skills necessary to obtain a "sustainable competitive advantage" were, in order, reputation for quality, customer service and product support, name recognition, and the ability to retain good management and engineering staff. These factors were ranked higher than low-cost production, financial resources and technical superiority, even though many of the firms in Aaker's sample were high-technology manufacturers.

Let's end by going back to the beginning. AMA's David Fagiano did not open a Pandora's box. The box was opened by successful managers long ago. For Edward McCabe, the pride in his work and the respect of his customers and peers are what drive him; that drive incidentally has resulted in hundreds of millions of dollars in billings during his career. John McConnell, an ex-steel broker following a simple variant of the Golden Rule in the rough-and-tumble steel industry, has nurtured a firm of fiercely loyal employees that over the years has significantly outperformed the more sophisticated USX Corp. and Bethlehem Steel—companies which, by the way, have been led by CEOs with financial and accounting backgrounds. While he was at the helm of USAA, Robert McDermott attributed the financial success of the company to the fact that he was passionate about service and, accordingly, invested heavily in technology, workforce development and customer interface systems.

Those managers who live by the rule that their top priority is to make profits and enhance shareholder value will achieve precisely the opposite. Just give them time.

COMMITMENT 8:
FOCUS ON MARKET UNITS OF ONE

Committing to the customer as the top business priority is the first step. Thinking "one," or "market of one," means viewing each customer as an individual market with individual needs and individual idiosyncracies. The capacity to think and act "one" is an enormous advantage for leapfrogging the competition. In fact, vendors that believe they are engaged in simple product and service transactions will be a dying breed. Here is a story of a fence that was not a fence, but rather, a solution to a deeply felt need. Unfortunately, the supplier didn't see it that way ...

My wife and I learned a sobering fact recently. The No. 1 cause of death for toddlers in California is drowning in a home pool.

Since we live in California and happen to have both a two-year-old and a pool, my wife became, shall we say, concerned, and insisted that we supplement our existing pool cover with some additional protective barrier that would prevent our son from even venturing near the pool. This wasn't simple paranoia on her part. Our pediatrician told her that during the previous month a child drowned after having somehow penetrated a pool cover.

Anyway, we hired a reputable contractor to build a small fence in the appropriate area. After hearing our concerns regarding safety and aesthetics, he proposed a reasonably attractive four-foot-high flexible green mesh fence, which we all agreed would serve more as a temporary shield than as a permanent barrier. (We weren't prepared to build a 10-foot wall around the pool, but we figured that a discouraging fence coupled with an imposing pool cover would be the ticket.)

With all this in mind, my wife and I left our contractor alone for the day. When we returned, we were relieved that the new backyard addition wasn't an eyesore. And it appeared durable enough to withstand the pounding of even the most determined youngster.

So far, so good. But the next day I noticed that, since the fence was made of flexible mesh, there was a section near the gate where one could—with a bit of effort—bend and fold the bottom in such a way as to scoot underneath, if one had a very small frame.

Hmmmmm. Not good. We called the contractor, who explained that the mechanics of the swinging gate which he had installed prevented him from stretching the adjacent mesh to the same tension as the material comprising the rest of the fence. Hence, there was necessarily a slight bit of slack that could be exploited, but again, only with some effort.

The vendor-customer dynamics now shifted from logical to psychological. From our perspective, the fence was inadequate; it would have to be replaced or reengineered. The contractor's position was a bit different. He contended that he had spent an entire day building a fence reflecting the material, specifications and price to which we had explicitly agreed. One small section of the fence had a bit of inevitable slack, but overall, it met our criteria for safety and aesthetics.

Besides, he reminded us, a four-foot-high mesh fence was never intended to be impervious. From his perspective, he had met the customer's requirements. If we wanted any changes, he'd be glad to oblige, as long as we told him precisely what we wanted and paid him for his labor.

So far, this sounds like a typical, mundane conflict—the kind that's boring if you're not one of the protagonists, or that provides fodder for Judge Wapner's TV courtroom. But I propose that this divergence of opinion illustrates a fundamental problem that exists in vendor-customer interactions today. More important, it illustrates the kinds of nitty-gritty issues that tomorrow's provider of services will have to confront with increasing regularity.

You see, the contractor's position was not unlike most vendors' positions these days: "Look, Mr. or Ms. Customer, we agreed on the specs and the services, I did them, here's the bill." Or, as in this case, "We agreed on the fence, I built it, here's the bill." A straightforward business transaction.

The contractor in this story represents every vendor we've all dealt with: the house painter, the dentist, the banker, the engineer, the insurance agent, the retailer, the publisher, the manufacturer, the distributor. Indeed, the contractor represents *us* if *we* are the vendor. And, in the old order of business—that is, the status quo we've accepted until now—the contractor's point is defensible. After all, who's to say the customer is right? Who's to say the vendor should suffer just because the customer doesn't like what was ordered? There was no malice here. On the contrary, the contractor listened to us the customers, and he responded in good faith. Further, the final product would surely pass the test of quality; it was a well-built fence. Besides, let's face it: There are no sure things in business transactions.

Times, however, are changing. Increasingly, the customer is less interested in the tangibles of the deal (the specs, the final product, the actual services rendered) than in the intangibles—the original motive and desire for purchasing the services in the first place and the extent to which those deep motives and desires are met.

This is a subtle but crucial point for any business to take seriously. The customer is illustrated by the position of my wife who, with some prodding, would admit:

"I didn't necessarily want a fence in the first place. I wanted peace of mind so I wouldn't have to worry about my son. I thought I wanted a fence because that's all I could envision, but in reality, I wanted a solution to my problem. Now the problem still exists because I'm still worried that my child could find the soft spot and possibly scoot underneath the fence. So I'm stuck with having to watch him as if the fence didn't exist. Sure, I agreed to the fence; yes, I understand the mechanics of the gate; and yes, things are better in terms of probabilities. But I still don't have the peace of mind I anticipated when I got into this deal in the first place."

In the old order, this line of customer reasoning is whiny and unreasonable. In the old order, the vendor defends his or her position contractually, and the customer either takes his lumps or takes it to court. But I propose that in the new order—the emerging world of business—this scenario will have a different ending. Customers—individual and corporate—will be less patient with legalism and contractualism. Vendors that rely on them, however sincerely, will fall behind in the race toward competitive advantage.

Here's what's happening: Nowadays, customers are more demanding and fickle than ever before, with good reason. They're smarter and more aware. They have more and more choices, from a logarithmic increase among competing vendors all the way to the enormous self-help possibilities of the World Wide Web. *Hence, they will gravitate toward vendors who understand that business is no longer about buying and selling products and services. It is about addressing peoples' intangible motives and desires.* Read those last two sentences again, because 99 percent of businesses today are run with absolutely no understanding of this point.

In the new order of things—which are already starting to happen—what will count for customers is the *total experience they have with the vendor.* By "vendor," I mean both the organization and its representatives. The customer's appraisal of the total experience will be based on questions like:

- How easy is it to work with this vendor—before, during and after the sale?
- Does the vendor really, truly understand what I'm looking for?
- How responsive, caring and concerned is the vendor toward me and my particular problems?
- How willing is the vendor to probe and listen, and then adjust and contort, to my idiosyncratic demands?
- Does the vendor know me so well that he/she can anticipate what I might want before I do?
- How effective is the vendor in devising a creative solution to my real problems and unique needs?
- To what extent does the vendor seek my input and solicit my involvement toward working together to meet my needs?

In this scenario, the price and final tangible output are part of the total experience, to be sure, but not the only parts, and not necessarily the most important ones. Right now, customers are beginning to take their total experience seriously, and they're starting to judge vendors on that admittedly non-rational basis. They're saying: Wait a minute. Officially speaking, I got my fence built or my house painted or my teeth adjusted or my bank loan granted or my insurance done or the product delivered. But, by George, I'm not happy with how things went or how things turned out. In the past, I, the customer, didn't take that experience seriously. After all, business is a contractual arrangement. But no more. I do take it seriously now.

Simply "listening to the customer" and then responding will no longer be sufficient, because the customer may not be able to articulate what he or she really wants. In the future, the successful businessperson/contractor will act as a consultant, working with my wife and me to solve problems creatively. In doing so, he'll necessarily wind up doing things and partnering with other vendors in a manner he might personally find unorthodox (which, by the way, will expand his own skill base and networks).

Think about it. Suppose the contractor had approached the problem with the mind-set of a personal coach. He knows he brings to the party certain key skills and competencies in the building trade. Fine. But so do a jillion other contractors. His real value to us is his ability to use those skills in a manner that we the customers have never imagined and to form alliances with other vendors he may or may not have ever worked with before to help him achieve these goals.

Who knows? Maybe he would have created—on his own, with our help, or with the help of a new strategic partner—a creative type of child-proof, adult-friendly barrier that not only would have been foolproof, but one that he could have parlayed into a new service niche or a new product line. Either way, a new business spinoff and revenue stream. (As a matter of fact, my wife and I have since learned that a local contractor and a nurse have joined forces in a very lucrative "child-proofing" business).

Or maybe, in alliance with a creative landscape architect, he could have used his ingenuity to create a beautiful new natural child-proof barrier that we, the customers, didn't "ask" for initially, because we couldn't conceptualize it.

If this contractor applies imagination to solving our real problem, the consequences are powerful: He "wows" us with an innovative solution, he jacks up our loyalty (and resultant word-of-mouth marketing), he differentiates himself from other contractors, he augments his fee, he expands his skill base, he expands his network base and the scope of his business. In short, he perpetually redefines and reinvents his business because he's not limited by the products and services he thinks he sells. He's not limited by any mission statement that limits his business vision, either. His business is to apply his unique skills in an ingenious way to solve customer problems. Within those parameters, the nature of his business is perpetually changing, evolving and growing.

What I'm saying may sound weird today, but I predict that it will soon be conventional wisdom. A whole new world is emerging, one where the products and the services in your current portfolio are going to be less and less relevant. The products and services that you're clinging to are becoming commodities fast.

Fences? They're commodities. Bank loans? Commodities too. Personal computers? Long-distance telephone service? Custody of financial assets? Food-processing equipment? Gaming and gambling? Security systems for the home? Travel booking services? All commodities. (If you don't believe me, talk to the people who must survive in these businesses.)

The value-add and the way to differentiate yourself and capitalize on new opportunities—thereby the route to competitive advantage—lies in focusing wisdom, attention and resources toward addressing each customer's unique needs. The folks at Unisys Federal Systems Division tell me that even in the enormously big government sector they serve, they can no longer simply sell their traditional staple of mainframe computers. They've reconfigured their strategy and workforce in order to provide long-term customized information-technology solutions (like information systems engineering, telecommunications and network integration, software applications and facilities management) for each of their clients' specific needs. As part of this equation, they sell all sorts of mainframe as well as non-mainframe computer hardware—including competitors' products. Whatever it takes. Will Unisys be successful? We'll see. But the important point is that they're on the right track, for they understand that it's not the product that counts, but the customer's total experience.

Now hold on, you may say. This is all well and good if you can create services. But I'm dealing in mass-market products. I can't afford to think about my business in terms of each individual customer.

My response? Good luck—you'll need it in the next millennium. The rules are changing. Mass markets are withering in the face of the onslaught by global competition and technological advance. "Mass customization" and individual tailoring are replacing undifferentiated, standardized, commodity-like products. At the 1996 Comdex convention in Las Vegas, Netscape CEO Jim Barksdale said: "We are entering the third wave of the Internet. ... While the first waves of the Internet focused on users being able to easily find information, the mark of this third wave is that information finds the user. Our new products will have the intelligence to help you focus on the information you care about."

Netscape is not alone. Sun Microsystems and several small startups are now using Java programming to deliver individualized software programs, web pages, news updates and other specified data to each customer's personal computer. Dow-Jones allows individual subscribers to create their own on-line *Wall Street Journal*, individually tailored to the reader's unique specifications. Time Inc. is talking about a goal of four million separate issues of *Time* magazine, potentially, one per subscriber.

In the manufacturing arena, Levi-Strauss is using a range of technologies, including EDI, CAD-CAM and computerized fabric-cutting to pilot the concept of custom-built jeans. The customer tries on a sample pair of prototype jeans in a selected location, and the data is beamed to a facility where a robot makes the jeans to order. There's a three-week turnaround with a $10 to $20 price increment over a mass-produced off-the-rack pair of jeans.

In a similar way, 20 Matsushita employees in Japan can receive an individual customer's body specs from a prototype bicycle frame in a retail outlet, and then draw from a technology allowing 11 million variations of road and mountain bikes in 200 colors, in order to quickly produce the custom-built bicycle.

In the new world order, wrapped around these individualized products will come tailored customer service, from manufacturer to retailer and from retailer to end-user. The paradigms are shifting. Engineers at the 3M computer components facility in Austin, Texas, assert "How do we know what to make until we work it out with the customer first?"

You get the picture. Customized products, personalized service. The new world order will focus less on economies of scale and more on providing a perpetual stream of innovative solutions to—and with*—market units of one.

It won't be easy to transform oneself from a transaction-driven, commodity-oriented self-image to one based on the selling of customized expertise and solutions. Joe Costello, president of Cadence Design Systems, is on a personal mission to transform his company from a vendor of electronic design tools to one of customized services. Even though he can document that the fastest growth in earnings and margins are coming from this new way of addressing the business, he is still facing internal resistance.

---

* Individual customers (units of one) are huge potential sources of collaboration not only for customer service, but for product development and cost reduction efforts as well. More on this in Giant Steps IV and V.

"Everyone is used to the traditional structure and roles—marketing, R&D, application engineers, and sales. All of a sudden, we say we aren't selling just tools. That raises an identity crisis for many people in the company." Costello has found that the new organizational persona requires engineers to think like consultants and spend time on the front lines. It requires financial people to share data across the organization. In fact, it requires people in all functions and levels to share information openly, including with customers and suppliers. It requires people in sales to start thinking about after-sale relationships. It requires everyone to know the client's business, not merely Cadence's product line. This is a difficult transformation, to say the least. Costello reckons it will take at least two more years of constantly pounding away before the culture is completely changed.

Let's go back to our contractor. By insisting on implicit contracts and narrowing his view to agreements about fences, he's positioned himself as a commodity provider of commodity transactions. Whatever he gets paid today by us, he'll lose by a multiple tomorrow. No margins, no repeat business, no word-of-mouth marketing, no new alliances, no new business opportunities. He won't understand why; he'll blame politicians, immigrants, big government, big corporations. Maybe he'll pour more of his limited resources into advertising, which will put some quick and dirty window dressing salve on his undifferentiated service, and he'll be disappointed by the marginal impact that results. Or, he'll conclude that the only way to compete is by volume or price. Then he'll learn that volume—even if efficiently executed—makes little sense if mass markets are dying and that competing on price is akin to slow self-strangulation.

If you're truly committed to leapfrogging your competition, here is my suggestion: Plaster the message of Giant Step III on every business document, office wall and meeting agenda from now on. Let it drive every capital budgeting, personnel, product development and after-sale decision. It won't be easy, because you and I were incredibly intelligent in the old world but not particularly so in the new. But if we repeat this credo over and over again, we might finally start to believe it, and we just might start acting on it. We would then really wrap ourselves around each of our customers. They and our shareholders will thank us profusely.

GIANT STEP IV:

TRANSFORM YOUR ORGANIZATION INTO A WEB OF RELATIONSHIPS

In the premier issue of *Leader to Leader* (1996), Peter Drucker made the following observation:

> *"I met with a very big company not long ago—around 80 or so on the Fortune 500 list. They expect to be number 5 on that list in 10 years, and I shocked them by saying I don't think that list will exist, so that goal is meaningless. That list basically assumes that everything you do is under your roof and is owned by you and run by you. But already in many companies, most work is done through alliances, joint ventures, minority participation, and very informal agreements which no lawyer could possibly handle."*

I don't agree with Drucker that the Fortune 500 list will be meaningless, but the trend he's citing is unequivocal. In a knowledge economy, it is both naive and arrogant to assume that any one organization can lock up all the expertise and talent. Besides, in a world where speed and agility are paramount virtues, and where your goal is to leap—not waddle—over competitors, it's not smart to weigh yourself down with a heavy, often debt-laden vertically integrated structure.

As Tom Peters has noted, the key nowadays is not to own the resources, but to have access to them. Echoing this sentiment,

Frank Casale of the Outsourcing Institute observes: "Smart companies now want to have as small a work force as possible, be able to turn on a dime, and have access to world-class resources."

Given that technology has rendered time and place irrelevant (I can be anywhere and be connected with anyone and anything real-time), the light, agile, brain-based organization is one that can quickly connect with talent from any source in any pocket of the world for any project and any goal—and thereby create a value-adding web of relationships globally.

This is why Fuji—an expert in photographic film and paper—joins forces with Xerox—an expert in photocopy equipment services—to create mutual value: Each gains exposure in each other's national terrain, and just as important, Fuji learns American entrepreneurial skills and Xerox learns about being a "document" company. This is why software-database expert Oracle and credit-card authorization king VeriFone bring together their distinct pools of talent to capitalize on the emergence of digital cash and create an Internet payment system. This is why KT&D, a small, Delaware-based insurance agency, decided to outsource all its routine, in-house work (including claims processing, accounting and marketing) to a consultancy that was expert in those areas, leaving the professionals at KT&D to do what they do best: sell policies, create new lines of business and penetrate new sales territories.

This is why First Direct, the no-branch telephone bank owned by Midland Bank, can grow as fast as it has (650,000 customers in Great Britain since its launch in 1989; 12,000 new accounts monthly) and still stay lean, light and creative: It focuses on leveraging its intangible assets—exceptional telephone service, database marketing, predictive modeling of consumer behavior and rapid response to individual customers—while linking with a select set of very tangible outside vendors that provide immediate ancillary services including car insurance and home security systems as part of the deal.

British Telecom, prior to its recent merger with MCI, was simply one of many companies networked together in MCI's constellation of partners. MCI is basically an integrative software company that has traditionally outsourced services from paging to security systems, and functions from manufacturing to technology R&D, to its more than 100 carefully chosen partners. Likewise, Corning is considered one of the more successful American companies in putting together both quasi-permanent and temporary "virtual" alliances. Indeed, prudently positioned alliances are so central to Corning's strategy that the company, as one report concluded, considers itself "a network of organizations."

This philosophy allows any start-up anywhere to be a significant player. Black Rock Ventures, a $10-million golf club company, outsources marketing expertise for TV infomercials, contracts with Asian manufacturers to produce clubs, and links up with a couple of American contractors to assemble them. Another partner handles telemarketing, order fulfillment and customer service. Black Rock itself focuses on strategic direction and product development. So does Irvine Sensors, a fast-growing southern California specialty chip manufacturer that doesn't even do its own manufacturing. It sources its chip fabrication to a facility in San Jose, California, while a group in Korea does quality assurance and a group in Kuala Lumpur does packaging and worldwide shipping.

In a 1995 summit at the Massachusetts Institute of Technology, one participant described this trend as leading to an inevitable conclusion by the year 2020: "We imagine a world in which there are many, many firms with only one person, and many others with fewer than 15 people. These firms would come together in temporary combinations for various projects. Work is already organized like this for producing movies, organizing conventions, and constructing large buildings." And, might I add, for producing golf clubs, microchips, insurance and banking services, telecommunications and photocopy services and, frankly, just about anything you can think of.

This arrangement even extends to include competitors. General Colin Powell recently remarked that one of his most sobering realizations while Chairman of the Joint Chiefs was that in the hardball world of geopolitics, it's no longer a simple case of white hats (us, the good guys) vs. black hats (them, the Russians, the bad guys). The CIA and KGB now collaborate, as do NASA and the Russian Space Agency.

Competitors Rockwell, Northrop Grumman and Honeywell worked together with customer Boeing to help develop the new 777 aircraft. Sun Microsystems licenses Java to be included in arch-rival Microsoft's Internet browser Explorer; the result boosts the exposure of Java while enhancing the attractiveness of

Microsoft's product line. When I worked with Visa International, I was intrigued to learn that the banks which issue Visa consider themselves fierce competitors, but they actively cooperate with each other in raising the ease of product usage among merchants and customers.

For me, a real eye-opener occurred when I addressed the annual meeting of the trust divisions of the New York Bankers Association. The speaker prior to me was a senior representative of high-profile competitor Fidelity Investments, who openly shared his insights with his competitors in the audience. Why? Because his competitors in the audience sold Fidelity products as part of their overall portfolio. That's the nature of the beast nowadays. Schizophrenia rules. In any given moment, depending on the context, AT&T and Motorola are each others' customers, suppliers, competitors, or joint-venture partners. To expand upon General Powell's sentiments, competition is no longer good guys vs. bad guys. The relationships are far more incestuous than that.

Viewing the marketplace in terms of relationships also leads to a new way of viewing customers: No longer as endpoints of a transaction, but as viable, interacting partners with compatible goals, obligations and commitments. Silicon Graphics teams worked closely with teams from customer LucasFilm to generate new advances that allowed LucasFilm to create special effects for *Terminator 2* and *Jurassic Park*, among others, while Silicon Graphics wound up with a new technology to sell on the open market. Teams of plastics maker Nypro work closely with teams of customers Gillette and Johnson & Johnson, not only to improve Nypro's product and delivery quality, but also to improve each others' productivity on matters including inventory and logistics. Bill Gates is talking about selling not products, but "membership" to Microsoft, where electronic mediums such as the Internet will allow Microsoft to dialogue frequently with each of its customers, solicit their ideas and interests, respond quickly, and thereby create a viable, ongoing Microsoft community.

All in all, Giant Step IV has significant implications for any organization. Certainly, you want to keep and grow the core skills, competencies and talents that make you "world-class great." But you also want to ally yourself with a slew of enterprises (including certain competitors and customers) who are the most outstanding in the technologies and niches that you want to cultivate, and in the functions that you no longer want to keep in-house.

By embracing cooperative relationships with the cream of the crop (not necessarily the cheapest of the crop), organizations can sharply accelerate product development and market penetration, as well as significantly reduce operational and distribution costs— all vital tactics to nimbly vault over conventional wisdom and existing competition.

The picture of the leapfrogging organization will not be the solid, massed pyramid bolted to one locale and one way of doing things, but instead, an ever-multiplying, often-temporary set of overlapping web-like circles—spread everywhere, permeable and ephemeral. Savvy leaders will transform their organizations into value-adding networks, combinations, clusters and alliances, where each party brings to the table unique talent and expertise. Cultivating constructive relationships for the purpose of achieving extraordinary goals will be so important that it is safe to say that the value of your organization's relationships will be as important—if not more important—than the value of your organization's products.

One last point. The fuel of this Giant Step is *trust*. Not blind trust, but the kind of prudent trust that allows two partners to be open, inclusive and collaborative with one another—rather than operating within the typical arm's-length, legalistic, often adversarial context that describes so many "partnerships" today. I'm not just talking about relationships between two companies, but even within companies themselves. You don't have to go to inner cities to find gang warfare. In too many traditional organizations you'll find carefully protected "turf" and destructive inter-departmental confrontations. All this makes a mockery out of words like "teamwork," "partnerships" and "synergy."

In contrast, the thing that impresses me most about the exceptionally successful Merix Corporation is the trust that permeates the relationships there. At the Oregon-based circuit board subassembler, it's not unusual to see mixed groups spanning all functions and levels, receiving and sharing relevant data and working together as equals on company problems. This is as true with strategic issues as with operational ones.

At a recent three-day off-site, shop-floor representatives worked hand-in-hand with executives to chart a strategic path for Merix's future. The annual awards banquet at Merix revealed another extraordinary manifestation of trust. As two representatives of the Supplier of the Year came forward, CEO Deborah Coleman—who is second to none in promoting an open-door, informal culture—leaned over and whispered to me "Hell, I thought those two were *our* people."

And why should she have thought differently? Those suppliers were members of ongoing Merix project teams, they attended important Merix meetings, they were intimately involved in boosting Merix's fortunes. That's trust. That's a web of relationships. That's the openness that has helped propel Merix into a financial darling of the industry.

AT&T vice president William Moody, in a recent talk at the University of San Francisco, said that the whole issue of trust is receiving rapidly increasing attention at his company—for reasons similar to the ones outlined here. Moody is no fool, and he readily admits that not everyone is trustworthy. Yet he also observes that real trust is an all-or-none affair. The key with "outsiders," therefore, is to selectively choose people to collaborate with who you feel are trustworthy, and then act with total trust unless the other party violates it. The organization, argues Moody, has one of two choices: "Either you build systems that unleash trust or you build systems that diminish trust."

In most cases, it's the latter that predominate, and leaders like Moody are realizing that this must change. I gave a series of lectures at the Steel Service Center Institute last year. In the audiences were executives from every segment of the rough-and-tumble steel distribution system—from raw materials to finished product. Repeatedly, the topic that galvanized the most interest was this issue of trust. As one steel man told me, "In our business, trust is a joke. It's something you look up on page 45, paragraph 2, subsection 3 in a 50-page contract. We've got to learn how to trust other players in this business, or else we're all going to get killed. But people are afraid to take the first step."

Leaders must take that step, because the notion of distrustful webs is an oxymoron, a self-canceling phrase. Whether we're talking about joint ventures, activity-based accounting or virtual alliances, trust is the glue that binds. The days of rewarding a purchasing manager for jerking around and lying to a supplier in order to save a couple of bucks are over. Spaghetti-like relationships cemented by earned trust are one of the key catalysts for propelling an organization over competitors that are still operating in a turf-hoarding, arms-length, legally constricted "I am an island" context.

If you're sincere about transforming your organization from a pile of bricks and mortar into a web of value-adding relationships, you'll want to commit toward dealing differently with your key constituencies, including employees, customers, suppliers and strategic partners. Commitments 9, 10 and 11 provide a number of practical paths toward this goal:

- Get real about what it takes to build a team (Chapter/Commitment 9)
- Invite your competitors in, don't fence them out (Chapter/Commitment 10), and
- Bless thy complaining customer (Chapter/Commitment 11)

Commitment 9 puts the onus on relationship-building, whether internal or external. If you're really serious about creating value-enhancing partnerships with employees, customers, suppliers and so on, challenge yourself to apply the Commitment 9 criteria for cultivating real dream teams, not pseudo-teams. The words here are *cultivate*—which means grow, nourish, replenish—and *real*—which means genuinely bonded with common goals, philosophies, values and a sense of trust.

If you can meet the standards of this Commitment, you're already well on the road to transforming your organization into a web of relationships. The subsequent two Commitments, however, will give you even more ammunition.

Commitment 10 calls for developing a new perspective about your competitors. Commit to trashing the simplistic us-vs.-them mentality of the past. Respect your competitors, yes; monitor them, of course; but stop draining your creative energy by trying to come up with ways to "beat" them. Instead, use them as a spur to develop creative impulses that will grow your own business. And if competitors have special expertise or connections that can help, broaden your vision to include them in your strategic web rather than seal them out.

Commitment 11 challenges you with perhaps the most difficult Commitment of all: Deliberately create inviting, two-way, open communication webs with *complaining* customers. Yes, view your customers overall as partners. But reach out to the complainers in particular. Why? Because, as this chapter will demonstrate, the loudest complainers often hold the keys to greatest change, by surfacing important weaknesses and by prodding you to challenge the very way you run your business. Organizations that consciously create enticing webs to draw in dissatisfied customers will not only keep those customers (and other dissatisfied customers who don't complain), they will also propel themselves forward in ways that they may never have anticipated.

The first segment of Commitment 11 uses a story about a medical lab test to demonstrate the potential value-adding information that a dissatisfied customer *could have* provided if only he had been asked. The second segment shows you how to differentiate between a customer from hell—who you ought to "fire" pronto and toss out of your web—and a customer who's gone through hell—who you ought to bring in as a partner just as quickly. The third segment provides tips on the why's and how's of nourishing the complaint process—in effect, tips for bringing that complaining customer into your web.

COMMITMENT 9:
GET REAL ABOUT WHAT IT TAKES
TO BUILD A TEAM

> *Webs require intimate teamwork. Lots of it. If you're sincere about cultivating genuine teamwork among employees, customers, partners (maybe even competitors), ask yourself how your current teams stack up on the eight points described in this chapter. Even better, ask members of your organization's teams to grade themselves using these eight criteria, and then candidly discuss the results in a constructive, team-like way.*

"Team" is a big buzzword nowadays. Joint-venture teams, cross-functional teams, customer-vendor teams, virtual teams, project teams, quality teams, product development teams, "skunk-work" teams, top management teams, all sorts of teams. Teams, we are told, are the wave of the future—corporate salvation, in fact.

Yes, you catch a little sarcasm. The concept's right, but I'm skeptical of all the hype.

True, *real* teams form the foundation of webs, and they get extraordinary things done. But many so-called "teams" nowadays aren't really teams at all. They may be labeled as such, but they're often simply a collection of individual egos. The people in these collections may even call themselves a "team," but they neither operate nor feel like one.

Here, then, are eight signs to look for that will help you separate the real teams from pseudo-teams as you build webs within and beyond your organization. After you rate yourself, ponder the postscript on pages 130 and 131

1. **Consensus.**
   Do members of your "team" share the same overarching goals and the same sense of commitment to the group? Consider these questions:

- Do you all agree on the team's vision and purpose: why it exists, where it's going, what it's trying to do, what its core priorities are? Or do these issues generate confusion and uncertainty—maybe even conflict—among members?
- Are you all committed to the same values, such as: What do we stand for, how do we define success, what is ethical and fair behavior, and how should we behave toward each other? Or do the values that are ostensibly followed amount to so much lip service?
- Do people feel a sense of ownership in the group; do they feel like they're a genuine, involved, participating, egalitarian part of it, and do they feel that this ownership is an important part of their work life? Or are they noncommittal, grudging participants, perhaps because they feel that membership in the group is irrelevant to their performance, or perhaps because membership is mandated from above?

2. **Trust.**
   Do members of your "team" really trust each other? Ask yourself these questions:

   - Do people believe each other when communicating? Or are they a bit anxious that they are hearing partial truths and that hidden agendas exist?
   - Do they believe they can depend on and count on each other? Or do they feel that relying on others' goodwill and expertise is either naive or dangerous?
   - When people interact and communicate with one another, is *honesty* the operative descriptor, or are *manipulation* and *deceit* more appropriate?
   - Do team members feel safe with each other, or are they wary of each other's motives?
   - Do people feel confident about each other's professional capacities and efforts? Or do they feel uncomfortable, perhaps suspicious, so that they've got to scrutinize others' actions in order to get the "right" results?

3. **Candor.**
   How open are your "team" members with each other? Ask yourself these questions:

- Can they be open and straight with each other about concerns, anxieties, hopes, fears, joys, angers? Or do they wind up holding things in, muttering under their breath and throwing verbal darts at people behind their backs?
- Can they be forthright with each other about problems the team faces? Can they openly exchange criticisms of each other, the team as a whole, and the status quo in general—while simultaneously generating alternatives and reviewing ideas for the future? Or do they tend to pull their punches with each other, carefully sniffing the wind before communicating at all?
- Do they share their "wins" and "losses" (goal-attainment, setbacks, personal learning, personal reactions to events) with each other? Or do they camouflage these experiences for political reasons, while rationalizing negative outcomes with excuses and fingerpointing?
- Are the communications and information-exchange among people marked by words like *direct, frank, straightforward, undisguised, plainspoken?* Or just the opposite?

4. **Respect.**
   To what extent do members of your "team" feel—and demonstrate—that they hold each other in esteem? Consider:

   - Are people aware of the full set of each other's skills, experiences and expertise—including those that are not "officially" required by the job description? Or is there a myopic ignorance of people's full array of talents?
   - Do people genuinely—even naively—listen to each other's ideas and concerns? Or do they simply defend and promote their own preconceptions, with only a pretense of paying attention to what others believe?
   - Do people publicly honor and recognize each other's efforts and contributions? Or are accomplishments taken for granted?
   - Do people value each other's time? Or do they act in a way that suggests that others' time doesn't have much importance?
   - Do people hold agreements and promises among themselves as sacred? For example, if someone says he will

publicly support someone at a meeting, he does; if someone says she will show up for a meeting, she will—on time, and prepared. Or, are agreements and promises viewed expediently as "maybe—if it's convenient"?

5. **Caring.**
   Do people seem genuinely concerned about each other's personal welfare, as human beings? (Yes, this is a squishy-soft concept, but it's naive to think it's irrelevant to teamwork.) Again, some questions:

   • Do people show sympathy for each other when personal and professional problems arise, or empathy when occasions for joy arise? That is, are they sincere in asking concerned questions, writing little notes and cards, giving gifts on birthdays and anniversaries, or holding collections if personal finances are a problem?
   • Do people help each other succeed and grow, and then share in the excitement of each other's accomplishments? Or are such concerns deemed unnecessary or childish?
   • Do people transcend co-dependency, that is, do they hold each other to high standards of performance and provide each other with a four-fold combination of straight feedback, no-nonsense expectations, coaching and compassion? Or do they confuse caring for people with indulging them, thereby—in the name of "caring"—failing to insist on high standards or to coach poor performance and inappropriate behavior? Or even worse, do they justify a mistaken view of caring by inappropriately "rescuing" people whose behavior and performance consistently falls short of the mark?

6. **Collaboration.**
   Do people emphasize working together, behaving as if their own goals and those of others in the "team" were in harmony?

   • Do people act as if their own success will be enhanced by the success of the team, or do people act as if their own needs and those of the team are contradictory concepts?
   • Does individuality emerge as unique contributions to the team, or as egocentric self-aggrandizement?

- Do the individuals in the team share information, tools and other resources with each other? Or do they tend to hoard and protect turf?
- When the team is working together, is the dominant mode a search for "win-win" solutions, or is the dominant mode a "win-lose" perspective where team members are in subtle battle with each other for ostensibly scarce resources and rewards?
- When difficulties or crises occur, is the dominant response cooperative problem-analysis? Or is it cover-my-rear blame-analysis?
- Do team members make sure that every team member is included, is "in the know" and "in the loop"? Or does a laissez-faire, "I'm-not-my-brother's-keeper" mentality prevail?

7. **Meaningful recognition and rewards.**
   Do recognition and reward, formal and informal, reinforce "team" activities?

   - Are team members recognized and rewarded for contributing to the team purpose and charter, or do team members feel that they're better off pursuing their own personal agendas, even while outwardly participating?
   - Are recognition and rewards directly and significantly linked to team performance (achieving team goals)? Or are compensation and other goodies determined strictly by individual performance?
   - Are team members recognized and rewarded for helping and coaching team members? Or are such behaviors considered inconsequential when rewards are handed out?
   - Are team members recognized and rewarded for a willingness and ability to learn and practice new, important skills and knowledge? Or is training and development considered an occasional "soft" perk (or obligation), not carefully aligned with team priorities?

8. **Team influence, authority and business connectedness.**
   One can't separate team effectiveness from the total organizational environment within which it operates; hence, to what extent is the "team" integrated as an influential part of the business?

- Are team purpose and goals developed in close collaboration with key external and/or internal constituencies (for example, customers, suppliers, partners, senior managers, employees in other functions)? Or do team goals and activities occur in a social and strategic vacuum?
- Does the team have the authority to do what it was organized to do? Or is a lot of time wasted playing political games and trying to overcome massive bureaucracy?
- Is the team an integral part of the work done in the company? Or is the team an artificial limb plastered on top of the existing structure in order to suggest that management is "doing something"?
- Is the organization investing financial, managerial and time resources in the team, or does it let the team "sink or swim" with little support, hoping it somehow will survive?
- Does top management trust and respect decisions made by the team? Or does top management frequently second-guess and interfere in—or simply fail to act on—the recommendations made by the team?

Postscript

Okay, I'm the first to admit that these eight dimensions represent ideals, and that the questions themselves are stereotypical extremes. I know of no organization whose teams would score perfectly on these dimensions. I suspect that only at the Pearly Gates would we find people who would work in flawless harmony.

Even at fast-growing Johnsonville Foods in Sheboygan Falls, Wisconsin, a company that is peerless when it comes to being internally team-based, teams merely approximate rather than fully achieve the noble goals outlined above. That's noteworthy, because keep in mind that at Johnsonville, cross-functional teams (many staffed by employees with initially no more than a high school education) do all recruiting, hiring, performance evaluation and termination. They formulate, track and amend budgets. They make capital investment proposals, and they do necessary research and analysis. They are fully responsible for quality, including control and correction. They develop product prototypes and packaging. They develop and monitor productivity improvement measures. They interface with vendors, suppliers and customers as necessary. A few specialty teams are now involved in the strategic planning and positioning of the entire company. All this in a corporate environment that is fully supportive of team-based activities, as evidenced by the autonomy, resource accessibility and continual training opportunities that the teams enjoy.

So you might say that if Johnsonville can't score a perfect "10" on these questions, who can? But that's the wrong question to ask. Johnsonville is as successful a business as it is—and as effective a team-based organization as it is—precisely because it is moving aggressively in the direction of the eight dimensions above—and because it is committed to perpetual improvement on them.

In contrast, I reckon that most organizations, and their teams, are marked by movement in the other direction. I've tested this proposition empirically in organizations other than Johnsonville, by asking members of so-called teams to rate themselves on a 1–7 scale (1=very low, "negative" end; 7=very high, desirable end) on each dimension. The results have been mediocre at best—in the 3–4 range. Frequently, the scores have been so embarrassing, so appallingly low, that out of sensitivity to the "teams" involved I've stopped conducting my informal research altogether.

Instead, I ask team members to evaluate themselves honestly on each dimension and share the data among themselves. And then to do it again and again and again. That's what I challenge you and your team colleagues to do. Remember, whether your team is made up of multiple functions or multiple organizations, real teams are not merely announced and labeled as such on a piece of paper. Nor are they groups that meet periodically. Real teams are cultivated and grown by their members—thoughtfully, persistently, and sometimes painfully. This applies even with alliances bristling with brilliant "core competencies."

I predict that the bold efforts of Compaq and Thomson to develop a hybrid PC/TV, and the revolutionary intent of Teledesic (the eye-opening Microsoft/McCaw/Boeing alliance) to launch satellites which would allow anyone, anywhere to access the Internet without a computer, will truly succeed only if the parties involved score well on these eight dimensions. Hence, if you're serious about creating value-adding webs, and if you know that teamwork is key to leapfrogging the competition, you won't shirk from using the eight dimensions as a means to monitor your progress. It's a never-ending job, but the results are worth it.

COMMITMENT 10:
INVITE YOUR COMPETITORS IN—
DON'T FENCE THEM OUT

Valentine's Day cards are probably seldom exchanged between executives of Sony and Philips, or Mercedes and Toyota, or Microsoft and Netscape. And you can be darn sure that every other Internet provider has been trying to capitalize on America Online's undercapacity woes, just as every other airline was poised to take immediate advantage of American Airlines' labor problems earlier this year. In short, you don't have to love your competitors, but you'd be doing yourself a great service if you judiciously included some of the better ones in your web. The flip side is that obsessing on "beating" your competitors will hurt you even more than it will them. Read on.

Healthy competition is natural and inevitable in thriving economies; it's what makes capitalism such a powerful economic force. It is so important that the exhaustive research of Harvard's Michael Porter allowed him to conclude that "vigorous domestic rivalry" is the primary determinant of any nation's economic strength within the international community.

In real life, however, many executives spend big bucks and time obsessing about beating, pulverizing or eliminating their competition. But this path leads to neither progress nor prosperity.

I have in front of me a *Wall Street Journal* article that describes how a senior executive of a large corporation "barks" (very appropriate word) the following: "I want my people to destroy our competitors, I want them to kill and crush them." In my own consulting practice, I've frequently heard these words used as strategic objectives. It all sounds tough and virile, but let me briefly propose three reasons why this sort of macho posturing is both counterproductive and outdated.

1. *When managers focus on squashing competitors, they are operating from neither a position of power nor a position of innovation.*

   The key to competitive advantage is to create new opportunities and lead the market rather than pay undue attention to what today's established competitors are doing. A strategy that is preoccupied with "beating" competitors is reactive, fear-based and myopic. It is reactive because management decisions by definition revolve around what others are currently doing; in effect, management that obsesses about beating competitors necessarily allows others to define the game and make the first moves.

   Besides, since unexpected sources of competition are incessantly cropping up, an organization with a "kill the competitor" mind-set is forever frenetically and pathetically doomed to run around, spending its creative energy trying to stamp out new fires.

   A "crush-the-competitor" priority is also fear-based because the driving force for organizational motivation and teamwork is negative: to somehow liquidate a so-called dangerous alien (the competitor) before "it" destroys us. On both an organizational and a personal level, this approach is anxiety-laden and exhausting.

   Finally, a preoccupation with "beating" the competitor is myopic because the organization inevitably operates under the delusion that there are limited possibilities (death to the competitor) rather than a full range of exciting unchartered ones. Put it all together and it's easy to see what happened to America Online, CompuServe and Prodigy. These three companies were so focused on beating each other that their strategic moves revolved almost entirely against each other. They each subscribed to the content-based, captive-audience business model, and they matched each other's moves in that arena. Meanwhile, Netscape and Microsoft developed the browsers which allowed customers to create their own Internet content, bypassing the "big three" altogether. The recent woes of AOL, CompuServe and Prodigy are simply the latest arc of a downward business cycle.

   As mentioned in earlier chapters, cutting-edge companies are primarily interested in changing the rules of the entire game with fresh, unique market offerings. Review business history of the past 20 years and consider the breakthrough impact of Schwab's discount brokerage services, Dell Computer's price-friendly/mail-order/after-sale service mix, Hewlett-Packard's Laser Jet printers, and Merrill Lynch's early asset management account offerings. You'll probably conclude, as I did, that successful companies like these are less obsessed with "killing" established players and products than in carving out new niches and creating hitherto nonexistent possibilities for their own businesses. Bottom line: the focus on beating competitors reflects narrow thinking—and narrow thinking will inevitably yield narrow results.

2. *When managers are preoccupied with destroying competitors, they are likely to unintentionally create an internal corporate culture in which "beating others"—even when those "others" are inside the organization—becomes more valued than achievement or innovation.*

Yes, I know the official party line: Concentrating on smashing the competitor will presumably coalesce us into a tight collaborative corporate team. But I wonder. When the primary strategic goal is to attain a killer victory over someone else, it seems just as reasonable to conclude that a win-lose mind-set will trickle down in such a way that the target goal transcends competitors.

That is, the corporate culture is just as likely to become laced with a "beat the other guy" priority, where people subtly learn the importance of seeking victory over others, period. Like victory over another colleague or another department within the same organization. The wealth of research findings that social psychologist Alfie Kohn has collected over the years strongly suggest that under these circumstances, genuine performance and innovation, on either a team or individual basis, will take on a secondary status to that of smashing the competitor—in this case, anyone external or internal who is perceived as a threat to one's self-interest.

In short, it is difficult to promote collaboration and trust internally while preaching the opposite externally. Look at the in-house gang warfare currently taking place in many organizations and you'll see what I mean.

3. *When managers overemphasize the idea of beating competitors, they become oblivious to something more important: that
   some of these competitors can provide valuable sources of
   strategic opportunity as allies.*
   Indeed, in today's helter-skelter brain-based global economy, a
   failure to seek alliances that pool expertise and resources—
   even with traditional rivals—can be lethal.

   Here's why. When it comes to competition, I've already
   noted that the world is no longer a simple good guy vs. bad guy
   affair. It's a much more tangled and ambiguous theater, as I
   found out when I downloaded my latest version of Microsoft's
   Explorer using my Netscape Navigator! Or consider: A number
   of local daily newspapers—from the Waco *Herald Tribune* to the
   Chicago *Tribune*—are currently delivering the national edition of
   The New York Times to their interested subscribers. The *Times*
   typically pays the local paper around 25 cents for each home
   delivery (50 cents on Sunday). This allows the local dailies to
   spread their fixed costs and raise their gross margins, while the
   Times capitalizes on established distribution systems to build its
   own revenue stream. *Times'* executives now view these other
   dailies as complementary, not as competition.

   A similar sentiment exists between CBS and NBC: CBS
   "shock jock" Don Imus is carried by MSNBC, augmenting the
   revenues of both companies. When CBS's 1996 show *Ink*
   bombed, ABC was not particularly overjoyed. Why? ABC has a
   stake in DreamWorks, which produces *Ink*. As an ABC executive
   commented: "It's planned schizophrenia. The rules are different."

   Yes indeed, they are, which means you can't automatically
   exclude competitors from your web. When Netscape and
   America Online recently agreed to produce compatible products,
   strategic alliance consultant David Raphael of Belmont,
   California-based Marcar Consulting told me: "They've figured out
   that they stand to make a lot more profit from standardization
   than from killing each other." You'll always be facing competition
   from somewhere, but you're more likely to leapfrog over it if you
   can selectively and collaboratively draw resources from any and
   all world-class players, including carefully selected competitors.

   In the brutal terrain of jet engine manufacturing, General
   Electric has joined forces with Pratt & Whitney to develop an
   engine for the Boeing 777-600 series aircraft which will be

launched in the year 2000. Raphael notes that if both companies pursued the traditional course of "crushing" each other in pursuit of 777-600 contracts, each company could anticipate $200 to $300 million in operating profits over the next 10 years. But Raphael's calculations indicate that this alliance will generate $900 million in operating profits over the same time period. Split two ways, that means a winning $450 million for each partner.

Further, the alliance will allow GE to attain the standard Chairman Jack Welch imposes on all GE businesses, which is to be No. 1 or No. 2 in the sectors in which it plays. Without this alliance—especially given Rolls-Royce's entry—it is unlikely that GE would attain this standard. Finally the alliance allows both parties to consolidate their experience and expertise toward creating a radically new type of engine. GE and Pratt & Whitney thus leapfrog over today's competitive feuding by collaboratively developing new technologies and infrastructures that will no doubt serve both of them well in the years to come in other markets.

Two notable quotes provide a useful perspective on this issue. One, from Harvard's Paul Lawrence, writing for a 1997 American Management Association circular: "It is imperative for future managers to understand cooperative business alliances because, in the decades to come, managers will either be part of an alliance or be competing with one."

Combine that thought with this one, from Stewart Alsop, writing in the September 30, 1996 issue of *Fortune* magazine: "[In] today's computer business [*author's note*: who nowadays isn't in the computer business?], alliances with other companies—including competitors—are often more important than good relationships with customers."

In short, adopting a new inclusive mindset allows you to see the world of "competitors" anew. Raphael's advice in this matter is straightforward. If you want to collaborate with competitors, first, be open to possibilities, and simultaneously be careful. Second, start with a highly focused scope, a project. That's what Hewlett-Packard and Corning typically do with their respective partners (and what GE and Pratt & Whitney are doing). And third, build trust and success, and grow the partnership incrementally. Finally, never forget that partnerships—like marriages—require time and persistence.

I think Rafael is right on target, and I would add to his list. I have found that differences in corporate cultures, systems and technologies, geographical distance and, increasingly, disparate language, religion and social mores must be ironed out. Permeating the entire partnership, and muddying the waters further, an air of distrust and sometimes mutual fear frequently exists and must be overcome, regardless of whether the partners previously were competitors or not. To do all of this, persistence is clearly a must.

The bottom line: Choose the competitors that are world-class players in areas in which you're not, focus on establishing mutually enhancing goals, follow the eight "dream team" rules cited in Commitment 9, and something magical and paradoxical occurs: Competitors wind up helping *you* leapfrog the competition.

These, then, are the reasons why the whole "crushing" mentality is a dead-end, which itself is a testament to a couple of larger trends in business today. Crushing becomes particularly self-defeating in a world that is becoming more and more interdependent. In an interdependent economy, our self-interests and destinies are dependent on others. Accordingly, the quality of relationships that one establishes with customers, vendors, suppliers and partners becomes a key strategic success factor. Collaboration, candor and trust within these relationships become strategic imperatives. In this kind of world, organizations that insist on playing the role of squinty-eyed, fast-shooting cowboy or goon-like Mafioso will not fare well.

Once we eliminate crushing from our planning repertoire and focus instead on leapfrogging, we are free to consider more sensible advice about dealing with competitors:

1. **Accept them**—They or others will always be there; that's the nature of free markets.
2. **Be aware of them**—Keep a general lookout, but don't get bogged down in the paralysis of incessant competitive analysis.
3. **Respect them**—Welcome them as spurs to your own motivation and efforts; remember that pride à la arrogance and a "not invented here" corporate culture are always precursors to a fall.
4. **Whenever possible, join them**—They may have valuable skills and networks you don't and vice versa; so dialogue with them, learn from them, and probe joint opportunities with them.

COMMITMENT 11:
BLESS THY COMPLAINING CUSTOMER

Are you following the principles of teamwork as Johnsonville Foods does? Are you including customers and suppliers in key meetings, as subassembler Merix does? Are you sharing databases with your customers, as plastics manufacturer Nypro does? Are you living with your customers on their premises, as healthcare specialist Interim Services does? Yes to all the above? Then let me test your courage and humility to the nth degree: Are you willing to include those vociferous, irritating, <u>complaining</u> customers of yours in your web? Here's why it's imperative to do so:

Every customer complaint is a golden nugget of information for any company, which is why managers should gratefully pounce on them. Managers can use complaints as fuel to improve current operations. They can use them as leverage to enhance product and service quality, and to educate personnel as to what's really important. They can analyze them to glean subtle clues for breakthroughs in the products and services themselves. That's because savvy managers know that customers who actually take the time to complain are as valuable to bottom-line financials as any MBA analyst or high-priced consultant.

To be sure, complainers are bothersome. But remember that each complaining customer is telling the vendor three things:

1. *My business and I are still wooable* if you personally show me you care about me and fix your mess (even though I say you've lost me, if I didn't care, I'd just walk).
2. *I represent others* (you ought to thank me; quieter customers who are just as disgruntled have silently moved on, or are looking to do so at the first opportunity).
3. *I am telling you the end result of glitches* in your systems and business philosophy (consider me a fire alarm that's warning you that whatever it is you're doing, you had better change, and fast!).

To demonstrate how a complaining customer can provide you with a wealth of strategic insight—if you listen—read this true story about a hospital that didn't listen. The lesson: Bring in this disgruntled customer as a part of your extended web. He's got plenty to say, plenty to advise, and on top of that, he's the one who's paying the bills. As you read this story, consider the value of having him share his experiences and opinions with your staff. Or invite him to join a project team aimed at radical improvement of operations.

My father recently underwent a series of lab tests administered by a local hospital. He would come home muttering after each hospital visit, and once back home, if asked how his tests were going, he would generously offer a few choice expletives about hospitals, physicians and the medical industry in general. One day, I spontaneously said: "Dad, you've been complaining about your tests all along. Tell me, in terms of quality, what makes a good lab test or, for that matter, a bad lab test?"

If I asked this question in the healthcare industry, I'd get answers framed in terms of accuracy, statistical reliability, clinical comprehensiveness, and so on. But I was more interested in the customer's perspective. Here are my father's responses along with my own commentary.

"Why do I have to wait days to get the results of a simple test when the results are really important to me? Am I to believe that they've got a bunch of people working day and night all that time on my sample?"

An eminently reasonable query. The Boston Consulting Group surveyed a diverse group of U.S. businesses and concluded that 95 to 99 percent of their internal activities have little or no relevance to the customer. For example, they found that it took on average 22 days to turn around a customer's application form in the insurance industry, yet the average amount of time spent internally on attending to any given application consumed a grand total of 17 minutes. Hence, the typical organization infrastructure—with its policies, sign-offs, meetings, reports, etc.—manages to take a 17-minute task and turn it into a 22-day affair. It was this sort of research that made Hammer and Champy's book a bestseller and sparked the reengineering craze.

"Quality and cycle time are like yin and yang," James Swallow of consultancy A.T. Kearney points out. "If you go after cycle time, you lower the water level in your lake, and suddenly all the rocks stick out—exposing the places where quality runs aground." Colin Gilmore, one of the heads of United Airlines' aircraft maintenance quality efforts, tells me that quality really took off when people began to focus on cycle times. "It's only when you ask people how we can reduce cycle time by 70 or 80 percent that they really become excited about creating an entirely new process. Asking for small cycle-time reductions means that people can get by with doing more of what they currently do. But calling for big reductions means you have to wipe the slate clean."

Excess waiting time is like excess inventory. It is a sign of misplaced strategic priorities, internal operational inefficiency, and poor relationships with colleagues and suppliers. It used to take Motorola three weeks to both process an order for certain customized pagers and have the manufactured product ready for shipment to the customer. Motorola reduced this time frame to two hours. How? By investing in flexible manufacturing systems, by maintaining close relationships with an elite group of suppliers that provide nearly real-time delivery, and by using technology to cut out as many in-house people as possible in the decision chain. A salesperson now plugs in the customer's order on a hand-held computer, and the data is transmitted electronically to the shop floor, where an "empowered employee" (that is, a functioning adult who can make a decision without being second-guessed) takes the information and starts the manufacturing process within minutes. That's quality.

"Why do I have to wait every time I go to the hospital?
If it's not the paperwork they make me fill out, there are six
other people scheduled for the same time."

This is the more personalized component of the waiting problem. A. Blanton Godfrey, CEO of the Juran Institute, once asked an audience of healthcare professionals the same question: "Why do you make patients fill out the same long forms for a lab test regardless of whether they stay on-site one hour or one week, regardless of whether it is a first-time visit or if the patient was with you three days earlier?"

Let's take it a step further. Why do your customers wait? For action in response to a complaint or suggestion? For a reply to a question or problem? For a service rep to call or arrive? For a new product or feature? For an invoice, a payment, an order or a document? To be connected to the right person who can help them, or simply to get through on the telephone without hearing a busy signal or being put on hold?

Why do your so-called internal customers wait? While working with one manufacturer, I asked the professionals who wrote the user manuals how much of their time was spent waiting. Their response: 75 percent. I found that figure remarkable until they explained that they waited for instructions from the sales and engineering groups. They waited for further instructions because they often didn't fully understand the initial instructions. They waited for both sales and engineering to review their work independently. They waited while sales and engineering had to coordinate their feedback because the independent feedback from the two groups was often contradictory, and so on. The notion that the people who write the user manuals could constructively be included with representatives of sales and engineering in cross-disciplinary teams with concurrent efforts apparently was too radical an idea for that corporate culture. Accordingly, they waited. And since problems like these do not occur in isolation, I know that many other groups in that company waited, which meant, ultimately, that real (paying) customers wound up waiting as well. In fact, speed to market was a major headache in this company.

Figure out a way for your customers to wait less and you will not only cut out a bundle of gross cost excesses but also create a loyal corps of customers who perceive your output as the highest in quality. Yet for some bizarre reason this advice is something that many "professional" managers don't "get." Nothing infuriates me more than standing in a slow line at a store, bank, airline ticket counter or hotel check-in, and watching managers in the background doing "managerial" things like shuffling papers, thoughtfully pondering the fate of the universe or studiously observing their employees at work rather than jumping in to help those employees reduce customers' queue times. Is this a quality issue? Is this an issue that will keep the company from leapfrogging the competition? You bet it is.

"Whenever I call the hospital and ask about the status of my file, why can't I get an answer from whomever answers

the phone? I get angry when they say that they don't have my file handy, or they don't know anything because they just came on duty, or—even worse—they can't give me an answer because their supervisor or the doctor isn't there to okay it."

My father happens to be a computer buff, so he has difficulty understanding why so many organizations haven't entered the 1990s yet. He is bewildered by the fact that paper and file folders are still *de rigueur*—along with their propensity for getting misplaced and being error-ridden—in so many organizations and that everyone on the payroll (especially anyone interacting with customers directly) is not trained to access a customer's file instantly with a touch of a keypad.

My father might take heart to know that Fidelity Investments privately attributes a sizable part of its success not to its investment predictions, but to clients' appreciation of the highly trained, well-paid professionals who answer the telephone and are so well-versed with Fidelity's products and organization that they can readily access any customer's file, answer most questions on the spot or immediately connect the customer to the precise person who can.

My father also is driven to the depths of frustration when the person on the other end of the line tells him that he or she can't answer a simple question without deferring to his or her "supervisor" or to the "doctor," neither of whom is ever available. The rationale, when one is given at all, is that the information is too proprietary or too sensitive. Rubbish. Too sensitive for whom? Remember, my father is the patient. Besides, he's not asking for sophisticated medical data that requires a combination M.D.-Ph.D. to explain or comprehend. He wants to know the status of his file and when he can expect some results.

It's easy to empathize with my father in his frustration. How often have we been driven to the verge of apoplexy when we are faced with some poor soul who cannot provide us with the most elementary information, or make the most common-sense decision, without getting a sign-off from his or her absent "superior"?

"If they tell me the results will be ready by next Monday, why aren't they? If a doctor tells me he'll call me between 8 and 10 on Tuesday morning, why doesn't he?"

Customers have long memories; they remember the tiniest commitments. Federal Express understands this as well as any company I've seen. A few years ago, Chairman Fred Smith said: "If a customer has a complaint or problem, we'll get back to him or her that day with a response, even if it's to say that we're still working on it. The sun doesn't go down without a customer getting a reply to the question."

Think about this equation: **CP = D/E**. *A customer's perception of quality is equal to what the vendor delivers relative to what the customer expects.* Poor-quality companies overpromise and underdeliver. High-quality companies promise a lot by virtue of demanding high standards of themselves, and they deliver even more. This is just as true for a promise to call back on Tuesday morning as it is for a guarantee of state-of-the-art product.

> *"It's their attitude. Take the way they talk to me. Why can't they be nicer? After all, I'm worried about my results; that's why I pester them. And when I do get the results, why can't they explain the specific numbers to me, rather than give me a patronizing response, as if I'm too stupid to understand the specifics? And if I call them on it, why do they label me a 'difficult' patient?"*

Pretty self-explanatory, isn't it? A few years ago, a client survey was done by one of the then-Big 8 accounting firms just prior to its merger with another then-Big 8 firm. The survey indicated that the two factors that most influenced their clients' satisfaction with the company's services had nothing to do with technical expertise in auditing or consulting. Instead, the factors were "empathy" and "personal concern shown to the client." I wonder how the button-down folks in that organization reacted to those results. I wonder how many "professional" managers even understand them.

Disney understands, which is one reason why its service quality is unparalleled. A non-Disney executive once told me a "Disney story" that deeply impressed him. It seems that a few children who were viewing a large fish tank at Disney World became upset because they thought some of the fish looked "unhappy." Their parents sheepishly brought this concern to the attention of one of the staff members. The staff member took the parents and the kids "backstage" to talk to one of the professionals who tended the tanks. He, in turn, spent two hours with the kids not only explaining to them why the faces of happy fish may have appeared unhappy to them, but also giving them a tour and showing them how he and his staff tend the tanks.

Do empathy and respect have a lot to do with the kind of quality necessary to leapfrog the competition? You bet they do.

As my father reached the end of his list, I was struck by the fact that he had forgotten something important. "Dad, I asked you to tell me about quality, but you haven't said a word about things like accuracy and reliability."

He looked at me with annoyance and snapped, "Obviously. That's a given; I take those things for granted."

He's right. We all do, don't we? We take for granted that the coffee at the coffee break will be palatable, that the airplane's engine performance will be flawless, that the paperwork on a loan will be accurate, that the gas will not knock, that the long-distance telephone reception will be clear, that the new CD player will play, that the blouse or wallpaper will not disintegrate within a year.

But when we judge the total quality of the products and services of these vendors, we go well beyond narrow, technical standards. In fact, we're terribly demanding and fickle, and terribly unfair to boot: Any vendor will tell you that it's really tough to provide zero-defect products and services, much less all the additional intangibles we demand, such as what my father expects from a high-quality lab test.

And yet, if we invite customers like my father into our web, three magical things occur. One, his dissatisfaction with us disintegrates. Two, he can help us unearth current problems and develop solutions that make a real difference to customers. Three, he and his story galvanize us with a sense of urgency—and enthusiasm—as we execute dramatic changes in our organization. All rather vital spurs to leapfrogging the competition, don't you agree?

> **Yes, customers can indeed be unfair, but in a turbulent global economy, where competition among vendors is frenzied and choices among customers are profuse, that's a fact of life. We can choose to ignore my father as a crank, or, as suggested above, invite him to be part of the hospital's management web. If you're still doubtful, read the next tale. And remember, truth can be stranger than fiction.**

Yes, Virginia, there are customers from hell. Kris Anderson of Performance Research Associates hit the bull's-eye when she said: "If you don't believe there is such a thing as a customer from hell, you must be a consultant or a CEO. No one who works with the public on a regular basis can doubt their existence." Starry-eyed souls who spout the line that "the customer is always right" are usually well-buffered from the bizarros of the world who the poor front-line folks periodically have to deal with.

Oh, yes, I know we're supposed to love all customers, but pray tell, how does one love a customer like Gerard Finneran? I read about Gerard in several publications, but I like *Esquire* magazine's account the best:

"Gerard Finneran, a 58-year-old investment-bank president from New York, was arrested for allegedly assaulting a flight attendant and defecating on a service cart while drunk during a flight from Buenos Aires to New York. According to the complaint, Finneran used 'linen napkins as toilet paper and wiped his hands on various service implements used by the crew' and then 'tracked feces throughout the aircraft'."

Or how about this one? A few years ago, I received a call late at night from the COO of a hospital I was working with at the time. He was perplexed. The hospital was moving aggressively towards a patient-oriented, patient-friendly culture. But a little problem had unexpectedly emerged. An elderly man had been admitted to the hospital, and his extended family had taken over the hospital lobby. By "taken over," I mean they were camping in the lobby, intimidating other customers, ignoring the hospital's half-hearted requests to cease and desist, and stealing anything not bolted to the floors. The COO asked me hesitatingly: 'Well, given our new culture, what I am supposed to do with these people?'

Might we agree that both the above cases are indeed customers from hell? If so, the COO's question is germane. How do we handle them?

I don't think love is the answer. In the first case, I know what I'd do if I were airline staff. I'd manacle the son-of-a-gun on the flight, then I'd see to it that he was arrested immediately upon touchdown. Then I'd prosecute the dickens out of him. Case closed.

In the second case, here's what I said to the beleaguered COO: "Are you out of your mind? Is your hospital trying to corner the thieves-and-rogues niche? If not, call in security and get 'em the hell out of your hospital immediately!" He agreed, with relief, and he acted. Case closed.

There is no excuse for tolerating individuals who are ugly, abusive, destructive or potentially violent with your staff. Customers from hell exist, and they must be dealt with firmly, fairly, quickly and unapologetically. Any other response is an insult to your employees and a double-insult to the vast majority of customers who are decent human beings.

My colleagues Ron Zemke and Chip Bell, also of Performance Research Associates, point out that there's a critical difference between *a customer from hell* and *a customer who's been through hell*. But they often look alike. Bell contends that since the number of customers who are truly malicious or evil is extremely rare, it's far better to first assume that they've been through hell. And if they really have been through hell, then you had better believe that other customers are going through hell, and you're going to wind up losing everyone's business. I would take it a step further: Each time you respond inappropriately to customers who have gone through hell, you push them closer to the door marked "customer from hell."

Bell agrees wholeheartedly that a true customer from hell ought to be fired pronto, but consistent with the prior chapter, a customer that has gone through hell is potentially one of your most value-adding partners—if you (and your company) really and truly listen to his or her concerns, and then respond appropriately, sincerely and dramatically.

This brings us to the latest tale of the weird. Last year, Jeremy Dorosin of Walnut Creek, California, joined the swelling ranks of customers enduring crummy experiences. (I use the phrase "swelling ranks" not merely from anecdotal impressions, but from hard empirical data from nationwide research efforts like the recent American Customer Satisfaction Index study. The ACSI results indicated that overall, customer satisfaction is heading south in the United States as companies—lip service to customer service notwithstanding—are slashing even modest investments in this direction and seem incapable of comprehending that customers' expectations of service are going up, not down. But I digress.)

Jeremy Dorosin says he purchased two defective espresso machines from a Starbucks Coffee outlet in the San Francisco Bay Area, and he was unhappy with the allegedly bureaucratic, impersonal way Starbucks handled his complaints.

Apparently, he was *very* unhappy. Most customers in his shoes would have either griped or silently seethed. Not Dorosin. What he did is the stuff of nightmares for any executive. He invested $10,000 for three prominent ads in *The Wall Street Journal.* Here is what one of them said:

HAD ANY PROBLEMS WITH STARBUCKS COFFEE?

Over 2,000 calls say you're not alone. 1-800-510-3483. Selected appropriate incoming letters of public opinion about this customer service problem with Starbucks will be published in an upcoming ad in this newspaper. Thanks for your tremendous support, J. Dorosin, One Mistreated Customer.

Mistreated Starbucks' Customers
2631 N. Mainstreet
Walnut Creek, CA 94596

The ad obviously touched a nerve, because the nationwide response was voluminous. Supportive phone calls and letters poured in from all over the country. Talk shows and pop magazines jumped on the story. So did the serious press: I was asked to comment on this new international crisis by CBS Nightly News. Chip Bell spoke on National Public Radio, and Ron Zemke was interviewed by *The Wall Street Journal* itself. Depending on which side of the fence you stood, Dorosin was either a saintly hero standing up for the abused common man, or a deranged devil willing to destroy a shining icon of corporate capitalism for his own egotism.

I don't believe either conclusion is accurate. In fact, I'm not interested in pursuing whether Dorosin was right or wrong; that's why I didn't call him for an interview even though he lives a stone's throw from me. My point is that the Dorosin-Starbucks' case represents the murky, uncertain terrain that companies often must confront, the ambiguous no-man's land—between the customer from hell and the customer who's been through hell. The more relevant question is this: Regardless of where Dorosin stood on this continuum, how should Starbucks have dealt with the situation?

Bell and I have great respect for Starbucks and, in the spirit of using a good company and an "extreme" customer to illustrate a valuable point, we put our heads together to suggest a few vital steps that Starbucks should have taken, but apparently didn't. Hopefully, these steps will help your organization cope with customer complaints more effectively—capitalize on them, in fact, as aids in leapfrogging the competition.

1. **Be empathetic.**
    The first and most important thing Starbucks should have done is to demonstrate humility, empathy and understanding as a way of telling Dorosin: "Your feelings are valid." Starbucks contends that its personnel acted "properly," that they followed "acceptable" procedures for handling complaints. Maybe so, but that's not the point. Complaining customers are often further alienated by what they perceive as legally "correct," but nevertheless insensitive, by-the-book, bureaucratic responses they receive when they are angry or distressed. When Dorosin complained, Starbucks' people didn't have to agree with his version of the facts. But they didn't have to hide behind "cover-thy-rear" procedures either.

    Given the fact that he was a regular customer, and given the minuscule dollar value of the machines he purchased (a couple hundred bucks) relative to that one store's daily sales, they could have said and done things to let him know that they were genuinely sorry for the trouble he experienced, and genuinely interested in solving the problem to his satisfaction, corporate policies and procedures be damned.

Companies that "get it" understand that this mind-set yields an enormous return on investment. Federal Express invests megabucks in teaching its front-line people how to defuse angry customers on the phone or face-to-face. Carl Sewell, owner of a fabulously successful Dallas-based car dealership and author of *Customers for Life* (Doubleday, 1990) says, "Why argue with a customer over a $25 item on the bill when you know that if you keep him as a loyal returnee, he'll spend between $300,000 and $400,000 with you over a lifetime, and tell his friends to boot?"

Who was right, Dorosin or Starbucks? Who cares? This isn't a math problem; it's a business problem. Should Starbucks have simply replaced the machines? With the right dose of empathy, I'm not even sure that would have been necessary, though places like Nordstrom or L.L. Bean (two companies with a fanatically loyal customer base) would have done so, no questions asked. More important, they wouldn't have done it grudgingly, but with sincere apology.

That's the validation that customers seek, especially when there's a screw-up. Customers will tolerate even the most intense foul-ups as long as they believe that the company really cares about their feelings. And as any lawyer will tell you, the big-time lawsuits come when people feel that they've been ignored or bureaucratically jerked around by impersonal, uncaring organizations.

This point is the preliminary step, and is a critical customer service issue. It's a necessary precursor to points No. 2 and 3, which are *leapfrogging* issues.

2. **Get him into your web.**
   This is the crux of the matter. Once the problem escalated, that is, once it moved from the Bay Area store to a nationwide *Wall Street Journal* ad, Starbucks' executives in Seattle should have leaped into dramatic action aimed at proactive recovery and inclusion. Ron Zemke has suggested that Starbucks could have hired a blimp to drag a big public apology around Dorosin's home and place of employment. That's plenty dramatic, to be sure, and has much more to commend it than the official stonewalling that Starbucks actually did.
   Dorosin's reaction to Starbucks' bureaucratese was, shall

we say, extreme. His new demands included a top-of-the-line Starbucks' espresso machine ($2,495), a two-page apology ad in the *Wall Street Journal* ($247,182), and a public pledge that Starbucks open a center for runaway youth in San Francisco ($???). Clearly unacceptable, but a dramatic-recovery response by Starbucks from the very beginning might well have precluded this degeneration of events.

If you really want to talk dramatic, here's what Starbucks' executives could have done the moment they saw the first Dorosin ad: One, muzzle their in-house legal and public relations attack dogs from focusing on official denial and blame-the-customer scapegoating. Two, have two or three senior people (why not the president?) fly down to meet with Dorosin personally; let's face it, anyone who is willing to spend that much money to take out ads must have something to say. By meeting with him and listening, listening, listening, the whole situation could have been defused quickly. Even more important, executives who've become removed from daily customer interfaces might have learned something very valuable about their customers, service, products and operations.

In fact, assuming that Dorosin did say something valuable, why not fly him to corporate headquarters and let him tell his story to corporate personnel who've been so busy fueling the rapid growth of Starbucks that they may have forgotten who brought them to the dance. In fact again, why not invite—and pay—Dorosin to join a task-force aimed at revamping procedures and training that apply to store personnel who might regularly deal with customer dissatisfaction?

In short, instead of considering the guy a simple nut case, why not assume that he's mad as hell about something, and that he's doing what a lot of other customers only fantasize about doing? And then why not include him, involve him, invite him into the web? By doing so, Starbucks would have taken his creative, manic energy and funneled it into a constructive consultative role to help figure out ways to solve these problems so that nobody else experiences them. (And, if you ever hear anyone say, "Hey, I can't be kissing up to every weirdo who spends $10,000 in ads in *The Wall Street Journal,*" point out to them how ridiculous they sound).

3. **Follow up, follow-up, follow-up.**

After No. 2 above, Starbucks could have sent Dorosin a certificate of thanks, and cash payment or freebie coupons as compensation for his efforts. Executives could have checked in with Dorosin a few months hence to insure that his subsequent experiences with Starbucks were not merely "satisfactory," but "outstanding." They could have further used his input to publicize this incident internally as a tool for training, store operations and corporate policy-making—all aimed at dramatically boosting customer service in general, coping with unhappy customers in a way that enhances their loyalty, and developing a few contingency "planned recovery" systems when things do break down. They could have publicized this entire incident externally so as to let the public know that Starbucks cares about its customers, Starbucks wants to partner with them, and Starbucks has got enough humility to admit that it might have wronged them.

Finally, executives could have used this incident to reflect on the possibility that an obsession with corporate growth might be overshadowing attention to the kind of customer experiences that are the "soul" that Starbucks began with.

Ron Zemke has written some wise words that apply to this situation: "Too often we worry about the cost of atonement and the repercussive consequences of paying for a customer's ire and displeasure. But ... the cost of trepidation is most certainly higher than the cost of consolation."

So, to reiterate the theme that we began with: Yes, indeed, there are customers from hell, and they'll come at you without provocation. Dump them politely but fast. Prosecute them if they go over the edge. Don't ever expect your front-line people to tolerate their abuses.

But remember, customers from hell are the rare exception to the rule. Before you label every angry complaining customer a villain, think about your dependence on these people, think about how valuable it would be to respond to them in empathetic, constructive, inclusionary, web-like ways, and think about what a pain in the neck we all are when we act the role of customers in our personal lives and are turned away, disappointed.

> *So now you're serious about bringing valued custom-*
> *ers—even complaining ones—into your web. Here are a*
> *few final tips on how best to proceed.*

Customers' perceptions are usually well-founded. You know this from your own experiences as a dissatisfied customer. Therefore, if you want to differentiate yourself in the marketplace and capitalize on customers' inputs, consider the following steps:

1. **Make it very easy for customers to complain.**
   I mean really easy. Have a well-publicized 24-hour 800 phone line with many extensions staffed by competent, well-trained, carefully selected individuals who are especially good at tracking and handling complaints. Create easy-to-fill-out survey cards with return postage on products, and mail them with invoices or other correspondence. Position suggestion boxes in as many sites as possible. Establish electronic accessibility to one of your central terminals. Make sure home phone numbers are on all business cards.

   If you're not sure whether you're hearing enough, periodically interview a sample of customers to find out how to make it easier for them to convey any problems or frustrations.

   Proactively solicit complaints. Customer service departments and toll-free customer assistance centers are not enough. You—yes, you—should call customers and ex-customers directly with a list of specific questions, and you should do so regularly. (More on this later.) Carefully probe what didn't work, what didn't go well, or what could have been done better. Hold regular focus groups; solicit specific, even "minor," sources of hassle and irritation. Don't hire consultants to do it for you. Every manager should be a part of at least one focus group a month.

   Learn from Milliken's (textiles) and Northwest Mutual Life's practice of flying in customers and putting them up on-site to air their views, or Stew Leonard's (grocery) bimonthly customer focus groups, attended by top management. Take the attitude of one California hospital CEO who makes it a point of visiting discharged patients at their homes, where they're secure and comfortable, in order to really get good feedback.

2. **Work like mad to respond to each and every complaint.**
Easier said than done. Begin by logging every customer complaint from all sources and insisting that everyone in management access that information in any decision making. Follow the lead of an L.L. Bean executive who said: "Track, by computer, every customer complaint. Update and follow up daily." Or Staples (office supplies), which tracks every complaint and uses those data to drive the adjustment of products, policies and guidelines.

Then take it a step further with the responsibility for follow-through. Once the information is available, somebody has to "own" each complainer, and see that the problem is fixed, customer satisfaction is assured, and appropriate changes are championed throughout the organization. Every manager's job description should include being that "somebody" regularly, every month.

Two key points here: First, complaints must be handled "fast and friendly." By *fast* I mean from the customer's time perspective, not from the legal department's. By *friendly* I mean that customers are delighted by the empathy which somebody in your organization shows for the hassles they have had to undergo. Ron Zemke's research indicates that nearly 40 percent of a customer's perception of service is influenced by how well the vendor responds to unforeseen problems. Employees at Ritz-Carlton and Dell Computer seem to "get" this, and it pays off at those organizations.

Second, the system (structure, policies, habits) must be fixed so that the glitch that caused the problem will not occur with a future customer. Fixing the system also will allow you to take advantage of the complaint to innovate in your product and service offerings. One 3M executive mentioned that more than 50 percent of the new product innovations in his division came from the ideas of complainers. Unsurprisingly, he geared a lot of his time to listening.

Remember, if you don't do No. 2, No. 1 is a waste of time. Stew Leonard Jr. once told me an interesting story. His grocery store has a large suggestion box that is usually filled to capacity by the end of the day. Every morning the information of the prior day is logged, and by late morning the list is on every manager's desk. Action is expected immediately; problems are to be solved that day, if possible. "A couple years ago we became complacent," Leonard remarked. "We began to make up the list every three or four days instead of every day. The volume of suggestions gradually went down. But our focus groups told us that dissatisfaction was going up. This was weird: We never told customers that we were not responding to the suggestion box every day, but somehow they figured it out. As soon as we went back to our once-a-day commitment, the suggestion box started to fill up again."

3. **Educate, educate, educate.**
    In orientation. In management-development sessions. In memos and briefings. In meetings and stump speeches. Teach people about the strategic and financial value of complaints, about the need for urgency in responding, and perhaps most important, that everyone owns the problem—not just the "customer service" people.

4. **Approach complaints as operational problems and strategic opportunities.**
    This means putting complaints in the category of research and information, not personal attacks. It means replacing blame analysis with problem analysis. It means viewing complaints in the Renaissance tradition, in which the critic was your ally, helping you to better focus on reality. A few years ago an executive at Intermountain Health Care told me that once his hospital literally relabeled "patient complaint" forms as "consultant reports," managers began to pay close attention to the information.

5. **Make complaints and complainers visible.**
    Post quantitative complaint data publicly (not just for your own people but, as First Chicago Bank does, so customers can see it too). Post raw unedited letters and phone call transcripts on bulletin boards. Reprint them in newsletters. Read and discuss them in meetings. Publicize responses to the complaints. Identify and laud the folks who did the responding. Invite complainers to address people in your organization and to work

with them on improvements. Pay them if necessary. Include a "customer panel" in every management retreat.

After conducting such panels with organizations as diverse as Northrup King (seeds) and Mercy Healthcare System, I've learned that the information is invaluable for meaningful management retreats, and that nothing grabs managers' attention like eyeballing a customer who lays it on the line.

6. **Adjust quality measures, performance review and compensation accordingly.**
What gets measured and rewarded gets done. Quality measures always should incorporate pervasive customer complaints. One manufacturer found its customers rated the product lower because the user manual was so poor. Federal Express' Service Quality Index yields a score based on the highest-to-lowest hassle factors as experienced by the customer.

Key questions for managers' performance evaluation and pay might include the following: How many complaints have you solicited? How many firefighting teams have you been on? How have you used the input of complainers to improve this organization? Rewarding managers for reducing complaints will only encourage cheating. What's desired is their discovering and acting on complaints.

7. **Reward complainers.**
These people can help your business prosper, and their advice is often priceless. Visible displays of your gratitude not only make good common sense, but also send a signal to them and to your organization. Consider thank-you notes and phone calls, small cash rewards, plaques and certificates, gifts, "consultant of the month" awards, feature stories in company newsletters, and periodic celebrations with complainers as guests of honor. Even better, reward them by officially inviting them to join your problem-solving teams.

8. **Stop calling them "complainers"!**
Or "difficult customers" or "customers from hell." And let's all stop saying they "complain," "gripe" or "bellyache." This clearly applies as much to me as to anyone else. Words are tools, so let's all begin by giving these outspoken souls their due. They

are critics, allies, consultants, guests of honor—anything as long as it reflects their contribution to the success of our organizations and our careers. For that reason, let's get them into our web—and fast!

In fact, as we end this Giant Step, let's note that if we can stretch ourselves to include so-called "complainers" in our web, there's no reason why we can't commit to getting *anyone*, anywhere who is world-class into our web as quickly as possible.

GIANT STEP V:

EAT CHANGE FOR BREAKFAST, SERVE IT UP FOR EVERY MEAL

I recently had a conversation with a CEO of a struggling $100-million company. He complained that every year he would wind up spending literally two months immersed in an abhorrent, wasteful budgeting process.

I pointed out that companies like Quad/Graphics place minimal emphasis on annual capital budgets, and instead use computer technology to crank out a daily income statement which goes immediately to decentralized business units (all with P&L accountability) which in turn use it as a daily guide for financing. I told the CEO that his own company was set up to do the same: His newly decentralized structure was in place, as was the information technology.

The logic was compelling: Quad/Graphics Chairman Harry Quadracchi asks, "Why is it that so many companies insist on having a 12-month budget, drawn up in November of one year, based on still-incomplete numbers, that will be the Bible for running the company as far away as December of the following year?" The CEO I conversed with ruefully admitted that he was spending nearly 20 percent of his fiscal year on this minutia rather than using the time to concentrate on growing his business.

"So," I said, "what are you going to do? Are you going to at least investigate the possibilities?" Embarrassed, he muttered something and quickly changed the subject. His response basically meant only one answer: negative. He was apparently more comfortable in the known routine of stooping for pennies than in the possibility of reaching up to grab the dollars overhead.

"Change" and the need for it is the hot issue nowadays. We talk about it a lot in management retreats, but back home, the audio of talk and the video of action are often at odds. Big batches of sound and fury are followed by tepid, tentative action or quick, short-lived fads. Fundamental overhaul is rare; a culture of constant renewal is even rarer. As Jim O'Toole of the Aspen Leadership Institute has noted, we often fall back on the "ideology of comfort and the tyranny of custom."

Organizations that leap over competitors stay limber, springy and forward-looking by living and breathing change; they eat it for breakfast, they prepare it for every meal. In these organizations, people in every nook and cranny on the payroll are expected to challenge organizational processes and premises in line with corporate vision and values. They are rewarded for proactively taking prudent risks on behalf of cost containment, customer enhancement and new business development. They take responsibility for changing their own jobs by streamlining what they currently do and grabbing new responsibilities as needed. They are comfortable—indeed energized—by a corporate environment where formal job descriptions are virtually nonexistent, where levels of authority and functional silos are minimal, where lines of communication can best be described as "spaghetti," and where "work" is organized around a set of multiple projects and multiple teams conducted in multiple locales.

This is the sort of environment that breeds iconoclastic thinking, irreverent perspectives and bold decisions—just the ingredients necessary to vault over the pack. It is that environment which Oticon CEO Lars Kolind explicitly credits for his organization's exceptional financial success and reshaping of the hearing-aid industry.

There's certainly been enough talk about change, and its corollary, "resistance to change." Talk without action weighs down the organization. It should be pretty obvious that no organization can leapfrog its competition without a culture that instigates big actions reflecting big change.

CEO Jim Thompson of the Vallen Corporation, who is transitioning his company from a seller of low margin industrial safety products to a purveyor of high-value industrial safety expertise, argues that "we have to change faster than the outside environment does." That's a tall order, and he's absolutely right. And this is where leadership comes into play. Vice President Brian Jones of plastics manufacturer Nypro put it nicely in Tom Peters' newsletter, "On Achieving Excellence":

"I went to business school, and they teach you fundamentals of management—direct, control, plan, cut costs. It's the wrong thing to teach. They should be teaching people what their job is, which is to reinvent the system within which people work."

In our book *Jumping the Curve*, Nick Imparato and I summarized our own research which supports Jones' sentiments. First, we reviewed the conventional wisdom which says that a manager's performance **(p)** can be predicted based on two factors, ability **(a)** and motivation **(m)**, the typical equation being **p = a x m**. In this equation, the higher the ability and the greater the motivation, the higher the performance.

But we noted the obvious: Many managers who ought to excel according to this equation in fact do not. That is, they may have a glowing resume and years of experience (lots of ability), and they may work diligently 24 hours a day (lots of motivation), but they still don't bring home the bacon.

So, we wondered, is it possible that there is a missing link in the traditional performance equation? The answer, we discovered, was yes. Our research showed that in today's marketplace, a third factor has emerged—one which not only augments performance, but which transforms "management" into "leadership." This third factor is nothing short of a redefinition of the manager-leader's role, and it is so important that we labeled it *"accuracy of role perception."*

Specifically, Imparato and I found that the horses to bet on are those individuals who consciously define their management role as agent of change in a world of new realities. We proposed a new performance equation: **p = a x m x a.r.p.** Note that the equation remains multiplicative; that is, an accuracy-of-role-perception **(a.r.p.)** level of zero means that the manager's performance is effectively wiped out, regardless of experience and good intentions. Doing the same old/same old, albeit with great skill and earnestness, is not a mark of a candidate getting set to leapfrog the competition. It is only within the context of stimulating a change process that ability and motivation take on new value-adding heights.

Since the publication of *Jumping the Curve*, I've come to believe that "agent" of change is no longer a strong enough label; *provocateur* of change might be a better descriptor. It's those managers who combine expertise, initiative and the personal responsibility to provoke change—regardless of whether or not their people are theoretically "ready" for it—who will most likely guide their organizations to leapfrog their competition.

Giant Step V is particularly crucial because most of us have sufficient skills and motivation to succeed as leaders. What we most often lack is the will, the perseverance, the obstinate pigheadedness to ruffle routines, disrupt complacency, challenge processes and cause constructive disequilibrium—and to do so every day because we believe that it's our job to do so. It's our leadership responsibility, even our fiduciary obligation. When we take all that on, we begin to understand the magnitude of Giant Step V. This section provides a few clues about what leaders can do to create an organization that does indeed serve up change for every meal.

First, managers who live Giant Step V are bone-honest: when they talk about making change, about mobilizing to leapfrog the competition, they walk the talk. They engender a sense of understanding (why the need to leapfrog); they impart a sense of urgency (what needs to change *now*); and they lead a daily discipline that is visibly consistent with the new priorities and values they are espousing.

Further, they not only delineate a stretch-the-envelope visionary direction for the organization, they ensure that it inspires everyone emotionally to make the leap of faith and that it becomes shared and "owned" by everyone. As part of this process, they carefully avoid the pitfalls of fads; they reject the idea of pat solutions and magic bullets. They are skeptical of any quick-fix programs and painless promises of salvation. They know that leapfrogging the competition requires all-hands courage, commitment, perseverance—and shared sacrifice.

Second, leaders who live Giant Step V have the self-insight and self-confidence to change themselves, not just their organization. While they are uncompromising in viewing their role as agents/provocateurs of change, they seek constant feedback from employees and customers alike, and they are not afraid to adjust their personal styles or short-term decisions when it helps the organization make big transitions toward big goals.

Finally, they are eternally vigilant against the danger of complacency and arrogance; in fact, they feel and induce a sense of urgency *especially* when the numbers look good. They know that after they do leapfrog the competition, a kiss of death is just staying put, as in, "Why fix it if it ain't broke?" Leapfrogging the competition requires eternal vigilance, which no doubt is why Intel CEO Andy Grove so aptly entitled his recent book, *Only the Paranoid Survive.*

It should be no surprise that dominant players like Microsoft, Intel and Gillette manage to avoid the dread disease of complacency, because the spirit of Grove's message is maniacally endorsed by CEOs Bill Gates, Andy Grove and Alfred Zelen, respectively. So if your company's numbers look good today, beware! There's always tomorrow. If you successfully leapfrog the competition tomorrow, beware again! There's always the day after tomorrow. Accepting and confronting that reality is at the core of Giant Step V.

This section discusses all these attributes and behaviors in some detail, and provides a fitting finale to the challenge facing any organization that wants to thrive in the emerging millennium. When all is said and done, carrying out these five Giant Steps requires leaders who themselves are not afraid of change; in fact, who relish it both personally and professionally. With leaders like this, transformation occurs, and our organizations are imbued with life, direction and hope.

The remainder of this book, discussing Giant Step V, is the most comprehensive and hence the lengthiest. The reason is two-fold. First, without a leader's unyielding commitment to carrying out Giant Step V, Steps I, II, III and IV will simply not occur. Second, in order to leap beyond the mass of conventional wisdom on "change" and "leadership," I believe it is necessary to confront some truly sacred cows in business today, and to explore in depth a number of necessary do's that aren't being done, as well as a number of don'ts that (unfortunately) are. If each of us can do that and simultaneously examine our own behavior with intellectual honesty, we will be able to perform this Giant Step. So let's continue in that spirit.

To seek change as the exciting strategic opportunity that it is— and thus serve it up with every meal—this section will show that one needs to embrace four personal Commitments:

1. Get honest, walk the talk (Chapter/Commitment 12)
2. Don't get snookered by fads-du-jour (Chapter/Commitment 13)
3. Sponge up daily doses of reality (Chapter/Commitment 14), and
4. Beware the danger of success (Chapter/Commitment 15)

The message of Commitment 12 is simple: If you want to make change in your organization, you've got to emulate the behavior you want to see. No more lip service. No more programs of the month. No more audio-video mismatches. Commitment 12 notes that the essence of leadership is visibly challenging the process—daily. It also provides two paths toward effectively doing so. One is a simple but powerful prescription I call "U2D2." The other is a compelling three-part declaration that gets to the nuts and bolts of transformational leadership.

The underlying theme of Commitment 13 is that if you are committed to leapfrogging the competition, you have to avoid management fads-du-jour. Like Sirens beckoning Ulysses, management fads entice all of us. And like those ancient ladies, they will destroy. To drive the point home, Commitment 13 presents the fall-out from three management approaches that have genuine merit as concepts, but which in practice have too often become destructive fads. I'm speaking about TQM, reengineering, and the mania of dealmaking for dealmaking's sake.

Commitment 14 warns us that even as we are making change, we must stay in touch. Supplementing the regular monthly interfaces with complaining customers, discussed earlier, this Commitment challenges us to enthusiastically seek a *daily* dose of reality from all key stakeholders—customers, employees and partners—and to insist that all our colleagues do the same. No more substituting laundered reports for face-to-face interactions with critical constituencies. No more surrounding ourselves with gilded trappings and yes-man gatekeepers for the purpose of seeking shelter from people with whom we ought to be rubbing our bellies.

We must continually soak up direct, unfiltered feedback from key constituencies in order to get a reality check on how we're doing vis-a-vis our strategic priorities. It is that unfiltered feedback which will fuel us to change far quicker than simply attending an off-site or reading yet another article entitled "Change or Die." This Commitment describes a path toward strategic listening with customers, and tells the story of an executive who consciously listened to his own employees with the same sentiment.

Commitment 15 is the wrap-up that reminds us that one of the best predictors of business failure is business success—because success in so many companies is followed by that intervening variable called complacency—or even worse, arrogance. As we saw in the earlier discussion of the Thomas Lawson Syndrome, business history has too often been littered with the carcasses of companies that believed their own press clippings. This chapter relates a more subtle fable, about one company that seemed to follow the right path toward listening, but in reality was too comfortable with itself to follow up on the information that emerged—until too late.

The message is clear: Beware the danger of success, even after you initially leapfrog the competition. There's always tomorrow's race, and then another the following day. Leapfrogging the competition is not a one-shot affair. That's what makes the business of business so fascinating and so compelling.

COMMITMENT 12:
GET HONEST, WALK THE TALK

Too often, executives and managers believe they can achieve meaningful change in their organizations while, on a personal level, maintaining their current behaviors, current schedules, and current calendars. It doesn't work. Leapfrogging the competition is a process that requires leaders who <u>personally</u> eat change for breakfast, every day. Building credibility, integrity—and hence success—into your change efforts starts at home.

Larry Lucarelli, a middle manager in a turbine engine repair company when I met him a few years ago, told me a revealing story:

> "I was brought in as a technical branch manager with 32 engineers reporting to me. My predecessor had been fired because 'nothing was happening' with engineering. I called a meeting and put it on the table: 'The rap on you guys is that you can't get anything done.' Their response was straight: 'You're right. We're putting out 30 percent of the work we could. We spend the rest of the time writing reports for other parts of the company.'
>
> "I told them, 'Okay, turn in all your reports to me. Just the originals. Don't make any copies.' At the end of the month I had about 12 inches worth of reports stacked on my desk, and I simply waited. One day someone in finance called me: 'Hey, I didn't get any numbers on your expenditures. I need that input for my cash-flow projections.' Within 10 minutes those numbers were on his desk. Nobody else ever called.
>
> "I asked some questions, and it turned out that the people getting those reports were simply filing them. If they had a question, they wouldn't even refer to those files. They'd call us. So within the first month, I replaced 12 inches of monthly paper with a one-paragraph report to the vice pres-

ident of finance and a two-page bullet progress report to everyone else. Productivity shot straight up."

There is a bulk of research out there that converges on one point: Effective leaders do what Lucarelli did—they challenge the status quo, and they do it every day. Different researchers use different terminology, but the message is the same.

In their seminal research described in *The Leadership Challenge* (Jossey-Bass 1987, 1995), Jim Kouzes and Barry Posner found that effective leaders continually challenged the process; ineffective leaders didn't. Harvard's Ronald Heifetz found that whereas management traditionally involves creating conditions of equilibrium, leadership involves creating dis-equilibrium. Noel Tichy of the University of Michigan found that leaders cause transformations. Research I conducted with colleague Linda Mukai found that effective middle managers are impatient with the status quo and constantly try new things—often without asking.

Leadership expert Warren Bennis notes that no subject has been more studied and less understood than leadership. True enough, but on this point the research is unequivocal. Leadership doesn't simply mean "accepting change" or "reducing resistance to change." Leadership means creating change, even when colleagues within the organization don't quite see the need for it. Three successful CEOs—Harry Quadracchi (Quad/Graphics), Bill McGowan (late of MCI), and Lars Kolind (Oticon)—independently voiced the same opinion: The job of the president, or any other leader, is not to be the chief organizer but the chief *disorganizer.*

Your first name doesn't have to be "CEO" in order to act like a leader. Opportunities abound in the shape of pockets of inefficiency, traditions and structure that add no value and reduce the firm's ability to compete effectively. Look at what Lucarelli did. How long had that debilitating paperwork process been going on unquestioned before he took action?

So if you're not already creating change, what can you do to act like a leader and start revving your organization to leapfrog the competition? Here are four suggestions:

1. **Start with simple stuff.**
   Basic irritants such as those engineers' reports are begging to be confronted. Or how about meetings? Insist on changes, like

reducing their length by 50 percent, for starters. How about challenging why many of these meetings even exist, or why their agendas have little to do with the company's strategic priorities, or why people perpetuate a corrupt system by attending meetings they know are worthless? Or why not start making meetings more productive by insisting that relevant "outsiders" (hopefully a soon-to-be misnomer) like customers, vendors or folks in other departments attend?

2. **Always ask "why?"**
Did you notice the prevalence of the word "why" in the above paragraph? Imagine the power of constantly, incessantly questioning every meeting, report, habit, rule, policy, system and process with that simple question: "Why are we doing this?" And unless the answer is a definitive explanation of how the current way is the best way to help the firm leapfrog the competition, keep on asking why. Ask that dumb question repeatedly and 75 percent of the time you'll unearth the real answer: "Because we've always done it this way." Not good enough.

3. **Expect everyone else to ask "why?"**
Teach them that this is important. Evaluate your people not on how well they perform their jobs, but on how much and how effectively they change their jobs. The definition of the Japanese word *kaizen* is useful. *Kai* means *change*. *Zen* means *better.* The whole phrase means "change it for the better," which becomes the responsibility of everyone on the payroll.

4. **Don't ask for permission.**
Prudently pick your battles, to be sure, but don't fall into the trap of playing it safe. It's true: No guts, no glory. This is not necessarily easy or risk-free stuff. Larry Lucarelli didn't ask for permission to do what he did. Was it risky? Perhaps, but as an AT&T manager said in explaining his reasons for challenging the process: "Yes, there is a risk in doing this. There is an even bigger risk in not doing this."

To summarize, we would be wise to remember the words of Albert Einstein: "The important thing is to not stop questioning."

For those aspiring to eat change for breakfast, that's the first item on the menu.

> *Now that you're ready to walk the talk, here's a pre-scription designed to stimulate change that may provide the antidote to the "how-to-get-started" blues.*

Despite all the books and seminars on making change that are consumed annually, a lot of folks in management positions are simply lousy at actually doing it. Fortunately, Dr. Harari (well, okay, I have a Ph.D., not an M.D.) has the antidote. To you, dear reader, I hereby offer the prescription for walking the talk: I call it U2D2. I speak with utter seriousness: Take U2D2 daily for the rest of your professional life and you will become a credible and transformational leader—which means, as discussed throughout this Giant Step, you will be able to create a corporate culture where change is devoured at every meal.

Before ingesting any prescription, a smart consumer like you demands to know its ingredients. The basic elements of U2D2 are *Understanding, Urgency, Direction* and *Discipline*. Let's review each in turn:

U1=UNDERSTANDING. Leaders are often ineffective at creating change because their people are in the dark. I cannot tell you how often I have spoken to employees and managers who are ignorant of the organization's market pressures, financial burdens and strategic dilemmas. That's a major reason why they're suspicious of change, or resistant to it.

Effective leaders work daily to ensure that everyone in the organization understands *why* perpetual change is necessary. They share the dangers and opportunities that confront the company, the steps that might be taken and why, and the sorts of contributions and behaviors that are required from everyone. They use all communication channels—newsletters, e-mail, bulletins, public forums, small group discussions, one-on-ones—to disseminate news and information about new competitors, new technologies, and new partnership opportunities. They discuss the numbers: sales, margins, cycle times, investor reactions, customer service issues, customer defections and quality data. They talk about trends in costs, earnings, returns and market share. They explore options and responses, both strategic and tactical. They invite response and feedback. They demand that written and electronic sources of direct communication be accessible to everyone.

By their own behavior, effective leaders personally demonstrate their commitment to keeping people "in the know." It might be Microsoft's Bill Gates, diligently responding to scores of personal e-mail messages daily, or AlliedSignal's Lawrence Bossidy honestly grappling with tough questions tossed his way in a no-holds-barred session with a group of workers on a factory floor. It might be Springfield Remanufacturing's Jack Stack regularly going over a multi-page financial statement with groups of blue-collar employees, or Atlantic City Medical Center's George Lynn holding freewheeling public "speakeasies." It might be Nellcor Puritan Bennett's Ray Larkin or Southwest Airlines' Herb Kelleher roaming their company sites in order to be personally accessible to anyone.

The idea behind these steps is simple. Information is power. You can't "empower" people to be accountable, creative and proactive unless they are "in the know." You can't generate teamwork and trust if information is hoarded. You won't generate ownership or commitment to any intervention if people don't "get" what you're trying to do, or why.

That's why *Understanding* is the first component of U2D2. When executives tell me that their most pressing frustration is getting people to "buy in" to certain interventions, I suspect that the executives are the only ones who really, truly understand why the interventions are critical.

U2=URGENCY. Effective leaders are repulsed by complacency. When they hear sentiments like, "If it ain't broke, don't fix it," they become alarmed. Effective leaders realize that today's numbers (earnings, market share, etc.) are simply a reflection of what the organization did yesterday. If the numbers are good today, the organization made the right moves yesterday. But since only the naive believe that tomorrow will look like today, only the doubly naive believe that perpetuating yesterday's moves will lead to tomorrow's successes.

Accordingly, injecting a sense of *Urgency* into the organization becomes a top priority for real leaders. Their ongoing preoccupation is shaking people out of their comfort zones. I read an article recently which said that if you live in South Central Los Angeles and you don't feel paranoid, you're crazy. Effective leaders demonstrate a healthy sense of paranoia for similar reasons. They couple it with liberal doses of excitement in the face of new business possibilities, based on the "data" of the *Understanding* phase.

They cap it all off with an unbridled passion for excellence in quality, service, innovation and teamwork. They realize that management is an emotional process, and that the information gained in the *Understanding* phase must be augmented with an enthusiasm to continuously improve and a passion to lead the market in some arena. This is why Bob Ulrich, when he headed retailer Target and more recently when he took over the helm at Dayton Hudson, has continued to hammer home his message, "Speed is life." Ulrich is alluding not only to the reduction of cycle times, although that clearly is critical; he's also referring to the importance of an all-hands *Urgency* to try things, to get on with things, to complete things, and to do so in a timely way.

One would think that if the organization's numbers are bad, the leader's task vis-à-vis *Urgency* will be easier. Sometimes that's the case, but often, when companies finally do take action in the face of bad numbers, it's a panic reaction, not *Urgency*. Panic is characterized by knee-jerk, cover-thy-rear behavior that temporarily douses immediate fires without moving the organization toward genuine transformation. It usually follows a long period of complacency. It's based primarily on raw fear, not a healthy excitement. It's mostly flame-broiled sizzle, not steak.

Astonishingly, even bad numbers often fail to ignite people to action. People's capacity to cling to behaviors that no longer work is extraordinary. Denial ("the numbers will be better next quarter"), sham action ("let's get another consultant's report") and just plain fear of moving beyond a comfort zone all collude to preclude genuine change.

Several years ago, Nellcor CEO Ray Larkin shared an insight with me while in the midst of a frustrating period in which he was attempting to stimulate change in the face of rising costs and product development problems: "One of the hardest things I learned was that the facts don't speak for themselves. People are capable of rationalizing the most damning facts. Data can't replace leadership." That's why *Urgency* must go hand in hand with *Understanding*.

Whether today's numbers are good or bad, effective managers fuel the fire. They continually challenge the process. As USC's Warren Bennis notes, they create outright dis-equilibrium. And in moving the team, these leaders are patient with those who struggle to change, while they are unapologetically impatient with career skeptics.

AlliedSignal CEO Lawrence Bossidy put it well in a *Harvard Business Review* article: "The leader's job is to help everyone see that the platform is burning, whether the flames are apparent or not."

D1=DIRECTION. Direction tells us who we are and where we're going. In ambiguous, unstable times, people need a sense of coherence in their work lives. Effective leaders place great emphasis on ensuring that people in their organizations feel, own and live an overarching vision, a common philosophy, an inspiring purpose, and a collective set of values and ideals.

Understanding and *Urgency* rev up people with reasons and fuel for change. *Direction* gives them the path and the vehicle to channel their creative energies. *Direction* is not simply a mission statement or a soundbite "vision." It is a perpetually evolving set of answers to questions like: What is our business? Where do we want it to go? What do we stand for? Who do we serve? But just as important: What makes us unique? Interesting? Controversial? Special? What are we world-class-great in doing? What markets and products will we be unequivocally preeminent in? How will we *amaze* customers?

Direction is exciting. As Sun Microsystems CEO Scott McNealy put it, "I want Sun to be controversial; [otherwise,] we have zero chance of profit."

In 1987,when then-CEO George Lynn launched PACE (Patients Are the Center of Everything) at the two hospitals which comprise the Atlantic City Medical Center, he was careful to avoid any semblance of soundbite or faddism. Daily problem-solving dialogues became *de rigueur* among managers and employees: Who exactly are our patients? What does it mean for us to say that patients are the center of everything? How do we ensure that patients are the center of everything? In order to realize our ideal, what changes do we need to make in our organization structure to achieve our priority? Our budgeting? Our leadership styles? Our physical architecture? Our relationships with physicians, and each other? Gradually, a picture of a hospital driven by patients emerged.

Direction provides people with an alternative to dissatisfaction with the present, as well as an alternative to passivity and despair. Just as important, *Direction* unifies and bonds people, providing them with the "big tent" of community heading down the same road. When *Direction* is shared, conflict yields healthy problem analysis, and diversity of opinion leads to innovative decision making. The reason is that everyone knows that disagreements are fueled by a common purpose. That is why the spirited debates within Atlantic City Medical Center were a sign of a healthy organization.

But when *Direction* is not shared, when overarching priorities, values and commitments are at loggerheads—then conflict breeds turfism and blame-analysis, and diversity leads to divisiveness. Organizations become fragmented. Confusion reigns: What are our priorities anyway? What are acceptable behaviors? What's okay to do? What are we really emphasizing around here? People become cynical, passive and unfocused. Self-protective power-plays and fiefdoms emerge.

Direction must rest on the foundation of *Understanding*. A *Direction* that does not reflect an accurate read of market realities may lead everyone on the same path, but the path leads over a cliff. For years, IBM's *Direction*—built on premises of mainframes, centralized corporate information systems, employment guarantees, and starched white shirts—carried the day. But as market realities shifted, the *Direction* became a liability. It needed to be renewed, which has been CEO Lou Gerstner's major accomplishment over the last three years. The *Direction* pioneered by George Lynn for Atlantic City Medical Center rested on an *Understanding* of the changing world of hospital administration, and on the *Urgency* that transformations in healthcare delivery were necessary right away.

D2=DISCIPLINE. This is not about punishment or kinky sex. It's about consistency and persistence in execution. It's about the leader's daily behavior and decisions being aligned with the *Direction.* It's about rejecting lip service, pseudo-support and expediency. In short, it's about honor and integrity.

Discipline is the daily grind that makes things happen and lets people know you're worthy of your word. For three years after the launch of PACE, I watched George Lynn sound like a broken record. He talked about PACE every day, in every meeting. He roamed both hospitals in the system, visiting housekeeping and nursing groups at 2 a.m. to talk about PACE and the importance of linking everyday behaviors to it. I once watched him politely turn down a request by the chairman of the hospital board to meet on a particular date because of a prior commitment with a group of front-line employees set to discuss the implications of PACE.

Lynn was relentless. He spurred his people to develop measures against which progress toward PACE could be monitored, and he held them accountable for their performance thereafter. Charts, graphs and key indices were omnipresent—tacked on walls, discussed in meetings—digested by all as the organization moved toward its big goals. Lynn himself reviewed business decisions in reports and meetings in terms of their "fit" with PACE.

As we first noted in *Jumping the Curve,* Lynn insisted that his managers analyze operational problems, personnel decisions and vendor relationships in terms of PACE. He told them that he wanted them to have the same emotional reaction to PACE that they have toward budget variances. He "stacked the deck" and helped create "small wins" (new project successes) by picking people who were visibly committed to PACE. He invested heavily in service quality training, and he enlisted the help of 3M as a partner and mentor. He blessed self-managed teams that were willing to try new initiatives consistent with PACE, and he promised that he would personally protect anyone from retaliation by any manager who was threatened by the process.

And he delivered. For Lynn, the fact that patient satisfaction scores, physician referrals, and operating margins improved steadily over the next two years reinforced the validity of the PACE *Direction*, and added fuel for yet more *Urgency* and more *Discipline*.

Lynn has since moved along from Atlantic City Medical Center to be CEO of AtlantiCare, a healthcare holding company of which the Medical Center is a subsidiary. Earlier this year, Lynn and I reminisced together about PACE. He noted with pride that the eleventh annual PACE retreat was coming up, and that PACE is still thoroughly ingrained in hospital strategy and operations. He also noted that the administrators of the two hospitals of the system—both of whom had grown up with PACE—are still fully committed to the process, even though the specifics of PACE have necessarily changed in response to the enormous changes in healthcare over the past decade.

Of the entire U2D2 process, Lynn told me that he found the *Discipline* phase the most personally taxing. "Continuing the grind is the hardest part of it," he said. But that's the essence of good *Discipline* and, all too often, it's where many of us fall short.

One last point: in his *Discipline* while at the helm of the Medical Center, Lynn was persistent but prudent; he was not a dogmatic bull in a china shop, running roughshod over people. There were times when he tactically stepped back, gave some leeway, held off. But as a result of everything else he did every day, it was clear to everyone that he never lost sight of his primary *Direction*, nor of its *Urgency*.

Study inspiring leaders like Mohandas Gandhi and Nelson Mandela and you will note occasions where they seemed to back off or compromise on specific decisions, thus incurring the wrath of their more extreme colleagues. But for Gandhi and Mandela, such actions were temporary and necessary blips on a long road; there was never the slightest doubt of their commitment to their ultimate cause.

Great business leaders are the same. When leaders with *Direction* and *Discipline* compromise, they are rightly seen as prudent and tactical. In contrast, when managers without *Direction* and *Discipline* compromise, they are rightly seen as opportunistic and weak. Of the two Ds, *Direction* points out the path, but it only comprises 20 percent of the battle. Daily *Discipline* is the 80 percent sweat equity, the day-in-day-out stuff that demonstrates authenticity and separates real leaders from the shams.

Well, there you have it: a prescription for walking the talk. Listen to the good doctor: Take U2D2 several times a day, every day, until you retire—and you will retire a successful change agent with a legacy of having helped your organization repeatedly leapfrog its competition.

> *To generate change, you need "juice" (read: "passion,"*
> *"soul"). You also need juice to wash down the U2D2.*
> *Here's a recipe on how to get it and what to do with it,*
> *and thereby further raise the level of your ability to*
> *walk the talk.*

I recently attended a management retreat of a $200-million company. There was nothing particularly unique about this retreat; the discussions revolved around predictable issues like financials, news updates, future plans and a little hoopla congratulating past achievements. And yet, when I left the meeting after delivering my speech, I had a gnawing sense that something was wrong, something that I've seen too often in organizations.

On one hand, the presentations of individual managers appeared to be, if not impressive, then at least defensible from a fiduciary perspective. Yet there was a certain flatness, a certain lack of energy and focus, in the air throughout the day. That is, people were attentive and polite, the discussions were rational and sober, the planning for the social events was cheerful—but nevertheless, I felt a distinct lack of "soul" permeating the atmosphere.

Why? After exploring my disquiet on the plane ride back home, I suddenly had an *aha!* I realized that what was missing in this discussion were three little concepts, each of which carries a powerful wallop for leaders who want to get honest and walk the talk.

My colleagues Jim Kouzes and Barry Posner have proposed that one of the defining attributes of potent leaders is their ability to *"inspire a shared vision."* This conclusion is right on the money, yet it is one that I believe has not received sufficient attention among practicing managers—precisely because it seems so obvious as to appear mundane. In fact, I propose that the failure to inspire a shared vision is what leaves a lot of management discussions— during retreats and in everyday work life—polite and rational, but fundamentally dry, unfocused, unexciting and ultimately irrelevant.

Here's what I mean. In this little phrase, "Inspire a shared vision," we've got three vital words to consider: *inspire, shared* and *vision*. These three little words are crucial in our quest to eat change for breakfast. Let's explore each one in turn.

VISION: The most ballyhooed of the words, of course, is *vision*. Earlier in this book, I suggested that for practical utility, "bifocal vision" is a more useful concept for catapulting one's strategy over conventional wisdom. Absolutely true. But in the current context, I suggest that there's no contradiction if we continue to use and elaborate on Kouzes' and Posner's terminology. We'll simply employ the term "vision" as a shorthand to reflect the organization's underlying philosophy, purpose, mindset and business theory. (Within that framework, by the way, aggressive bifocal visioning should occur daily.)

A good vision can generate an organization-wide coherence in strategic thinking, a convergence of minds in execution, and a compelling brand identity in the marketplace. The specific content of the vision depends on the particular organization and its industry. Naturally, the vision should describe a set of ideals and priorities, an exciting picture of the future, a sense of what makes the company special and unique, a core set of principles that define what the company stands for, and a broad set of compelling criteria that will help define organizational success.

Note that a good vision is much more comprehensive than a catchy phrase—or, for that matter, a catchy little paragraph developed in a retreat. At interconnect manufacturer Merix, the broad vision includes several components. The vision statements themselves talk about being the "best interconnect company in the world," "creating extraordinary value," "bringing together the best ideas," "building an enduring great company," being the "benchmark" for its market segment. The operating principles revolve around such issues as customer focus, personal accountability, people development, expertise and solutions, and so on. The values are detailed paragraphs about "customers as our principal focus," ethics and communication.

Likewise, the big Ritz-Carlton vision—complete with credo statements, service philosophy, customer tools and employee "basics" for exceptional guest service—revolves around the hub value, "We are ladies and gentlemen serving ladies and gentlemen."

SHARED: So far, so good. Now having acknowledged the importance of vision, let me state that in some ways it's the least important concept in the trilogy of *inspire, shared, vision*. The deceptive little word "shared" is the rainmaker. Key questions include:

Do people embrace the vision as the embodiment of the organization's purpose? Do they understand how their roles will change if they are to contribute to the vision's realization? Do they believe the vision drives leaders' decisions—and their own?

An enterprise can have the most insightful, perceptive, wonderful vision in the world, but if people throughout the organization don't fully understand it, buy into it, feel involved in it, feel supported by it, act on it—in short, own it—then the impact of the vision is marginal. Leapfrogging the competition won't work unless it is a collaborative, all-hands affair.

What this means is very simple: Let's assume your company has a vision—even a comprehensive vision that addresses the issues I outlined above. Suppose I go into your organization and pick 10 people at random—any department, any level, any job title, any site, any length of tenure. Further, suppose that I individually ask each of them questions such as, "What are the ideals of this organization, what does it stand for, what's special and unique about this company to your customers, what does this organization do better than anyone else, what is the core set of principles that define your organization?" and so on. Suppose I simply ask, "What is your company vision, what is its business philosophy?"

Now, here's the climactic question. Will I get the same response from everyone? For that matter, will I get any response other than "I don't know" or "I'm not sure?" And suppose I follow up with yet another question, such as, "To what extent do you embrace (live, own) this vision? To what extent do you talk about it and live by it in your day-to-day problem analysis and decision making?" What responses would I get from those 10 randomly chosen individuals?

I'm pretty sure I could predict the results at Merix. A recent employee survey, responded to by 85 percent of the then-750-person workforce, found that more than nine out of 10 respondents believed that senior management does in fact have a vision for the future, that they (respondents) were sufficiently informed about the company's mission and values, that senior management supports the company mission and values through action, and that their (respondents') direct manager supports the company mission and values through action.

In a recent seminar in Gothenburg, Sweden, I posed the "shared" vision challenge to a large audience that included about

30 managers from Markpoint, a printer manufacturer. Markpoint is one of the best managed, quality-oriented, employee-involved firms I have seen for a long time. In private discussions afterward, I was intrigued that Managing Director Torkild Jensen and his team were concerned by my comments. They were refreshingly candid in confessing that even in their team-based company, they could not be at all certain that all hands even understood the vision, much less agreed or felt ownership with it. I bring this up precisely because I consider Markpoint to be a role model in many ways, and hence it makes me wonder even more how most organizations would stack up on this "sharing" dimension.

I think the syndicated cartoon strip "Dilbert" provides the answer. In one strip, his boss hands him a piece of paper, and the following dialogue ensues:

Dilbert reprinted with permission of UFS Inc.

Sure, one always strives for high marks on both the "vision" and "share" dimensions. Nevertheless, I would argue that an imperfect vision, if universally shared and utilized, is much more powerful, and a much better predictor of business success than a perfect vision that is neither understood nor universally endorsed.

INSPIRE: This leads to the third element: *Inspire*. On one level, the word applies to the vision itself. All too often, the so-called vision is an amalgam of vanilla psychobabble like Dilbert's "Empowered employees working toward a common plan," or not much different than the neutered descriptions in the company's annual report or 10-K. "Our company makes widgets, we make world-class widgets, we're a good company, we treat our people well, and we want to make a profit." Yawn.

In contrast, effective visions stir people's emotions, they kindle excitement, they arouse and animate. They do this by challenging people to achieve what Stanford's James Collins and his colleagues call "big hairy audacious goals." The vision should provoke an image of grand possibilities and engender pride in standing head and shoulders above the rest of the mob in a crowded marketplace. To notify employees and customers that "the Ritz-Carlton experience enlivens the senses, instills well-being, and fulfills even the unexpected wishes and needs of our guests" is a lot more inspirational than a goal of simply running a good hotel. To challenge employees with the image of creating a new world in which every adult and child uses a computer in every home, in every office and in every schoolroom—as Apple and Microsoft have done in different contexts—is something that transcends the notion of manufacturing hardware and software—and it's inspirational, too.

But I think the idea of "inspire" goes a step further than the vision. It goes to the heart of leadership. "Inspire a shared vision" suggests that it is up to the leader to challenge, provoke, animate and stir people toward embracing the vision. The late Bill Graham built an exceptional organization, Bill Graham Presents, to promote, produce and manage rock concerts. In the hitherto chaotic, sleazy and sometimes violent world of rock concerts, Bill Graham Presents redefined the terrain with a mix of precision, control, professionalism, creativity and love, which is precisely why most major rock bands insisted on using Bill Graham Presents. It's also why customers knew that a Bill Graham Presents concert would be honest, clockwork-efficient, safe and enjoyable.

Graham was not universally liked, but he inspired the utmost respect in the industry and a fierce loyalty among his employees and clients. He had what people called "the mania"—an absolute passion, even fanaticism, for his craft—and an uncompromising image of the perfect rock concert. More important, he was able to inspire this mania among others. By role-modeling his own passion, by holding himself to higher-than-high professional standards, by fomenting creativity and pure fun as crucial strategic priorities, and by being willing to hire passionate people and turn them loose, he inspired the same sort of behavior from others—a legacy that has remained at Bill Graham Presents even after his death.

There's more. Leaders who inspire create coherence out of fragmentation, and with that coherence they raise the bar on what people believe is possible. Graham was able to make others on his staff understand that all the different little tasks they do have a bigger, compelling purpose: the creation of the ideal, the ruthlessly efficient, the technologically cutting-edge, the constantly innovative, the customer-thrilling rock concert.

The mania that he infused in his people is what Apple Fellow Guy Kawasaki refers to when he says that the goal of leaders is to turn their people into "raging, inexorable, thunder-lizard evangelists."

Without inspiration, even the good vision statements (and concomitant strategies) become sterile, soulless entities—intellectually interesting, perhaps, but not behaviorally arousing. Passionate leaders drive inspirational visions. Merix CEO Debi Coleman has publicly stated: "You have no right to manage unless you care passionately about what you are doing." Bill Graham would have agreed. So would Torkild Jensen; the polite, quietly intense Markpoint CEO is at this moment working passionately to spread vision across his company.

At Merix, excellence in total quality, supplier relations, customer partnerships, lifelong learning, career development and employee morale seem to permeate. Perhaps that explains the company's record profits, 20 percent to 30 percent annual growth rate and a recent story on trade publication *CircuiTree*, which put one simple line on the cover: "Merix—the World's Best."

Back to the anonymous company I visited at the beginning of this discussion. The talk and the ideas were all "correct," but there was no underlying framework that put life, soul and direction into them. Missing were a coherent, comprehensive vision, a shared understanding and ownership of that vision, and an energy of inspiration that permeated and drove the vision.

Three vital little words. *Inspire, shared, vision.* Vital to serving up change with every meal. Does your organization excel in them, or was it your company I was visiting before I sat down to write this chapter? Even more important, are you willing to mix these three vital concepts with a daily dose of U2D2 in order to get honest and walk the talk?

COMMITMENT 13:
DON'T GET SNOOKERED BY FADS-DU-JOUR

Warning: This is a politically incorrect chapter. I have already mentioned that too often, real change grinds to a halt because of the "don'ts" that we do. This next section describes some glaring "don'ts" and contrasts them with healthy alternatives. The chapter title should be a clue to what's coming: In the Age of Consultants, we're constantly being enticed by quick-fix, high-priced, one-size-fits all elixirs that offer, at best, a pseudo-guarantee of business success. They can be costly distractions from the hard work that really needs to be done. Let's dive into three of the most sacred fads: TQM, reengineering and dealmaking mania. The point is not to vilify, but to demonstrate that the process of creating real value-adding change leaps over reliance on silver-bullet techniques. As you read the next section on TQM, for example, feel free to interchange "TQM" with the name of any program-of-the-year (or of the month) that you've lived through, and you'll know why that program most likely failed to achieve the changes it was designed to bring about.

I don't know exactly when it happened, but somewhere, somehow, total quality management (tqm) segued into Total Quality Management (TQM). The former—think about the three words individually—pertains to what I consider to be just plain effective management: Creatively and eclectically doing whatever it takes and using any tools and methodologies (statistical, technological, financial, marketing, strategic, leadership) to create a quality organization, a quality product, a quality culture and quality people—all for the purpose of attaining organizational success.

The latter—"TQM"—is a product in and of itself. There are literally hundreds of versions of this product in the marketplace, each designed, sold, delivered and defended by different batches of consultants, staff professionals and academics. And therein lies the problem.

Put together all the independent research conducted by consulting firms Arthur D. Little, Ernst & Young, A.T. Kearney and McKinsey & Co., and you come up with the conclusion that only about one-fifth—at best one-third—of TQM programs in the United States and Europe have achieved noteworthy improvements in quality, productivity, competitiveness or financial returns. This is a frightening conclusion given the hype that has accompanied TQM for years. It's even more serious given the fact that three-quarters of reasonably sized American firms claim to have invested in some form of TQM.

The findings themselves no longer surprise me, and that doesn't make me special. Managers are beginning to realize TQM is not synonymous with quality. Quality is essential for organizational success and competitive advantage. TQM is only one of many possible means to attain quality. In other words, quality is sacred; TQM is not. There's another difference: Quality is about unbending focus, passion, iron discipline and a way of life for all hands. TQM is about statistics, jargon, committees and quality departments.

Yes, of course, the two concepts sometimes converge, but there are at least 10 reasons why they are likely not to—not even in organizational environments that desperately cry out for quality improvements.

1. *TQM focuses people's attention on internal processes rather than on external results.*
   Despite all the lip service to the contrary, the actual day-to-day mechanics of most TQM programs hypnotize—if not require—managers and nonmanagers to become internally focused, even as all the action is happening externally. People become preoccupied with internal performance measurements, conformance indices and technical specifications. Paying attention to these data can be a useful part of *Discipline*, as noted earlier. But a *preoccupation* with them inevitably diminishes managers' attention to external factors such as constantly shifting customer preferences, technological breakthroughs, and new competitors capitalizing on them.

   TQM programs attempt to standardize and routinize internal processes with a carefully developed set of measurements and methodology. This is fine if the world outside is routine and standard, but it is not. Customer preferences and choices are constantly evolving and changing, and therefore, product and service offerings must be constantly evolving and changing as well.

Thus, what an internally focused company actually does may result in a product or service that, in the eyes of the customer, is outdated, blandly conventional, insufficient or just plain irrelevant. As one manager said: "Before we invested in TQM, the rap on our company was that we churned out poorly made products that customers didn't want. Now, after TQM, things have changed. We now churn out well-made products that customers don't want."

2. *TQM focuses on minimum standards.*
    Zero-defects products and no-rework efficiency are laudable goals, and they must be pursued. If TQM can help, well and good. But today those are minimal standards. Attaining them means you get to play in the arena; they're not guarantees of success. Unfortunately, TQM seduces many people into believing that minimum standards define quality. They do not. In today's frenzied global economy, quality also includes the capacity to offer customers things that add excitement, ease and value to their lives. Quality means offering your customers products, services and personal experiences with your company that they will find easy, useful, intriguing and even fun. In customers' definitions of quality, zero defects is merely one small part of that package.

    Tom Peters has a wonderful analogy on this point. Remember the scene in the film *Amadeus* when young Mozart plays before Emperor Joseph II? First he plays a mechanically perfect and uninspiring score written by his nemesis Salieri; then he begins to improvise, and suddenly the music soars and the listener is immediately stirred. Salieri's music was zero-defects TQM music. Sure, Mozart could play TQM music; without the technical proficiency to do so, he wouldn't have been allowed to sit at the piano in the first place. But if that's all he could do—if he couldn't add value to the notes with creativity, flair and beauty—Mozart's name and music wouldn't be what they are two hundred years after his death.

    We need to go beyond minimal standards. Meeting specs, making things that work, and delivering on time is the staple of

TQM, but nowadays, these essentials are just the cost of entry. In an article published by *BrandWeek* in March 1996, and appropriately entitled, "Quality Does Not Equal Loyalty," author Jon Berry suggests that as customers assume mechanical quality in car manufacturing, issues including styling, comfort and handing become more relevant. A *Consumer Reports* article notes that "Americans are building nice average cars but few 'gee-whiz-look-at-this' cars." TQM programs do not effectively confront the emotional "gee-whiz" or "wow!" factors—what Paul Sherlock of Raychem once labeled the "bewitch" and "bedazzle" effects—that are so essential to customer loyalty nowadays.

3.   *TQM develops its own cumbersome bureaucracy.*
Many TQM programs implicitly assume (in fact, consultants market them as such) that quality is an orderly, sequential, linear and predictable process. To a small extent it is. But ask any executive who's been successful in engineering a quality turnaround, and he or she will tell you that real total quality emerges from a chaotic, disruptive, passionate process that rips open the guts of any organization and rebuilds it from the bottom up.

If one accepts the myth of order and predictability, however, as most TQM programs do, it is natural to build an orderly, predictable bureaucracy around it. Of course, we don't call it a bureaucracy; we merely create reams of paper and sign-offs, a formal hierarchy of councils and committees, a plethora of meetings and techniques that must be adhered to, and a steadily growing staff that does little but monitor—some would say police—it all.

This has little to do with energetic, lithe, market-driven quality. Quite the opposite. Moreover, many people start viewing the whole concept of quality as a number-crunching paper chase or as a "whip." In one company, an hourly worker told me he was so fed up with the paperwork that "I sign off on the crap because I don't want to hassle with it anymore." In another company, a line manager of a successful operation begged me to tell corporate to "stop force-feeding their formula on us; they don't know what we do and they don't listen!"

The Florida Power & Light company is a case that TQM adherents once loved to cite. True, it won the 1989 Deming award, but despite a quality department of 85 full-time individuals monitoring 1,900 quality teams immersed in a highly statistical "quality review" system, the gains in quality were actually pretty modest. The gains in employee depression and stress were much more impressive. One outsider remarked that people seemed more interested in the appearance of quality and jumping through the internal TQM hoops than on quality itself. Today, Florida Power & Light's quality bureaucracy has shrunk dramatically. Similarly, British Telecom has dismantled its quality bureaucracy and "focused on the customer" instead. What a novel idea.

4. *TQM delegates quality to quality czars and experts rather than to real people.*
   This is a big one. Quality can't be delegated. It must be assumed and lived by everyone on the payroll. It must be central to company strategy, operations and individual job roles. I remember sitting at a dinner with a manager from Milliken, the South Carolina-based textile manufacturer and Baldrige winner that has been appropriately cited for a customer-obsessed, companywide quality process. We both had presented speeches to an audience of pharmaceutical manufacturers earlier that day, and as we ate, we were approached by a participant who told us that her company had recently created a quality-improvement department and she had just been appointed (or should I say anointed) director. She asked us if we had any sage advice.

   The Milliken fellow and I looked at each other, eyebrows raised. "Uh-oh," I said. He nodded, querying, "I wonder who's going to be responsible for quality?" We took turns explaining to the participant that it sounded like she was being set up to be a staff department charged with making quality happen while others—senior line managers, middle managers and nonmanagers—could go about their business absolved from authentic and complete accountability for "total quality management."

   It's true that the first thing many TQM programs do is anoint somebody or some group within the company as the grand pooh-bah of quality. This is a problem. Xerox and Honda define quality as "the way to do business." They're right, but does one then need a director or department in charge of the way to do business? If quality truly is the centerpiece of doing business, *it becomes everyone's responsibility and the corner-stone of strategy and operations.* The problem with quality departments, quality directors, quality councils, and the like, is that they slowly become isolated from the realities of strategy and day-to-day operations while simultaneously taking on the brunt of responsibility for the destiny of quality. Steve Young, one of the A.T. Kearney study authors, was blunt: "You don't need a director of quality."

5. *TQM does not demand radical organizational reform.*
You've heard this one before: If your organization is weighted down with excess management layers, bloat in corporate staff and a proliferation of functional fiefdoms, all the TQM training in the world won't jack up your quality. The plain fact of life is that authentic quality improvements demand the flattening of structures, the liberation of line management from corporate control, the freeing of front-line people from upper management and the meltdown of functional foxholes.

The last point is crucial: Cross-disciplinary, cross-departmental efforts, which include "outsiders" like customers and suppliers, must become the institutionalized norm as "the way we do things around here." Interdisciplinary collaboration must replace a system in which one department does its thing and then throws it over the wall. Studies reveal that quality improvements using fully empowered, self-contained cross-functional teams show 200 to 600 percent improvement over their traditional functional pass-off counterparts.

The problem is that while TQM gives these issues lip service, it rarely confronts them head-on. Too often in TQM, tough, painful, structural changes play second fiddle to the more visible carnival of motivational balloons and wall posters, innumerable classes with big binders and slick presentations with fancy graphics.

6. *TQM does not demand changes in management compensation.*
How much more straightforward can I be? When quality indices become important determinants of management compensation, as they have been at Motorola, Ford and Federal Express, then people really start taking quality seriously. Usually, since TQM genially divorces itself from compensation

issues, the audio of TQM and the video of pay don't match up, and the integrity of the quality process suffers, which means, of course, that ultimately the company's financials suffer.

7. *TQM does not demand entirely new relationships with outside partners.*
Since TQM is inner-directed and since it needs to avoid confronting the issue of radical structural change, it's not surprising that the organization's "intangible" relationships with suppliers, joint-venture partners and other company business units are not highlighted. Nowadays, with so much work being subcontracted and outsourced, often globally, and with the need for lightning-fast, top-quality turnaround work, new, nonadversarial relationships among partners become crucial for total quality. These new relationships are based on soft, squishy concepts like trust, honesty, inclusion, mutual support and candid, nonlegalistic expectations of both parties' responsibilities. These intangible relationships are absolutely essential to quality.

This is why companies as diverse as Baxter, Ford, GTE, Milliken and Xerox are no longer willing to jerk around suppliers in order to save a few dimes. Instead, they are pruning down their supplier lists dramatically. They are bringing in the survivors as long-term partners, giving them training, sharing data and cost savings, allowing them to access central databases via electronic data interchanges, and working collaboratively with them on common problems, new ideas and potential opportunities.

The same applies to sister facilities (plants, labs, offices, etc.) within firms, and to joint-venture partners. All too often, the bloody turf warfare among these siblings and "partners" would be amusing if it weren't so tragic. One can't simply declare partnership or synergy and then have it magically appear. Like any relationship, it has to be worked on with trust and caring. If a real relationship doesn't exist, neither will quality.

8. *TQM appeals to faddism, egotism and quick-fixism.*
On the surface I'm being too harsh on TQM on this point. After all, is TQM responsible for American managers' preoccupation with quick, pseudo-painless, no-harm-to-the-P&L results? Is TQM responsible for many managers' inability to deal with a

process that by definition is never-ending? Is TQM responsible for many executives' obsession with winning the Baldrige for reasons of personal aggrandizement and corporate public relations rather than as a reward for real quality improvements?

No, of course not. But let me go out on a limb and suggest that in their efforts to sell TQM seminars and programs, too many vendors have subtly pandered, perhaps inadvertently, to these myopic traits. I've seen representatives of well-known consulting and seminar outfits promote their own companies and wares by presenting a fantasy picture of a clean, orderly, straightforward, eminently logical, user-easy path to success, with some ego-gratifying quickie results promised for good measure. Good marketing it may be, but good quality it ain't.

9. *TQM drains entrepreneurship and innovation from corporate culture.*
The foundation of TQM is "continuous improvement." Continuous improvements on current operations and products are necessary, to be sure. But obsessing internally until one achieves a zero-defects "do-it-right-the-first-time" routine is a dangerous luxury that often slows down new breakthrough developments in products and services. It is the latter that is the cornerstone of business success.

We appear to be faced with a paradox which I described earlier in this book. On one hand, a company must pursue constant improvement toward perfection in what it is doing now. On the other hand, a company must encourage risk and tolerate errors in pursuit of the destruction of the status quo (products, systems, technologies) and the creation of the new. Typical TQM, at best, only addresses the first part of the equation, and then often myopically, as noted in points one and two. It does not address the second part of the equation at all, which means that the organization's capacity for entrepreneurship and innovation become seriously impaired.

I can't emphasize this point enough. For a company that wants to survive against the onslaught of myriad global competitors, routine is death. Distinguished Japanese scholar Ikujiro Nonaka proposes that business success in the future will be dependent on management's ability to "induce and amplify organizational chaos." Peter Drucker argues that successful organizations will be "destabilizers ... organized for innovation." Like economist Joseph Schumpeter, Drucker defines innovation as "creative destruction."

The reason that Microsoft's stock market value is two to three times that of Boeing and General Motors, even though Microsoft's sales and physical assets are a fraction of those giants, is that investors anticipate that Microsoft's earnings will be higher. And the reason they anticipate higher earnings is that, as discussed earlier, Microsoft consistently and creatively destroys its current offerings and replaces them with new products and features that customers will gobble up.

Apropos of "zero defects," Microsoft's newly released products are famous for the bugs still inherent in them. Naturally, the company zealously pursues constant improvement toward the elimination of those bugs, but its top priority is to accelerate the development cycle for new user-friendly products. It is that market-driven entrepreneurship and innovation that drives up market value, not an obsession with doing it right the first time.

10. *TQM has no place for love.*

By this outrageous statement, I mean that when all is said and done, TQM attempts to make quality happen via an analytically detached, sterile, mechanical path. What's often missing, frankly, is emotion and soul. Go out and look at all the earnest individuals diligently following the step-by-step processes they've learned in TQM (and, for that matter, customer-service) training classes, and ask yourself: Where's the love of our product and our customer? Where's the joy of the pursuit of excellence? Where's the passion in the doing and the creating? Where's the fun in being here? Where's the rage and agony in the slightest snag in product or service quality? If you can't find evidence of these, you probably won't find real quality, either.

Dr. Frankenstein learned that humans are more than anatomically correct bodies; Herr Salieri learned that music is more than correct notes. Similarly, we all are learning that quality is more than correct processes.

A few years ago, in Tom Peters' newsletter "On Achieving Excellence" (now renamed "Fast Forward"), business writer Paul Cohen wrote extensively about Maine-based Thos. Moser

Cabinetmakers. This 90-person company is winning the loyalty of a growing army of highly demanding consumers around the country with its array of exceptional products and services. Moser quality is superb, even though statistical process control charts and quality committees are conspicuously absent. Thomas Moser explains his company's approach to quality by noting that, first, most products on the market today "lack soul" and, second, "There's a set of values resident in our furniture that attracts customers. They're not just buying something to sit in, something well made and well designed, or something the neighbors will envy. Those are all motivations, but there is a strong emotional component to the objects themselves that motivates people to buy."

Moser goes on to say that what his company brings to the picture is *soul*, including creative craftsmanship of "absolute integrity," and an in-house delivery service (itself a profit center) that guarantees gentle, caring, precise, on-time delivery across the country. Small wonder that Moser can say with all sincerity, "We don't sell furniture." Not your usual TQM lingo.

And while the words may be a bit hyperbolic, even I—an ex-professor of statistics and psychometrics—can buy the spirit that led Max DePree, the highly respected chairman of Herman Miller, to say: "Managers who only understand methodologies and quantification are modern-day eunuchs."

Dear reader, with these 10 points, I hope I have not placed myself on your hate-mail list. Keep in mind that I didn't create the findings unearthed by Arthur D. Little, McKinsey, et al. I am merely trying to explain those findings and why TQM programs with which you are personally familiar might still be stuck in first gear.

To be sure, even traditional TQM can provide a genuine service when it gets people sensitized to the concept of quality, when it helps people get disciplined in their efforts to attain higher quality, when it offers people some pragmatic tools to help them in that process, and when it injects some commonality in language and goals into the company culture. But too often, when one strips away the hype, what TQM really does is at best a small part of quality, at worst a distraction from the real thing.

And what is that real thing? As customers and investors, we know. Ultimately, the only success that matters is whether the organization itself thrives. Writing in *Management Review* in June, 1992, Tamara Erickson of Arthur D. Little conceded that TQM might lead to improvement in narrowly defined processes where customers are known and efforts easily measured. However, as she cogently observed, "Automobile manufacturers strive to improve fuel efficiency. Detergent makers become intent on improving the whitening power of their products. While these certainly are not unwise targets for improvement, they are unlikely to move a second-tier firm into a leadership position."

And, of course, market leadership, as described in this book, is what leapfrogging the competition is all about.

Let's move to another prominent management product. Is it too early to place a "Reengineering, R.I.P." tombstone in the business-fad graveyard? Probably. Besides, reengineering—as originally envisioned—had real merit. It was when the faddists took over that reengineering began to be viewed as a magic cure-all elixir. If you want to leapfrog the competition, keep the following caveats in mind with regard to any change process.

Is reengineering really dead? It depends. If it is revered, as it often is, as a guaranteed blueprint for organizational success, as a magic vehicle that miraculously circumvents the vagaries of today's turbulent global economy, then it's been dead a long time. In fact, it was never alive. It came into the world of management hype stillborn, even as its apologists continued to worship it.

On the other hand, if reengineering is viewed as a set of common-sense ideas about revamping operations so as to improve efficiency, then it's as alive as any intervention that seeks to remove clutter and stupidity from organizational processes. But even with this more modest, realistic perspective, most organizations that have launched reengineering have managed to kill it. More on this shortly.

First, a little history. In 1990, Thomas Davenport and James Short published an article in *Sloan Management Review,* titled

"The New Industrial Engineering: Information Technology and Business Process Redesign." The article, as the title suggests, articulated means by which processes could be overhauled by capitalizing on advances in technology so as to, among other things, improve cross-functional efforts. That same summer, Michael Hammer published a sexier piece in the *Harvard Business Review*, with the provocative title "Reengineering Work: Don't Automate, Obliterate."

This article extended the thoughts of Davenport and Short by specifically calling for outright elimination of functional fiefdoms and, for good measure, many of the sacrosanct steps in conventional work flow. It promoted the idea of using information technology to link processes—like product development or customer service—that sliced across functional groupings, so that workflow was organized around those integrated processes, not around typically discrete functional fiefdoms. The article was well-written and pragmatic, and it was very persuasive. The requests for reprints were overwhelming.

But not as overwhelming as the response to the tome, *Reengineering the Corporation*, by Hammer and his colleague James Champy. This book expanded the conceptual rationale for reengineering and provided the kinds of stories that made executives salivate. Like the story of IBM's credit issuance department, which somehow managed to reduced its turnaround cycle time from seven days to four hours (!!!) while increasing the volume of transactions by a factor of one hundred (that's one hundred times, not one hundred percent), all this with fewer personnel.

Examples like these rolled off the pages of Hammer and Champy's book. Can you imagine the excitement they caused? The sheer possibilities blew managers' minds. Reading the book was a religious encounter for some, an erotic experience for others. Finally, salvation had come. The magic bullet. The cure for all woes. The simple step-by-step to-do list that would transform any organization into a model of leanness, productivity and market leadership. It was a dream come true.

No, it was just a dream. As with TQM and other fads, the people who most benefited from what Davenport now derisively calls the "Reengineering Industrial Complex" were the external consultants and the in-house staff apostles. As Davenport writes in *Fast Company* magazine: "How did a modest insight become the world's leading management fad? How did reengineering go from a decent idea to a $51 *billion* [my emphasis] industry?"

The answer is simple. As long as people are willing to pay for quick fixes and snake oil, someone will be out there selling them. Eventually, reality sinks in. Today, the $51 billion industry is itself downsizing dramatically, a delicious irony.

Managers are gradually realizing that the underlying premises of reengineering (like eliminating counterproductive organizational barriers and process steps) are eminently sensible, but they've always been around. Further, the premises of reengineering are easy to understand in principle, but damnably difficult to execute in practice. That's why the research findings on the actual efficacy of reengineering interventions are sobering, to say the least. Studies indicate that 85 percent of interventions just plain and outright "fail." Even the follow-up research of CSC Index (the original Champy purveyor of consulting services) concludes that about two-thirds of interventions have yielded "mediocre, marginal or failed results." Wow.

Here's the reality flash: Reengineering died not because there's anything "wrong" with it. Quite the contrary; reengineering is one (though not the only) sensible way for leaders to rethink their business and overhaul their organization. The reason reengineering failed is the same reason that any change intervention fails: Poor preparation, poor follow-through, poor business acumen, and a marked dearth of foresight, courage and persistence from executives. In short, rotten execution.

Rather than belabor this point any further, let's strike a more positive note by examining the flip side. Suppose you're enamored with the possibilities of reengineering, or suppose your organization has already committed to it. What can you do to help insure its success? I propose four steps that are rarely followed with passion and commitment, but if they were, they would circumvent any premature death of reengineering. Indeed, these four steps would truly help you and your organization realize the genuine potential of this intervention—and, for that matter, any composite of interventions necessary to leapfrog the competition.

1. **Link all reengineering efforts to the dynamic external marketplace.**
   As in TQM, many reengineering efforts fail because people focus their attention internally. They forget that their primary

concern ought to be responding to what's "out there." They stolidly focus on the minutia of reengineering protocols even as consumer preferences shift and new competitors with new technologies enter the fray, thus rendering the reengineering activities useless. All the reengineering in the world won't revitalize a product line or a technology that is becoming obsolete.

Think about our discussions in Giant Step I. In the world of consumer electronics, reengineering your organization won't help much if it's wedded to analog technology while the market leaders are moving toward digital interactivity. In the world of pop music distribution, reengineering your organization won't help in the long run if new no-name competitors are launching avenues for artists to record their own music, put it on the Net, and sell it there. In the retail banking arena, reengineering the organization will only buy you a little time if companies are successful in jointly developing mediums for digital cash payments that will allow buyers and sellers to bypass today's retail banking sector altogether.

Think also about our discussions in Giant Steps II and III. If you're in the transportation business, reengineering your centralized truck route system won't help you compete against folks like industrial packaging distributor Conifer Crent, which is in the process of eliminating centralized routes altogether. As mentioned earlier, Conifer Crent is developing a system where self-managed cells of truckers, sales and service people "own" a set of customers, and are able to deliver any volume of customized industrial packaging to anyone, anytime.

The point is, if you're going to reengineer, make sure your efforts aren't merely perpetuating a system that's dying. The most efficiently produced buggywhip is still a buggywhip. When leaders focus externally, they understand which internal interventions make sense to pursue and which don't. In the examples above, they focus their reengineering efforts on ways to capitalize on digital technology, on Internet distribution, on electronic commerce, on self-managed transportation cells—because that's where the external marketplace is heading, and that's what it takes to delight increasingly fickle customers. In short, let the marketplace drive the direction of reengineering efforts, not a consultant with a set of standardized "to-do" protocols.

2. **Go 100 percent.**

Your efforts are doomed to either mediocrity or failure if you apply reengineering to only one process, or you implement it in such a way that current processes are merely tweaked. In a 1990 conference, Michael Hammer himself suggested that the "theology of incrementalism makes it difficult to establish the appropriate climate for reengineering." That's why Nellcor Puritan Bennett CEO Ray Larkin argues that one would be wise to avoid goals that are attainable using current processes. The trick, he says, is to shoot for goals that are clearly impossible using current processes, which will force people to scrap the old system and invent a new one if they want to be successful.

A few years ago, Larkin proposed a series of so-called impossible goals for Nellcor, like getting inventory turns from 3 percent to 20 percent, and reducing service turnaround time on a major product line from three weeks to one day. The key, says Larkin, is to first genially agree with everyone's inevitably furious reaction that the goals are impossible. Then comes the important part: Give people free rein to form project teams to dismantle the existing process and put one in that will meet those goals.

What happens? Well, as they mercilessly scrutinize operations, people first discover that there's no point in making more efficient what shouldn't be done at all. They begin to scrap steps and systems altogether. Then they discover that they can design entirely new ways of attacking work that will allow quantum leaps in performance and productivity. Larkin is so committed to this process that he asserts that giving people modest goals is both "insulting and demeaning."

3. **Concentrate on the human side of the intervention, not the technological.**

Reengineering involves automation and technology, to be sure, but it is not equivalent to them. Reengineering may even require some staff cuts, but that is not its primary goal—nor, argues Davenport, was it ever meant to be a primary goal.

To quote the *Economist:* "The 'soft' side of reengineering (winning over the workers) is even more important than the 'hard' side (such as installing new computers)."

Davenport is even more adamant. Again, in *Fast Company*, he asserts that reengineering is only valuable to the extent that " ... it helps people do their work better and differently. Companies are still throwing money at technology—instead of working with the people in the organization to infuse technology."

There's a wonderful little story in the March 18, 1996, issue of *Fortune* magazine about a volunteer work group in Hewlett-Packard's North American distribution organization. In a short time-frame of nine months, this work group managed to completely reengineer the creaky, slow process by which product reached the customer. Among other things, the group reshaped a process which involved 70 separate computer systems and indeterminable byzantine steps into a single, uni- fied database covering everything from customer order through credit check, manufacturing, warehousing, shipping and invoicing.

But what was unique about this group is that reengineering wasn't "done" to them. In fact, nothing was done to them. The team leaders went out of their way to step aside, not provide pat answers, and—amazingly enough—not have any sort of "organi- zation" at all. That is, team members did not have any formally defined responsibilities; it was up to them to figure out—individu- ally and as a team—what to investigate, what to ask, what to work on, what to strive for. To quote Julie Anderson, one of the team leaders: "We took things away: no supervisors, no hierar- chy, no titles on our business cards, no job descriptions, no plans, no step-by-step milestones of progress."

The team leaders provided training, tools, support and encouragement. The idea was to reduce the myopia and defen- siveness that comes from formally assigned responsibilities, and to create a sense of personal ownership. People used their own wit and wisdom to challenge the process and come up with a rad- ically different alternative.

Now that's what reengineering ought to be about. How many organizations have tried to implement it that way? No wonder the track record is so dismal.

4. **Emphasize the foresight, passion, courage, fortitude and dynamism of leadership.**

If there's anything that requires leadership, reengineering

does. When times are calm and stable, "management" will suffice. Whenever big change is needed, however, leadership becomes vital. Reengineering can work if leaders demonstrate five fundamental attributes:

- **Foresight**—They paint a compelling, exciting picture of what reengineering is, and what it can do to grow the company and the individual. This means, of course, that the picture is more imaginative than simply cutting costs, more inspiring than just reducing payroll.
- **Passion**—They are genuinely excited by the possibilities, they demonstrate that excitement every day, and they work hard to infuse everyone with the same feelings.
- **Courage**—They are not afraid to tackle sacred cows, they are not afraid to question, to challenge complacency, to ruffle feathers, to create discomfort with the status quo, and to provoke people to move beyond their comfort zone. Neither are they afraid to publicly apply the principles of reengineering to their own jobs.
- **Fortitude**—They are tenacious, and bulldog-persistent. They do not give up in the face of initial skepticism and reluctance from the troops. They push on, they slog, they demonstrate their day-in-day-out commitment in every meeting, every question, every report, every review. They set an example, because they understand that unless they demonstrate personal change in their own daily behavior, their credibility will be seriously jeopardized.
- **Dynamism**—They assume that reengineering is not an event, a "program," or a one-shot deal. Rather, they understand that nothing remains stable or static, and that the relentless questioning and reinventing of everything that is essential to reengineering will in fact be a permanent fact of life. Reinventing our work will never end, they say with relish.

The leader thus has a crucial role in visualizing a completely different organization, articulating that foresight to others, doggedly pursuing it, and helping prepare others to jump in and join the effort. Without real leadership, reengineering—or any intervention—is reduced to a soul-less technique or a short-term fad du jour, neither of which will yield anything other than marginal impact.

So there you have it: four reasons why reengineering can succeed, or the mirror perspective: four reasons why it died in so many organizations that tried it. If you want to breathe life into the corpse, or, more positively, if you really want to pursue a full transformation and leapfrog the competition, I believe that these four pathways will serve as good medicine for your organization.

> *An even more controversial fad is the art of dealmaking. First, a caveat: I am not against mergers and acquisitions. I love it when two top performers meld to reinvent the marketplace in a way neither could have done either alone or in a joint venture. But often, dealmaking becomes a compulsive eating disorder rationalized by fancy labels like "synergy." Meanwhile, "vision," in the words of strategy gurus Gary Hamel and C.K. Prahalad, becomes "window dressing for a CEO's ego-driven acquisition binge." When that happens, you can kiss off any hope of leapfrogging the competition. Here's why:*

"In these days when there seems to be a compulsive urge to acquire other companies. ..."

These are the first words of a business text published in ... 1968. Today, that compulsive urge has reached epidemic proportions. Huge companies are gobbling up each other as if there's no tomorrow. Disney and Cap Cities/ABC. Connor Peripherals and Seagate. British Telecom and MCI. Chase and Chemical. Westinghouse and CBS. International Paper and Federal Paper Board. Boeing and Lockheed. Morgan Stanley and Dean Witter. U.S. Robotics and 3Com. The list goes on and on.

The press, excited by the carnage, splashes the news of the next deal every day. Self-anointed pundits dutifully bless the feeding frenzy as a sound, even necessary, corporate strategy and predict that in a few years there will be only two or three players left in every industry.

Excuse me, but could I please inject a little reality flash here?

Forget for a moment the specific examples cited above. Let's simply concentrate on what it takes to leapfrog the competition.

Where exactly is the logic that says that two ineptly run, bumbling corporations that join forces will somehow give birth to a sparkling, inspiring hybrid? Where is the logic that says two turgid, bureaucratic companies that consolidate their balance sheets will magically transform themselves into a fleet, flexible, entrepreneurial entity? Or that two companies that have individually managed to generate flat earnings and declining share in their current markets will somehow be able to right all wrongs by jumping into bed together?

Oh, I've heard the buzzword answers: synergy, cost-savings, economies of scale, cross-business opportunities, distribution channels for products, products for distribution channels, et cetera et cetera.

But if that's the case, then please answer a few more questions. Why are so many mergers that trumpet the above as strategic rationales such outright failures? Why did Warren Buffett write in the 1995 annual report of Berkshire Hathaway: "We believe most deals do damage to the shareholders of the acquiring companies"? Why did an October 20, 1995 *Business Week* special report (titled: "The Case Against Mergers"; subtitled: "Even in the '90s, most still fail to deliver") conclude: "The surge of consolidations and combinations is occurring in the face of strong evidence that mergers and acquisitions, at least over the past 35 years or so, have hurt more than helped companies and shareholders"?

I'm looking for answers. Why has the much-ballyhooed "synergy" used to justify Viacom's purchase of Blockbuster turned out, to use the February 21, 1997 *Wall Street Journal's* language, to be "illusory" and "sour"? Why did the acquisition mania of advertiser Saatchi & Saatchi wind up emasculating it? Why, over the past decade, have CEOs who have come on board in companies as diverse as Chrysler, American Express, Quaker Oats and CBS quickly moved to divest themselves of those wonderful businesses that their predecessors had so thoughtfully provided them?

And more recently, why have companies such as Sears, AT&T and PepsiCo voluntarily chosen to break up? Why is the once-vaunted "synergy" between Pepsi Cola, Pizza Hut, KFC and Taco Bell now considered a "liability" by the very people who until recently strongly supported their consolidation under one PepsiCo umbrella? Why did AT&T CEO Bob Allen remark that his managers were spending way too much time and resources tracking, controlling and integrating the vast cacophony of businesses that AT&T was involved in?

Look, I'm not a Luddite, and I don't live in a fantasy world. Lest anyone misunderstand, I state unequivocally that I'm not "against" mergers and acquisitions. Well-managed firms such as 3M, Johnson & Johnson, Microsoft, Compaq, Wal-Mart and Hewlett-Packard have for years grown shareholder value with rare, small, prudent acquisitions that fit nicely into a larger strategic context aimed at addressing tomorrow's marketplace. The key words in the last sentence, by the way, are "rare," "small," "prudent" and "aimed at tomorrow's marketplace"—which immediately lets out 90 percent of the activities going on today.

I've said it throughout this book: In the emerging brain-based economy, it's not simply the biggest organizations that will thrive, but the most agile and future-oriented. It's intangibles like speed and imagination that will grow your business and allow you to leapfrog the competition.

The face of business is changing so rapidly that consolidating the weight of two big companies today often dooms them toward slowness, caution and yesterday's product line. You don't need to have a crystal ball in order to predict that executives will tenaciously justify prior big-bucks investments, even if those decisions make little sense in emerging markets. You don't need to be an econometrics genius to figure out that rosy projections of post-merger share and earnings are built on today's realities, ignoring the entrée of new technologies and vendors that render those realities obsolete.

For example, a senior executive of a major East Coast bank conceded to me that, by and large, the M&A track record in the banking industry was miserable. He went further. Describing his own bank's acquisition activity, he said: "Even under the best of circumstances, what's the point of investing all this money in obtaining a new chain of branches when all the trends suggest that branches themselves will become less and less valuable as assets? We don't need to use our resources to buy our competitors' assets. We've got to put our attention and capital into preparing for the future, not get ourselves locked into old ways of doing things." He was referring to the burgeoning movement in debit cards, digital cash, electronic transactions and home banking—all of which render dubious the traditional thinking about the importance of adding up bricks and mortar in retail banking.

I think he's right. If you're going to go the M&A route, at least ensure that you're marrying someone who will help you succeed in tomorrow's economy. Be very careful that you don't get stuck in today's. As they say at phone companies Tele (Finland) and Telia (Sweden), what's the point of flinging big bucks at consolidating traditional long-distance providers if their services are becoming a commodity and the new breakthroughs are in cellular, data transmission and on-line services? If you're in the travel-agency business, what's the point of buying up today's bricks-and-mortar properties if tomorrow's wave will see travelers booking their trips right off the Internet?

In every industry, fast, creative new entrants are jumping into the fray. They drag the marketplace into a new paradigm precisely because they are not hampered by the yoke of heavy assets, sunk costs, and historical baggage. The very idea that megamergers will put everyone but a few players out of business is a sad delusion.

Cui bono? Who benefits? Who benefits from all this M&A mania? The record is clear that it's not shareholders. It's certainly not employees, either. To those who suggest otherwise, I say get out of the boardroom and stop reading the press releases. Go talk to the shell-shocked, overwhelmed, uncertain, hyperanxious troops who have to pick up the pieces after the ink is dry and the champagne is drunk. The unraveling of lots of publicly ballyhooed M&As—from Matsushita/MCA to Price/Costco—is due to the inability of executives to execute (or sometimes even take seriously) the hard grinding day-to-day work necessary to meld disparate people, cultures, and systems.

Cui bono? To those who suggest that the deals are made for the benefit of the customer, I throw up my hands and leave them to their *Alice in Wonderland* world. Will customers get faster, more reliable, more customized, more innovative "knock-your-socks-off" service after a deal? Fat chance in most cases. While the big new hybrids obsess on servicing their debt, the smaller, speedier unencumbered companies redefine the playing field with new customer-pleasing services. That's why in the banking industry, one *Los Angeles Times* headline hit the bull's eye: "Mega-Mergers Have Small Banks Clapping Their Hands."

It was the smaller, Progressive car insurance company—not the big, merged insurance giants—that initiated 24-hour service and an 80 percent reduction in customer waiting time for a post-collision visit from an adjustor. One report on the values of consolidation in the insurance business ("squeeze out costs," "modernize operating systems," blah, blah, blah) fails to explain a recent American Customer Satisfaction Index survey of seven major sectors of the economy, which concluded that the biggest drop in customer satisfaction was in the insurance business.

Yet the naivete (or is it "arrogance"?) of big companies which blithely assumes that customers and key employees will automatically stick around after the merger so as to fit nicely into the statistical projections is frankly unbelievable. If customer loyalty were a sure thing, then Kmart's diversification into specialty boutique retailing would have been a rousing success—just add up all those customers in all the new market segments—rather than the disaster it actually was.

Sure, somebody does indeed benefit from the carnage. The investment bankers, consultants and corporate lawyers have a vested interest in making the deal—any deal—and then scramming with the check in pursuit of fresh blood while the heat gets put on the poor practicing manager to actually make the new "synergy" work in practice. Similarly, the top executives of the two blushing merger-spouses usually structure things to insure that they themselves make out like bandits however things turn out.

But I think there's something even deeper and more interesting going on. There are, in fact, a few compelling reasons for all this M&A frenzy. Unfortunately, those reasons have little to do with coherent strategy or business acumen.

One is executives' futile quick-fix desire for stability and predictability. Big companies are starting to feel the pinch that smaller companies have been confronting for years. They're getting battered like never before. Hitherto predictable markets are becoming unpredictable through overcrowding of products and vendors. All of which means that relying on cost, scale and experience curves in the quest for business success (the typical ingredients of M&A deals) is no longer a viable option.

But rather than confront the need for leaps in paradigms, many short-sighted executives insist on taking a route that seems quicker and safer: "insure" success by buying it. So if you're an AT&T and want to get into the integrated telecommunications-computer business quickly, the solution is simple: Buy NCR. Bingo. On paper, it looks plausible. In practice, a strategic disaster. After years of bleeding NCR, AT&T finally unloaded the acquisition, and only then did a liberated NCR turn around, even declaring a profit last year.

Doing the familiar is no longer safe. You can't hide from the vagaries of the market by simply getting bigger. You can't buy success. You can't eliminate competitors. New ones, hardy ones, pesky ones come out of the woodwork daily with offerings we never even conceived of. Neither can you win by playing with the old rules of volume and cost. As former Secretary of Labor Robert Reich correctly noted: "Worldwide competition continues to compress profits on anything that is uniform, routine and stable."

Nevertheless, the search for the quick, predictable fix continues, even if successive results contradict each other. Today's acquisition for "synergy" is followed by tomorrow's divestiture in order to "get back to core businesses," which is then followed by tomorrow's merger for "operational efficiency," which in turn is followed by tomorrow's break-up to "get back to basics" and, well, you get the idea. There's no bold long-term vision, there's no sense of coherent purpose.

There's another real reason for all this M&A frenzy: It's called ego. I wish I were a shrink so I could really give this the attention it fully deserves. But consider: You're a proud CEO. You see other players in your industry making deals and growing twice their size overnight—seemingly painlessly. You see all the press clippings, and the fawning adulation and enormous compensation they're getting. Your ego is bruised. You're tempted. Your last name doesn't have to be Freud to understand that "my assets are bigger than your assets" has a thrilling psychological appeal.

As usual, the best word on all this comes from Peter Drucker. In the September 22, 1990 issue of *Time* magazine he spoke of why M&A seems to be the corporate strategy of choice. "I will tell you a secret," confided Drucker. "Dealmaking beats working. Dealmaking is exciting and fun, and working is grubby. Running anything is primarily an enormous amount of grubby detail work and very little excitement, so dealmaking is kind of romantic, sexy. That's why you have deals that make no sense."

There's a fundamental axiom in biology that also applies to organizations: Two dinosaurs mating will have a tough time giving birth to a gazelle. Nevertheless, they keep on trying. The deals keep on hatching as some magic cure-all. Are you a company like Daiwa bank, faced with minor inconveniences such as financial catastrophe, scandal and criminal indictments? Have no fear: "Merger may be the answer" (from Reuters). Are you a big airline with hostile labor-management relations, inefficient hub-spoke systems, and disgruntled business travelers? No problem. The solution involves "considering mergers" (from *The Wall Street Journal*). There's no end in sight to the delusions.

So I ask: Is there anyone out there who'll raise a voice to declare that the emperor has no clothes? That's a rhetorical question, of course, but it brings us right back to the precepts of Giant Step V. Yes, there are times when it is prudent to do a merger or acquisition; in fact, there are times when it would be foolish not to. But when dealmaking takes on a life of its own, when it becomes the primary hope for organizational renewal, or when it gets to the point that it "beats working," then you can be sure that the changes it begets will be value-detracting in the long haul.

Let's keep that in mind the next time a whiz-kid dangles the magic elixir of consolidation as our salvation. And as we end this politically incorrect chapter, let's remember something even more important: Transcending all fads du jour—no matter how well-packaged or well-hyped—is an absolute necessity for leapfrogging the competition.

COMMITMENT 14:
SPONGE UP DAILY DOSES OF REALITY

Although it may linguistically be a paradox, you need to be "grounded" to best leapfrog the competition. That is, you've got to be intimate with all aspects of the marketplace if your leap is going to take place in precisely the right direction and at precisely the right time. To be intimate, you've got to really know your stakeholders—from customers to employees to suppliers to partners. And to know them, you've got to get reality checks from all these sources every day.

I remember visiting a facility of a hospital supply company that was deep into TQM. A significant development project had to be scrapped; it turned out that the engineers—all of whom had attended myriad TQM workshops—had never been to a surgery unit to view the application of their products.

That's why sponging up daily doses of reality—in this case from customers—is so important. It lets you know what's on their minds. It provides you with their reactions and feedback to what you're doing. It fosters urgency, action and accountability. It generates a lot of interesting new "what-if?" ideas. It helps guide your leaps.

Sponging up daily doses of reality requires—minimally—what Tom Peters has called "naive listening." By listening, I do not mean the slow, expensive, detached, over-generalized surveys that are read only by a special few in the company, and acted on by even fewer. True listening involves humble, open "taking-things-in" from the perspective of a learner. True listening entails focused, two-way collaborative interactions, face-to-face whenever possible.

In the March 10, 1997 issue of *Forbes*, Peter Drucker argues that managers spend so much time perusing computer-generated output that they actually become less well-informed about the outside world, "if only because they believe that the data on the computer printouts are *ipso facto* information."

Drucker's solution? "I tell my clients that it is absolutely imperative that they spend a few weeks each year outside their own business and actively working in the marketplace. ... The best way is for the chief executive officer to take the place of a salesman twice a year for two weeks."

I'd go a step further. Naive listening to "plain, old," ordinary customers ought to be part of everybody's job, every day. It doesn't matter whether you're an engineer, a purchasing manager, a secretary, an analyst, an IS specialist or a controller, you ought to be spending time on customer sites, in customer focus groups, at trade shows, on sales calls, and on the toll-free line—listening, absorbing, probing, questioning and jotting down ideas. At software specialist Intuit, everyone on the payroll takes shifts in answering customer inquiries on the phone. Software engineers periodically follow selected new customers home (literally) to observe the ease (or dis-ease) with which they try out new finance or tax packages.

At industrial and retail packager Conifer Crent, executives as well as sales people carry pagers linked to key customers. The corporate culture is such that a pager going off has top priority, even when it means interrupting a meeting conducted by president Jonathan Perdue himself.

A few years ago, Cadillac's turnaround from a defect-ridden hog to a high-performance work of elegance was attributed in no small part to two steps taken by the GM division. First, dealerships became "listening posts" with immediate access to the company headquarters whenever vital customer feedback needed to be communicated. Second, executives began to call five randomly chosen buyers each week.

Good things happen when everyone takes on the responsibility of sponging up daily doses of reality. Imagine this possibility: Every manager in your company receives the name of at least one randomly chosen customer every day in order to call or visit and ask a few simple questions about his or her experiences with your product and company. For good measure, the manager is then responsible for seeing to it that any problems or suggestions that emerge during these discussions are followed up with action right away, *and* that the organizational systems that caused the problem or which inhibit implementation of good ideas are attacked ruthlessly. Imagine the impact of everyone doing this every day. The task need not require a big chunk of time, but it will force everyone to make some important changes to their current calendars, with good reason. People will quickly get very clear about how they're spending that daily calendar time, and they'll get doubly clear on what's really value-adding behavior in their worklife and what isn't.

The idea is for everyone to make time to interact—and get feedback—from customers every day. And since customers change every day, listening to them—really listening to them—will force you to eat change with every meal. The plat du jour may vary, but the meal will prove tremendously satisfying as what you learn helps position you to leapfrog the competition.

Sponging up daily doses of reality becomes a vibrant part of the corporate culture, a way of staying in touch with today's customers and getting important clues about tomorrow's. Sponging up daily doses of reality not only helps guide our trajectory as we leapfrog the competition, but it helps insure that we don't jump too far beyond our customers. This is an issue that's germane in any industry, but high-technology firms face it constantly as they pump out new generations of awe-inspiring products with extraordinary rapidity (one manager of a Silicon Valley firm described his company's products as "out of date before they're out of the carton"). Regardless of our industry, we want to "pull" and "stretch" our customers along with us per Giant Steps I through IV, but getting daily personal contacts with customers helps insure that we don't make the alternate error of leaping way ahead of their ability or desire to stay with us.

All of this is why sponging up daily doses of reality should be a necessary part of everyone's daily job requirement. No more: "I'm too busy (or important) for that." No more: "That's the job of the customer service department." No more: "Well, I deal with 'internal' customers." No more. The message must be clearly sent: It's everyone's job to soak up daily doses of reality with real, paying customers.

A few suggestions on how to accomplish this:

1. Every organization can identify multiple categories of customers. You need to sponge up reality from each, but keep your priorities in mind. I throw my hat in with colleague Bob Le Duc, who tells his clients: "Ignore the end user at your own peril."

2. A big addendum to Number 1: The only customers that count are external customers. Internal customers, *sayonara.* Companies can no longer afford to carry the overhead of jobs,

functions and activities that are buffered from external (read: real) customers who pay the bills. As the manager of a corporate group in one airline carrier told me: "The 'internal customer' schtick is a cop-out because as long as you or I satisfy the next internal person in the chain, we don't have to worry whether what we have done has any positive impact on the paying customer. In fact, we can easily say, 'I am not responsible for what happens in the marketplace; my job is to serve my internal customer.'"

The solution for anyone not immediately linked to customers? Figure out ways to join forces with colleagues who are directly serving external customers. Start with project teams, cross-disciplinary efforts and educational forums. Let me repeat the message: If you're not currently sponging up a daily dose of reality from external customers, get started right away.

3. If everyone's sponging up reality in different ways and times, the information you gain should be consolidated and made available to everyone. Otherwise, the learning and follow-up actions of one individual or group will be unknown to others. What a waste of valuable knowledge! What a depressing cap on collective brainpower!

    Hence, develop a variety of mediums by which people can share the knowledge they've picked up. Throw the daily doses you've sponged up into a centralized database or expert system accessible by all. At Buckman Labs, the K'Netix system fits this bill seven days a week, 24 hours a day. You can be at home with your PC, or you can be at one of the many Buckman sites around the world. It doesn't matter. You can be connected right away to a massive database that is user-friendly and provides the information you need, and which is automatically updated whenever you or anyone else adds information to the file.

    Let's not overlook low-tech methods. Newsletters, educational forums, small meetings, one-on-ones, public celebrations all play a role here. The important thing is to share the daily dose of reality as widely as possible.

4. Sponging up daily doses of reality means more than merely absorbing and accessing information, it means acting on it. If it's a customer complaint, do something about it and do some-

thing about the system that caused it and which will, presumably, cause it again. If it's ideas, observations or suggestions, get a pilot rolling.

Ideally, if people follow these steps, what emerges is not merely a passive "listen to the customer" scenario, but an active, *collaboration* with customers on win-win teams focused on a common cause, like cost reductions, improved service delivery, and new product development. When EDS project teams work hand-in-hand with client project teams, when Nypro teams work hand-in-hand with customer teams, that's when daily doses of reality naturally permeate the organization. That's when fresh, new ideas percolate regularly. That's when you and your customers help each other leapfrog the competition.

Now that you've read these suggestions on sponging up reality from customers, read them again and substitute "suppliers," "partners," and other valued stakeholders. And don't forget your in-house people. In fact, sponging up daily doses of reality from employees is so important that you might want to keep this simple question in mind:

"How'm I doin'?"
Among the interesting things ex-New York City mayor Ed Koch used to do was to ask citizens a simple question: *"How'm I doin'?"* The fact that Mayor Koch would continue to ask that question is one reason he remained popular with many New Yorkers despite the emergence of some embarrassing scandals during the final years of his tenure.

What is the significance of that simple little question? Certainly, voters like to have their opinions solicited in a direct, personal manner. So do employees and customers, for that matter. But I think there is something else going on. Most of us run our careers assuming—or hoping—that we're doing just fine with our employees, bosses, colleagues, customers, regulators and any other relevant constituency. Sometimes we're right, sometimes we're wrong. But is it wise to run our careers like a crap shoot? Common sense suggests that if we can gather valid feedback about ourselves, we are more likely to adjust our behavior so as to be more effective in influencing people and achieving our goals. Certainly, multirater or 360-degree feedback is helpful in this regard; however, asking six people to fill out a static questionnaire once a year or so is hardly sufficient. A lot more probing is needed, and it needs to take place much more often.

Yet it is an interesting anomaly in organizational life that even as we hunger for useful information to help our performance, few of us ask for specific feedback about ourselves in the direct and personal way that Mayor Koch did. And to complete the conspiracy of silence, people who do have the information we need often don't provide it to us. They remain quiet, especially if the news is bad. But if we are shielded from negative information, we do not confront what needs to be confronted.

Eventually, we wind up facing distressing situations that could have been avoided, like a customer or valued employee leaving us "without warning," or a cash-flow crisis that erupts "out of the blue," or an "unheard of" competitor who enters our industry with a new technology, or a "surprising" performance review from our boss or from the investment community. The flip side is that without specific feedback, we sometimes wind up tormenting ourselves when we suspect that something is wrong: We worry at work and at home trying to guess what the problem might be and what we ought to do about it.

Things aren't much better when considering positive information. One could argue that positive feedback is an endangered species in many organizations. It's a curious cultural norm that people often are remarkably reticent about giving someone concrete feedback (including praise) when he or she is doing something right. But if we are shielded from information that is positive, we may inadvertently stop doing the right things. If nobody tells us that we're on the right track, we lose important insights that could augment our performance, not to mention our self-esteem.

The bottom line is, you've got to ask. If you wait for employees or customers or anyone else to tell you what you're doing well or not well, you'll be waiting a long time. If you want to avoid land mines and seize opportunities, patience is not necessarily a virtue. I am reminded of a favorite cartoon of mine. Two big, mangy vultures are sitting on a branch overlooking a deserted landscape. One vulture says to the other, "Patience, my ass. I'm gonna go kill something." Instead of assuming timely feedback will come to you, go out and get it.

Paul Stewart did. In 1990, Paul was director of clinical services at Merle West Medical Center in Klamath Falls, Oregon. He read an article that my colleague Linda Mukai and I wrote for *Management Review* entitled "A New Decade Demands a New Breed of Manager" (August, 1990). At the end of the article, we challenged readers to ask their colleagues—including subordinates—to fill out a 15-point questionnaire that rated their competencies as managers.

Stewart read the article and quickly modified the questionnaire to a customized version, which he then administered to his department *(see box on next page)*. He asked them to evaluate him on the 15 questions. For example, in Question 1, a score of "1" means that the statement to the left most accurately describes Paul's management style; a score of "5" means that the statement to the right is more accurate.

Here's how to evaluate the scoring: For questions numbered 1, 2, 4, 8, 10, 13, 14, and 15, simply add up the scores. For questions 3, 5, 6, 7, 9, 11 and 12, flip the scale so that a score of 1 becomes 5, 2 becomes 4, 4 becomes 2 and 5 becomes 1. As Linda Mukai and I wrote, "A score of 60 means you have the mind-set of an effective manager. If you scored below 45, you have some work to do." Paul Stewart scored 56.5 (the sum of the average scores for each question); a good score with some room for improvement.

I wasn't surprised that Paul fared well. I've noticed a curious paradox: Poorer managers are the ones who really need feedback from all sorts of people inside and outside the organization. However, they are much less likely than effective managers to solicit such feedback and more likely not to hear such feedback even if it is given. In fact, it's not uncommon for poorer managers to shoot messengers of bad news, thus ensuring that they will not receive valuable information in the future.

Paul Stewart—one of the better managers, according to the questionnaire results and his reputation in the hospital—found that in terms of statistical averages, he received high marks on virtually every question. But disturbing to him was that the range of scores was uncomfortably wide; that is, a look at the actual distribution of

HOW EFFECTIVE AM I AS A MANAGER?
Circle One

1. He'll wait until things settle down.   1 2 3 4 5   He really likes change.

2. Most of his staff meetings are about internal procedures and budgeting.   1 2 3 4 5   He feels top management should make the first move.

3. If there's a way, he'll find it.   1 2 3 4 5   He feels top management should make the first move.

4. He'll wait for orders from above.   1 2 3 4 5   He wants to get things done right away.

5. He seeks responsibilities beyond his job description.   1 2 3 4 5   He fulfills his job description.

6. He asks himself "How can I enhance revenue? Add value?"   1 2 3 4 5   He focuses on staying within budget and making plans.

7. He feels his people should "challenge the system."   1 2 3 4 5   He carefully reviews his subordinates' work.

8. If he hasn't been told yes, he can't do it.   1 2 3 4 5   If he hasn't been told no, he can do it.

9. He takes responsibility for his failures.   1 2 3 4 5   He usually makes excuses for his failures.

10. He won't take risks because he might fail.   1 2 3 4 5   He takes risks even though he might fail.

11. He feels we need to do things faster.   1 2 3 4 5   He feels we can't turn things around that fast.

12. He wants to know what other departments are doing and what their needs are.   1 2 3 4 5   He protects his own departments.

13. He talks mainly to those people who are formally linked to him.   1 2 3 4 5   He'll go beyond the organizational chart to share information and resources.

14. "Leave me and my people alone and let us get our job done."   1 2 3 4 5   He'll cross departmental lines to get the job done.

15. He truly trusts only a few people within the hospital.   1 2 3 4 5   He volunteers to share ideas and resources with people in other departments.

raw scores revealed that some subordinates rated him a "1," others a "2," others a "3," and so on. Paul was bothered by the lack of consensus. "I've got some work to do," he confessed, and proceeded to dig into it further by talking directly to his people about the results. Thus, he gained further clarity about how he comes across to his people, and improved his management skills in the process.

The moral of this story is absurdly simple. Solicit feedback about your performance sincerely, regularly and personally. Canvass people's ideas and suggestions too. I am not suggesting that you become an insecure obsessive puppet whose strings are pulled by others. Nor am I suggesting that you give up your goals and principles if somebody disagrees. Rather, I am proposing that your organization's interests and your interests are best served when you judiciously gather information about yourself, for by accumulating information, you accumulate power.

You don't need a consultant to do this for you. Remember that too often the definition of a consultant is someone who takes your wristwatch, tells you what time it is, and then bills you. Apart from the cost, third parties can keep you buffered from the realities you must personally confront.

The number one leadership principle delineated by the U.S. Army is "Know yourself and seek self-improvement." One sentence explaining this principle is revealing: "If you really want to know about yourself, ask another leader who is the same grade and who sees you work as a leader." I believe that you should ask a wider array of constituencies, but the Army's point is well taken: This is a responsibility you shouldn't delegate or abdicate to a third party.

Paul Stewart developed his own questionnaire, and followed up on it with group meetings of his direct reports. He has continued this feedback process ever since. He has learned that nothing replaces the personal eyeball-to-eyeball "how'm I doin'?", be it with direct reports in a meeting, with a customer on the latter's premises, with a supplier at a trade show or with a colleague (or boss) over lunch.

In summary, whether you're dealing with employees, customers, suppliers, partners, investors, regulators or any other valued constituency, keep these quick points in mind:

1. *Ask straight.*
   Probe for specifics if you think something important is lurking under the surface. You may have to do this for a while before

people trust you enough to open up, but persist. Show yourself worthy of the information you need.

2. *Ask only if you really want to hear some candid replies.*
If you don't want to hear bad news with the good, or if you're not prepared to follow up and do something about the bad news, asking is even worse than not asking.

3. *Don't worry about asking too often.*
I know you'll use common sense. Besides, you know that the real problem in management is not that managers ask too frequently. Most managers don't ask at all, and if they do, they ask far too infrequently, far too obliquely, or far too formally (the once-a-millennium attitude survey) to make the process meaningful.

The late Sam Walton defined good management in terms of *listening.* It's an art that reflects integrity and requires practice. Do yourself a favor and don't wait for feedback to come to you. Develop your own personal listening strategy and persevere in implementing it.

And if you need a little personal incentive, you might be interested to know that a year after he started his survey, at the ripe young age of 35, Paul Stewart was promoted to CEO of Merle West Medical Center, a position he continues to hold today.

COMMITMENT 15:
BEWARE THE DANGER OF SUCCESS

> *You've faithfully executed the first 14 Commitments. You're leapfrogging your competition. All is well—or is it? There's one final hurdle you must continuously confront. ...*

In business today, daily surprises mock careful planning and can sabotage your company's hard-earned reputation. The only guarantee is that there are no more guarantees. Companies that were heroes yesterday are not necessarily heroes today (witness the difficulty faced by brand-name institutions like Apple, Westinghouse and TWA). But at least those companies are still around. As noted earlier, nearly 50 percent of the 1980 Fortune 500 no longer even exist—having been consolidated, or de-consolidated, or masticated into unrecognizable bits, or just plain Chapter 11-liquidated into oblivion.

Either companies keep up with the market or they're relegated to has-been status, regardless of their glowing history, puffy public relations press, or awesome balance sheet size. So-called "excellent" companies are not immune from these cold realities either. Remember back in 1985 when a cover story of *Business Week* blared out "Who's Excellent Now?" The article updated some of the "excellent" companies described in Tom Peters' and Bob Waterman's 1982 *In Search of Excellence* and found that 13 of them were having serious problems in the merely three years following publication of the bestseller.

The story was sensational, suggesting that Peters and Waterman were all wet with their eight principles of excellence. But a careful look at the data, including the trends and charts provided in the cover story itself, made it clear that those companies stumbled because they *deviated* from the eight principles which had made them excellent in the first place. In short, they got fat, dumb and happy. They believed their own hype, and worse, they believed the hype made them impervious to market realities.

In a similar vein, of the organizations cited in the first edition of *The 100 Best Companies to Work for in America*, written by Robert Levering and Milton Moskowitz in 1984, only about 50 percent made it to the second edition published in the early '90s. Some companies didn't make it for obvious reasons, like they no longer exist (People's Express, for example). But others failed to make the grade because either their standards have slipped or employees' standards for healthy work environments have risen. I suspect both trends are occurring simultaneously. Again the marketplace—in this case the marketplace for labor talent—is the great equalizer.

The bottom line is that no company is so big or so "excellent" that its finances or reputation can't be toppled. Excellence—or success—is not a static concept. Business is a long-running motion picture with perpetual ups and downs, not a still-life snapshot reflecting a fantasy of permanence. No company is "entitled" to success tomorrow just because it is hailed by investors and management gurus today.

Here's where it gets interesting. Companies that fail as a result of blatantly poor management are a dime a dozen, but what is more intriguing is when failure occurs on the other side of the coin, that is, when failure follows success and ostensibly good management. This occurs more often than we care to admit. Look at the history of individual companies and you'll find that a good predictor of today's business *failure* is yesterday's business *success*, because almost inevitably there are some little intervening variables in between—like complacency, arrogance and smugness.

Let me illustrate with a story about a certain company that understandably requests anonymity. A few years ago, this company was a $30-million organization doing exceptional things in the areas of customer responsiveness, new service innovations and successful niche targeting, which no doubt helped explain its 25-percent annual growth rate over the prior five-year period. A few years ago, management sincerely believed it had licked the complacency/arrogance problem. Senior managers understood that their customers were very demanding and that the firm's ambitious business goals could not be attained unless all hands—including non-management employees—were committed to those goals and empowered to do whatever it took to achieve them.

Accordingly, management spent a lot of time and money creating a good work environment for employees, an environment that not only satisfied their financial needs (the company paid darn well) but also allowed them the opportunity to take on many exciting responsibilities and new customer-driven projects hitherto reserved for management.

Sounds great so far, right? It certainly appeared that way a few years ago. The company was written up very positively in newspapers and received cover stories in trade publications. Its financials were solid. Employee and customer turnover was low. Everything appeared to be hunky-dory.

Until I sat in on an extraordinary series of in-house sessions, that is. Each session involved a cross-departmental, diagonal slice of employees and managers from corporate and field divisions. The purpose of the sessions was for employees to tell senior managers face-to-face how well or poorly the latter were doing in creating the "right" environment, that is, an environment that enhanced both employee morale and productivity, and one that contributed to the goal of total customer responsiveness. These goals were part of the organization's mission statement and values. Hence the sessions were geared to letting employees tell management how well the company was living the mission and values, how honestly management was "walking the talk," and what needed to be done to rectify gaps.

I commended the senior managers for their "how'm I doin'?" courage. How many companies do you know in which top managers even attend forums like this, much less initiate them?

On the other hand, I thought that the members of the top management team initially felt pretty confident, even a bit cocky. They assumed they wouldn't learn too much from these meetings. After all, this was a company noted for doing all of these wonderful, progressive, "excellent" things, like focusing on the customer, keeping the organization flat, sharing financials with employees, and so on. Besides, by most formal measurements of organizational success, and the low employee turnover rate, things seemed to be moving forward swimmingly.

The managers were wrong. Did they get an earful! Here they thought they were doing everything right, but somewhere, somehow, they had taken their eyes off the ball. After the sessions, I summarized the employees' comments into five categories, and here they are:

1. *Management doesn't listen.*

   Employees argued that they frequently proposed improvements in operations, service features and company marketing efforts. They argued that they also frequently voiced concern about company policies that inhibited their ability to innovate and serve the customer.

   They pointed out that managers frequently heard but did not listen. The evidence of this assertion? *"Nothing is ever done. There's no follow through. Managers say, 'Yeah, good idea,' but they often say they have to take it under advisement and then they just drop the ball."*

   Employees felt increasingly frustrated and noted that the organization's effectiveness and integrity suffered as a result, Even worse, they argued that senior management knew very well which middle managers were especially culpable in this regard, yet senior management did nothing about it. This meant that all the good intentions were perceived as just that: good intentions, not to be confused with hard business decision-making.

2. *Budgets are used as excuses.*

   Employees argued that, on one hand, management encouraged them to be innovative and come up with new ideas for cost efficiency and customer responsiveness. On the other hand, middle and senior managers often told employees that new ideas—even little ones—would have to be shelved; "the budget" wouldn't allow a test or implementation of the ideas. Employees argued this all-too-frequent response signified that the top organizational priority was apparently, "Keep your nose clean, don't make waves."

   They suggested that managers themselves should be willing to take some risks in reinforcing innovation and investing for the future rather than holding up "the budget" as something so sacred. Or, minimally, they suggested that managers take on the responsibility of coaching employees who have creative ideas on how to modify or sell the idea so that it would be approved.

3. *Data and numbers replace real information.*

   True, management shared budget and sales data, as well as income statements, with employees. Employees thought that was dandy, but they argued that being inundated with sheets of financials missed the point. Rather, they needed to understand the significance of those numbers. They wanted to know what management thought about the numbers and why. They wanted to know how management used those numbers in formulating policy and capital budgeting decisions. They wanted to know how the numbers impacted management's strategic goals and priorities.

Just as important, they wanted to be included in discussions on these topics. In short, they wanted impersonal data transformed into real knowledge. They said that if this were done, they would be better equipped to accept and execute company strategy and policies and, more important, they themselves would be better equipped to make fast, "right" decisions consistent with company values and priorities.

4. *Delegation is spurious.*
Employees applauded management's goal of turning more and more operational responsibilities to them. But they noted that, often, delegation was a sham for one of two reasons. First, delegation was sometimes just another word for "dumping." In their quest for total customer service, managers and sales people made big commitments to customers, and then "dumped" all the work on employees who sometimes had to work all night to meet the deadlines and specifications negotiated by managers. Or, in their efforts to keep the organization lean and trim, management often would not hire additional people, and frequently they did not replace those who left the firm.

Rather than reengineering the work processes to eliminate as many unnecessary old activities as possible, management would simply dump the old workload requirement of two or three people on some poor survivor in the name of "empowerment." This, said employees, was a prescription for burnout and cynicism.

Second, employees felt that too often managers' implicit unspoken message was *"I'm empowering you, but you had better run it by me anyway,"* or *"I'm delegating this to you, but do it the way I would have, or just do it the way it's always been done."* Or, as per criticism Number 1, *"I'm empowering you, but I have to take your idea under advisement."* Employees argued that these messages made "empowerment" something to be avoided.

5. *No recognition or appreciation exists.*
    Employees acknowledged the fairness—even generosity—of their paychecks. They appreciated the friendly, informal corporate culture. They endorsed the company's emphasis on customer service. But they felt that it wouldn't hurt managers to show some form of sincere personal gratitude when employees knocked themselves out in meeting deadlines or made creative contributions that translated into the company's bottom line. Employees said that frequently their heroic efforts on behalf of the company and its customers were not even acknowledged by managers. Employees often felt used and taken for granted.

Managers were surprised—indeed, stunned—by this feedback. Some were more than a little dismayed. I pointed out that they were fortunate to have learned important lessons. They learned that just because there's no crisis doesn't mean that things are okay; critical problems are invariably brewing and festering. They learned that despite their progressive management, there is always room for improvement. They learned that their people were not complaining or whining for selfish reasons; rather, they were turned on and demanding more opportunities and (nonfinancial) rewards for contributing to the company's well-being. How exciting! I saw the situation as a terrific opportunity for quantum improvement.

I also warned of potential dangers. It was clear that the senior managers' progressive styles of management raised employees' expectations not only for the company, but for their own work lives as well. I warned management that if, after conducting these dramatic forums, they reverted back to employee criticism Number 1—that is, "management doesn't listen"—employees' insecurities, disillusionment, cynicism and anger could potentially skyrocket, more so than if management had done nothing.

I urged management to quickly and visibly react to the important feedback they received. I urged management to hold more forums and to work in partnership with their employees to collaboratively alleviate the problems they raised. Finally, I wondered aloud if similar surprises would occur if management held the same forums with customers; I urged management to consider doing so.

Those on the senior management team assured me they would.

They didn't. Things stayed the same. Despite the smallness of the company, management remained blissfully ignorant of realities in the trenches. They looked at the numbers and concluded that the gravy train would run forever. They were wrong.

And so management got another surprise. A year later the company saw a rash of good people beginning to leave the company. These were some of the best and brightest, the ones who became the most easily disillusioned. Some of them joined competitors; a couple became competitors themselves by starting their own businesses and offering new and better services. Management saw a deterioration in the capacity of the company to deliver fast, efficient, customized services. Among those who remained, morale dropped and fresh ideas withered, all of which began to adversely impact the monthlies.

The board grew restive and began to rein in some of the more progressive management interventions in favor of more conventional controls and bureaucratic processes. This, in turn, exacerbated employee disillusionment and turnover—in fact, it generated some management disillusionment and turnover—all of which, in turn, further depressed customer responsiveness, and so on, and so on. Within just a one-year span, the lovely numbers had dropped precipitously and the company had turned from star to goat. No more cover stories in magazines.

Once again, management learned some painful lessons. One, the success-to-failure lifecycle for organizations used to be decades; in today's madcap world it can be just a few years, months or weeks. (Think about Compaq Computer, which went from champ to chump to champ within an 18-month cycle around 1990.)

Second, the numbers that a company achieves today—say, market share or earnings—are a consequence of what management did *yesterday*. But *tomorrow's* numbers are a reflection of what management does *today*. There's always a delayed reaction in the marketplace. And what may have been good management yesterday—hence, good numbers today—is often *not* what is good management today—hence bad numbers tomorrow. In short, no guarantees, no entitlements.

The update: A now smaller, humbler company has painfully pulled itself out of the morass by focusing management attention on some of the things it should have done two years previously.

Will the company be a success story again? I can't predict. No person or algorithm can. New surprises are undoubtedly just around the corner. But from talking to the new CEO, I can assure you that management has learned the most important lesson of all: *Beware the danger of success.* It now truly appreciates the old Chinese curse: "May you get what you wish for."

Business success is what every manager wishes for, of course. But managers must never forget that eternal vigilance and immediate aggressive response are necessary to combat the complacency, arrogance, smugness and protectionism of old practices that seem to be inevitable by-products of that success.

How do you think you and your company stack up on this issue? Always keep this issue close at hand, in your hip pocket, as you navigate Giant Steps I through V.

Why end this book with a reminder to beware the dangers of success? Because if you embark on these Five Giant Steps and the Commitments needed to fulfill them, I believe you will leapfrog your competition and do so quite effectively. You'll be very successful. So much so that you might be tempted to catch your breath and relax. Don't. People catch up to those who are sitting back. And nowadays, life cycle times are shrinking exponentially, be they cycle times of products, technologies—or organizations themselves. One leap is no longer sufficient. Recently, Lars Nyberg, CEO of NCR, astutely commented on his company's rather dramatic transition from a "dog" label while in the AT&T fold to a revival entity boasting both independence and profitability: "This is no time to declare victory. The challenges only increase as we look to grow the business."

So beware the danger of success. Keep on leapfrogging. It'll certainly propel your organization's fortunes. And on a personal level, I guarantee that it'll spice up your worklife, your intellect, your reputation and your pocketbook. I wish you the best of luck.

A SHORT EPILOGUE:
PUTTING IT INTO PERSPECTIVE

In 1455, the Gutenberg Bible came off a crude printing press, signaling a momentous shift in society and in history. The invention of movable type gradually precipitated a widespread availability of books to the masses, and ultimately, the democratization of information.

Yet as James O'Donnell, professor of classic studies at the University of Pennsylvania, points out in his website, not everyone was initially thrilled with this new technology. Many took the position expressed by Vespasiano de Bisticci, who wrote in 1490 that in his library, "All books were superlatively good and written with the pen; had there been one printed book, it would have been ashamed in such company."

Perhaps the most vociferous criticisms came from Benedictine monks, many of whom were scribes who wrote out the books by hand. The patron saint of critics, O'Donnell notes, was the Benedictine abbot Johannes Tithemius, who argued the following:

- Printed books (which use paper) would not last nearly as long as manuscripts prepared on skin.
- Print is uglier than the beauty and art gracing the pages of illuminated manuscripts.
- Print is more defective because printers make more errors than do scribes.

Tithemius was right on all three counts. His criticisms were articulate, reasonable and valid. They were also irrelevant. The new technology had unleashed a momentous force with its own life; a force that others capitalized on and took to new heights. The world would never be the same again.

My colleague Stanley Nel, dean of arts and sciences at the University of San Francisco, believes that Tithemius was not simply standing up as a union shop steward or a corporate protectionist against the impact of the new technology on the livelihood of the Benedictines. "At a much deeper level," Nel says, "he was mourning the passing of an age and a way of life."

I believe Nel is correct, and that the same issue is germane today. In response to the convulsive changes in today's marketplace, all of us can and perhaps should mourn the passing of an age in which we are knowledgeable and comfortable, an age in which we can point to wonderful memories. But as Nel points out, we are then left with one of two choices. "We can fight to protect our privilege and keep our comforts. Or we can give thanks that we will be able to participate in the coming revolution."

This latter sentiment underlies the spirit in which I wrote this book. The five Giant Steps tell us how to leapfrog the competition, of course. But their real value is that they do so by providing us tools to capitalize on forces as momentous as the ones faced by the Benedictines and, using Nel's sentiment, by empowering us to do so with gratitude and grace.

The revolution that Nel correctly alludes to is already here. EDS Chairman Les Alberthal notes that "the rate of change is occurring faster than we can comprehend." We can't delay the changes, we can't hold back the tide; we can't build a fortress against inevitabilities.

As I write this epilogue in April 1997, the hot news is about Dolly the cloned sheep. In the wake of the experimental results that have rocked the scientific community, social pundits are making sweeping predictions about a cold, sterile, Huxley-like "brave new world" where human beings are manufactured like widgets. Politicians are calling for bans on research. Just like the fears which emerged when heart transplants and artificial hearts became real possibilities, similar anxieties are being raised today.

But it's not merely that banning inquiry is futile; it's that we really have no idea what the cloning experiments will yield for society. Gutenberg himself simply wanted a more efficient means to print Bibles; he had no idea of the enormous ripple effect that his invention would unleash. Similarly, the ultimate impact of the cloning research is presently unknown. It will emerge from efforts of those who are willing to embrace—not reject—the available knowledge in order to leapfrog over today's conventional wisdom. Some observers predict that the real impact of this train of investigation might be the eradication of world hunger, or perhaps the development of gene chips that will revolutionize the entire field of medicine—for the better, I might add.

I happen to believe that moral discourse and debate about any societal transformation is a good thing. But as the Gutenberg/Tithemius story indicates, we can't deny transformation, nor can we even predict the onslaught of changes that are coming around the corner in every sector of the economy. What we can do is search for them, seize them as they emerge, and shape them toward re-inventing our businesses and creating new value for our customers and investors. The five Giant Steps will help us do precisely that.

The five Giant Steps are a blueprint, but it is the 15 Commitments described in these pages that will make or break the execution of that blueprint. Since you've read this far, I suspect that you are quite excited about embarking on this new journey. Let me reassure you that there is every reason for optimism. The terrain of the emerging economy is wide open, available to anyone. The playing field is leveled. It's a great time to be in business.

Keep in mind also that organizational renewal and success do not occur serendipitously. What's required in chaotic times like these are real leaders—people like you—to mold the future, sustain efforts, and keep promises alive. I believe this book will greatly assist you in that quest.

General Colin Powell has correctly argued that in both commercial and military endeavors, "optimism is a force multiplier." Hopefully, these five Giant Steps have provided you with the information and ammunition to set forth optimistically in a direction that can only be described as thrilling, a path which will lead your organization to soar, and your own career to attain new heights that your competitors—see them way down below?—can only dream about.

Index